Exceptional America

& Pocock — America's "experiment in escaping corruption" (mm 544); our belief that we had escaped → "exceptional" (note of...)

— but & we didn't escape

Major Concepts in Politics and Political Theory

Garrett Ward Sheldon
General Editor

Vol. 14

PETER LANG
New York • Washington, D.C./Baltimore • Boston
Bern • Frankfurt am Main • Berlin • Vienna • Paris

Philip Abbott

Exceptional America

Newness and National Identity

PETER LANG
New York • Washington, D.C./Baltimore • Boston
Bern • Frankfurt am Main • Berlin • Vienna • Paris

Library of Congress Cataloging-in-Publication Data

Abbott, Philip.
Exceptional America: newness and national identity / Philip Abbott.
p. cm. — (Major concepts in politics and political theory; vol. 14)
Includes bibliographical references (p.   ) and index.
1. National characteristics, American—History—Sources.
2. United States—Civilization—Sources. 3. United States—
Politics and government—Sources. I. Title. II. Series.
E169.1.A116   973—dc21   98-49947
ISBN 0-8204-3912-6
ISSN 1059-3535

Die Deutsche Bibliothek-CIP-Einheitsaufnahme

Abbott, Philip:
Exceptional America: newness and national identity / Philip Abbott.
— New York; Washington, D.C./Baltimore; Boston; Bern;
Frankfurt am Main; Berlin; Vienna; Paris: Lang.
(Major concepts in politics and political theory; Vol. 14)
ISBN 0-8204-3912-6

Cover design by Nona Reuter

The paper in this book meets the guidelines for permanence and durability
of the Committee on Production Guidelines for Book Longevity
of the Council of Library Resources.

© 1999 Peter Lang Publishing, Inc., New York

Printed in the United States of America

To: Megan E. Abbott
and
Joshua Alden Gaylord

"Anyone not in your family is a stranger."
—Don Corleone

Contents

Preface

Just after the "velvet revolution," I visited a Czech university recently liberated from Communist rule. As a visitor, my eyes focused upon the ornate medieval buildings and stolid Soviet party and government offices. Unlike Prague, which was already sprouting casinos and McDonald's, Palecki University and the surrounding town seemed frozen in this ungainly mixture of two worlds. But there was also a palpable air of exhilaration among both students and faculty. A faculty member pulled out from his desk a copy of Jack Kerouac's *On the Road* which he had reread many times over the years. "We do not have American space but now we have American newness!" he said. This professor, who was actually an expert on Ludwig Wittgenstein, was well aware of Kerouac's marginality in terms of American culture and his critique of American society but what he had plucked from this book was the sense of adventure and possibility. Moreover, it was this perception of American identity as newness, and his identification with it, that became the central part of my memory of the visit. I have lost contact with the faculty at Palecki. I suspect that this fascination with newness and its connection with America has deteriorated or changed. But it did cause me to wonder how a culture that is perpetually engaged with the idea of the new, functions across time. Though I did not include Kerouac in this volume, I have arranged a series of works that confront this exceptional notion of national identity. Academics have often been suspicious of the concept of American Exceptionalism and Americans at large have had their own doubts but it is this very preoccupation with our difference, defined as newness, that, I argue, makes us who we are by how we talk.

I am grateful for many people who have generously commented on this book in whole or part: Joanna Scott, Christopher Duncan, Garrett Ward Sheldon, David F. Ericson, Mark Roeloff, George Graham, Carol Nackenhoff. Versions of various chapters have appeared in *Political Research Quarterly, Review of Politics, Amerikastudien, The So-*

cial Science Journal. I am especially indebted to my wife, Patricia, for her abiding warm support. I dedicate this effort to my daughter, Megan, and her spouse, Josh, as they begin marriage and career.

Philip Abbott
Detroit, Michigan

Chapter 1

Introduction
We Are How We Talk

Simply stated, "American Exceptionalism" is a theory that asserts that certain American institutions and practices are so distinctively American that a specific, discrete set of explanations are required to understand them. The explanations themselves are numerous: the absence of feudalism, religious diversity, the peculiar character of the Revolution, fortuitous circumstances surrounding early political development, the genius of the founding fathers, the conjunction of race and ethnicity, cheap land, early suffrage for white males and the separation of work and residence are some of them. American exceptionalists differ widely in their assignment of relative weight and cause and effect.[1]

American Exceptionalism is a difficult and complex theory not because it is itself incoherent but because it has so many different uses. Certainly a central function forms an obstacle in terms of the construction of a diverse tradition of political thought. For if whole sets of institutions and practices are incompatible with the American experience, "un-American" in their brute ideological utilization, then a whole range of discourse and policy alternatives are irrelevant. On the other hand, if the American experience is an exceptional one, then Americans are liberated from the tragedies and unsolved dilemmas faced by other nations in history. Thus, on the one hand, borrowing from Mannheim's formulation, nothing is possible in the way of political experimentation except individual initiative, and on the other, everything is possible. Louis Hartz captured exquisitely the subtle dual employment of these tropes by political elites when he described their dual employment as "charm and terror."[2] Accept "Americanism" and bounteous benefits follow; reject it and risk marginality. These two interpretations of American Exceptionalism, one ideological and one

utopian in their respective policy implications, certainly do not exhaust the interpretations of the theory, but they do constitute a central aspect. In fact, as I argue, the most effective and inventive of
American political theorists have been able to selectively combine both
of these interpretations.

One other major complication is the fact that since the first commitment to American Exceptionalism in Winthrop's evocation of the
"city on the hill," in moments of crisis many American political actors
have themselves questioned the viability of the theory. Thus in the
1780s John Adams asked if America was on the same path toward
corruption that other nations had traveled, and in 1932, FDR in his
Commonwealth Club speech articulated a political theory for a society in which the "dream of an economic machine" had been shat-
tered.[3] In fact the delineation of the "Europeanization" (or "Third-
Worldization") of America has been a recurring feature of American
political discourse. Even within the last twenty years, the "end of American exceptionalism" has been declared because of economic decline,
racial consciousness, and the end of the Cold War.[4] Tom Engelhart's
recent analysis, for example, forms part of this new edition of this
subgenre: "Is there an imaginable 'America' without enemies and without the story of their slaughter and our triumph? Can there be a new
story Americans will tell about and to themselves, no less to the world,
that might sustain them as citizens and selves? So far only warring
fragments of race, gender, religion, and ethnicity have risen to fill the
space emptied of victory culture. Whether those fragments of 'identity' presage some longer term collapse or something new remains
unknown."[5] Thus, American exceptionalists frequently bifurcate their
accounts into exceptionalist and post-exceptionalist phases.

Another set of variables also needs to be added in order to outline
the basic structure of the concept and its function in the history of
American political discourse. Exceptionalists who emphasize the ideological or utopian aspects of the concept engage in a set of evaluations that can be called celebratory or critical. Thus, if America is
immune to the thought and practices of other nations, one can com-
memorate or bemoan this condition, and similarly so with the utopian
variation. For example, Daniel Boorstin argued that architectonic theory
was an efflorescence of European culture. Americans had substituted
this theorizing for a sense of "giveness." For Boorstin, however, this
tendency to abstract principles of political life led to the characteristic
tyrannies of our age. It was America's good fortune to have been able

to avoid the desire to "make our society into the graven image of any man's political philosophy."[6] Most conservatives and socialists, however, when they do accept the theory of American Exceptionalism, emphasize its confining character. "How can you Buy American when making the case against rationalism in politics?" once asked William F. Buckley and what can one expect from a country, asked Leon Samson in 1932, in which Thomas Paine, who would be a conservative in France, is a leftist in America and in which the New Deal functions as a "substitute socialism"?[7] The foremost contemporary theorist in this tradition is, of course, Louis Hartz, who wrote the brilliant *cri de coeur* that traced the "tyranny" of Locke throughout the history of American political theory.

Celebratory utopianism is almost a given in partisan discourse but perhaps more significantly it forms a central portion of self-identity for Americans. Leslie Fiedler describes this core aspect of American culture when he states that "to be an American (unlike being English or French or whatever) is precisely to imagine a destiny rather than to inherit one; since we have always been, insofar as we are Americans at all, inhabitants of myth rather than history, . . . "[8] That America is the most free, most powerful, richest country on earth are expressions of national achievement and individual self-confidence that have been given theoretical perorations by social scientists and historians such as David M. Potter, Seymour Lipset, and C. Vann Woodward. Thus, for example, Potter wrote: "Europe cannot think of altering the relationship between the various levels of society without assuming a class struggle; but America has altered and can alter these relationships without necessarily treating one class as a victim or even, in an ultimate sense, the antagonist of another. . . . Few Americans feel entirely at ease with the slogan 'Soak the Rich,' but the phrase 'Deal me in' springs spontaneously and joyously to American lips."[9]

Those, however, who accept the premise that conditions of American development permit the resolution of problems thought to be unsolvable by other nations *and* mark the discrepancy between ideal and reality, use American Exceptionalism as a weapon for reform or even revolution. "We shall not be peasants," was the slogan of the farmers who supported Shay's Rebellion; "We are daughters of freemen," was the slogan of the Lowell textile strikers. "Do you mean, citizens, to mock me by asking me to speak" on the Fourth of July, asked Frederick Douglass.[10]

Closely related to these bifurcations is the distinction contained within the designation "exceptional" itself. For if America is different, so are the Netherlands, France, Russia, Japan, Mexico, and others. For example, what nation other than the Netherlands invented itself literally and politically at the same moment? The Dutch reclaimed the sea and fought a war of independence almost simultaneously.[11] Or, what nation other than Germany failed to incorporate Enlightenment principles into its political culture when they lie right in its midst?[12] Or, what nation other than Russia inverted the path of economic development that proceeded so spectacularly from feudalism, to socialism, and then (perhaps) to capitalism? What other nation than Mexico had a longer and more violent revolution with such limited results?[13] Or, what other nation has preserved post-feudal values and was the first non-Western country to industrialize and become economically affluent?[14]

For the American exceptionalist, however, great distinctions such as these are magnified and/or multiplied so that exceptional (different, distinctive) becomes *exceptional* (unique, superior, extraordinary). Thus, while many nations have undergone civil war and many nations have confronted challenges to democratization, in America, according to Lincoln, the outcome of the conflict represented the "last, great hope on earth." Or, for Tocqueville, while the extent of political authority varied historically and by country, in America the condition produced a kind of "statelessness."

Stated as cultural injunction (but also replicated as political science), the patterns of exceptionalist discourse include: Class consciousness is muted in America and there is no socialism/ deference (boo!/hurrah!); "America, love it or leave it!"; "How can this happen in America?"; "Unless we do (or do not) do 'x' soon, we will be just like Europe/ Latin America/other nations in history!" The task of political theory, as most Americans have seen it, is to explain how America is a redeemed nation or to show how urgently it requires redemption.

Faced with these constraints, it is not surprising that so many students of American politics and culture should strive so resolutely to deny American Exceptionalism. But however successfully these challenges might be in qualifying particulars (didn't the American revolution really have a reign of terror and a thermidor?[15]; didn't America really have a tradition of class politics?[16]; was feudalism really absent in America?[17]; don't other nations have frontiers?[18]; didn't America have an early form of the welfare state?[19]; isn't American political discourse broader than that described as the Lockean consensus?[20]; or in their indictments of the consequences of American Exceptionalism [it encourages provincialism or in the words of a recent critic, "universalizes. . . by parochialization"])[21] they have little impact on the concept generically or, more significantly, as we hope to show, their arguments begin to assume the characteristics of exceptionalist discourse itself.

Once we try to make this position clear with brief analyses of two recent critics of exceptionalism and their historical antecedents, I take the theory for granted in the following way. Drawing upon the above categorizations of bifurcations in the theory, I plan to broaden the debate by offering the proposition that discourse in American political culture is *itself* a foundation of American Exceptionalism through an examination of central historical texts. For is it not possible that we have "become the way we talk" more than we "talk the way we have become"?

In each work, I argue that American Exceptionalism, though with very different emphases and purposes, forms a structure by which authors delineate their own vision of America. American exceptionalism is an ideal discourse for this project of reconstruction because it contains two core elements, "newness," which provides an authorization for the freedom to reorganize the polity upon eclectic foundations, and "enclosure" (often conceptualized as "oldness"), which provides a route by which new boundaries are created and justified as essential to the national identity. Thus, each theorist signifies his project as central to American identity and specifies threats to this conceptualization in the same terms. From the standpoint of American Exceptionalism, American history can thus be seen in terms of patterns in which enclosures encased in popular memory are broken through the evocation of newness, and then enclosed once again.

Newness has long been recognized as the essential feature of American Exceptionalism by Americans and onlookers alike. It suffuses Tocqueville's analysis (America required a "new political science . . . for a world itself quite new"[22]) as well as Baudrillard'" ("America is the original version of modernity. We [Europeans] are the dubbed or subtitled version.[23]") For José Martí, the Oklahoma land rush was emblematic of the nation as a whole. The whole country was "like a camp on the march. This is how the wilderness has been settled here, and how the wonder called the United States has come into being."[24] Even a writer like Thoreau, whose whole persona is a critique of American failures, writes of America as a "new Rome in the West."[25] Revolutionaries must always confront the new, but who can compare to Jefferson's evocation: "Our revolution commenced on more favorable ground [than the European's]. We had no occasion to search into musty records, to hunt up royal parchments, or to investigate the lawes and institutions of a semi-barbarous ancestry."[26]

These few citations cannot capture, however, how spectacular are American political texts in their employment of the new. For while these examples suggest newness as unprecedented, the writers we shall survey also tell us about newness as experiment, as boldness, as originality, as freshness, as innovation, as novelty, as energy, as the current, as youthfulness, as excitement, as vigor, as brand-new. All these tropes can, of course, readily collapse into the new but they also express nuances that are employed with a virtuosity that deserves re-telling.

Partially hidden though in the fireworks of the new are dire invocations of newness as negative: newness as inexperience, as the unfamiliar, as rash, as infantile, as strange, as unusual, as newfangled, as greenness, as crudeness, as unseasoned, as untried, as unversed. Likewise, while there are plenty of references to oldness as timeworn, as hoary, as antiquated, as archaic, as old-fashioned, as outdated, as stale, and as passé, there are frequent resorts to the old as venerable, as reliable, as enduring, as trusted and tried, and as abiding.

It is certainly true that the new has a distinct advantage in American political thought. A writer like—Jefferson, for example—can achieve fame and affection for arguments derived from newness. Reliance totally upon oldness, unalloyed with the new in any combination, is unlikely to meet the test of American Exceptionalism. In fact, I shall argue that American political theorists are compelled to explore the new and argue their cases in terms of the new. Nevertheless, it is rare among the great American political texts to fail to acknowledge oldness and to fail to consider the new as negative. Thus we can see patterns of the old and the new in our national texts that grasp at the new and seek to seal or enclose it. We can say that American Exceptionalism is a process that alters and reaffirms national identity. Hegel may have been correct to say that had there been forests left in Germany in 1789 there would have been no French revolution,[27] but it takes a culture that glories in the new to pluck out the possibilities (and also to disguise the unrealizable) from national events in such a way that perpetuates and emphasizes its uniqueness.

Students of American political thought have long remarked on the exceptional nature of its texts, often with the sense of regret or commemoration that is characteristic of different versions of exceptionalism. Political thought in America is rarely dialectical; its range of concerns is narrow, its arguments appear incomplete, we have been told. Even those who have focused their efforts upon discovering or rediscovering neglected texts remark upon their own distinctiveness. I do not wish to completely deny these ideological assessments of textual exceptionalism but will try to emphasize the active contribution of American political theorists in advancing, rather than just reflecting, American exceptionalism. In other words, I intend to examine the proposition that America is exceptional because its texts are exceptional. In many respects these works do, in fact, also reach the status of the *exceptional.* though not always in the ways portrayed by American exceptionalists or their critics.

Here then are the exceptional/*exceptional* texts we shall review: *Magnalia Christi Americana;* the *Federalist Papers*; *Notes on the State of Virginia*; the *Declaration of Independence*; Lincoln's Inaugurals and other speeches; *Walden*; *Winter in Taos*; *Democracy in America*; *The Souls of Black Folk*; *I'll Take My Stand*; Martin Luther King's "Have a Dream" and other speeches; *The Unpossessed*; *Oasis*; *Vida*.

Two of these exceptional/*exceptional* texts constitute a *sine qua non* of American identity, the Declaration of Independence and the *Federalist Papers*. As sacred texts, they illustrate how nearly immune their version of exceptionalism can be, even when challenged by figures as exceptional as Lincoln and King. While the text itself is not widely read (for reasons that I hope to show are centrally related to the appeal to the new), Jefferson's *Notes on the State of Virginia* states American sensibilities toward politics in ways that are unexcelled. *Walden* gives voice to American longings for the personal as place, as does Luhan's *Winter in Taos*, very much a lost text, in similar but in decidedly, though currently unfashionable, feminist ways. *Magnalia* stands as a prime example of the kind of eclectic and imaginative periodization of America in world history that continues even among exceptionalism's critics. *Democracy in America* represents a validation of our newness, making Tocqueville the inverse of theorizations of difference that constitute one of the central complaints of critical exceptionalists. *The Souls of Black Folk* and *I'll Take My Stand* are indeed exceptional statements of difference that we shall try to show are locked and entangled within a larger exceptionalism. *The Unpossessed, The Oasis,* and *Vida* deserve attention as texts of regret, especially since their sense of loss has itself been lost.

I have entitled many of these texts, or clusters of them, in terms of affect and relation (as glorious, sacred, beloved, renewed, regretful, entangled, merged) to concentrate attention upon their accomplishments in the formation and perpetuation of our identity as an exceptional nation. Let me briefly highlight the ways in which the authors of these texts employ newness and encase it in order to produce such potent sentiments.

There is no more direct way to convey newness than to promote a founding. Western political thought is, of course, marked by writers who proudly and boldly attempt to found or refound politics as conventionally understood. There are, to offer a few examples, Machiavelli's focus on the "new" prince, Hobbes' promise of a new method, Marx's challenge to philosophers to change the world in *Theses on Feurbach*, and Nietzsche's chilling calls for a new man. Students of political thought have noted how attention to foundings, methodological as well as historical, is a feature of modernity. In American political thought, however, the founding is a constant feature of political discourse and is, at the same time, partially secluded. The exceptional exemplar here, of course, is the *Federalist Papers*. As we shall examine, Publius was uncommonly deft at both proclaiming the exceptional nature of his founding and also in insisting that his efforts were conservative. In fact, it is the *Federalist Papers* that sets the pattern for the American reliance upon founding. For, given the uncommon glory of America's founding as recorded by Publius—its nonviolent nature, its reliance upon reason, its preservation of freedom—who could demand any other? On the other hand, if American politics begins with the exceptional founding then all political changes can be conceptualized on these terms. Histories of repeated failed foundings—efforts that Publius darkly warned his readers of—are not part of American political culture. Failure to initiate new beginnings can produce a range of reactions. Humility or cynicism, even nihilist risk-taking, are possibilities, but not the sense of redemption within grasp that one finds in America. Not only are there the requisite numerous evocations of the new in partisan politics (the revolution of 1800, New Nationalism, New Freedom, New Deal, Morning in America), but there is also a national history measured by new foundings. Mather spoke of a new Israel, Jefferson of constitutional revisals, Lincoln of a new birth of freedom, Thoreau of a new way of life, King of a new equality, and the Southern Agrarians of their own experiment which they insisted was unfairly discredited. Yet these foundings are always justified in terms of *containment*

confirming, extending, restoring or consolidating the old. Foundings are proclaimed and invariably connected to the "Founding."

Sometimes the relationship is complex and contested. Where does the *Declaration of Independence*, for example, stand in relation to the *Constitution*? For the *Declaration* too is a foundational text and it is one with an adamant moral injunction that the *Constitution* did or did not fully encapsulate. The question is further complicated by the contested grant of the right of refounding in the *Declaration*. The "right to alter or abolish" governments was, according to Lincoln at least, erased by the constitutional founding, but others have not read the text as such. Martin Luther King, in fact, argued that Lincoln's reading of the *Declaration* constituted a "promissory note" unredeemed that sanctioned a form of rebellion. The *Declaration* thus remains as an authorization to defound or refound. America may have avoided the trauma of total revolution that formed Tocqueville's definition of America, but also a repeating time bomb appears in its place. Tocqueville's image of France as a nation driven to contest or expand its revolutionary heritage is exceptionally exempted for America. On the other hand, in place of this huge Tocquevillian absence is a periodic authorization (given validation by the beloved Jefferson himself). The monumental statement of the *Declaration* thus requires in American culture repeated reinterpretations, just as monumental, that must be at least partially secluded since the text itself cannot be openly altered. The *Declaration* as constituting a merged text has produced exceptional/*exceptional* readings by Lincoln and King that were incredibly difficult exercises.

Sometimes the relationship between founding and Founding is less hidden than openly denied though inadvertently validated. Thoreau brazenly rejected the Founding as he understood it, but at the same time employed the *Declaration*'s authorization to advance his own project. Walden in 1845 is a very different place from Philadelphia in 1776, but the spirit of great projects, filled in with new elements, is still present. So too is Luhan's project in which an ersatz understanding of Native American culture is captured and added to her effort. Thus the sense of place that both Thoreau and Luhan thought absent in America but important enough to require refounding, is given an exceptional reading in which all the moral burdens of history are absent and, some might argue, the self becomes the sovereign nation.

These burdens are not so readily cast-off by other writers. *The Souls of Black Folk* and *I'll Take My Stand* are texts that are saturated with a sense of injustice. Critics of American Exceptionalism often note the anomalous condition of the African American and the white Southerner. These critiques, as we shall show, creep back to an exceptionalist position either in a critical (how can we tolerate racism in America?) or an ideological form (what place is there for an aristocrat in America?). But there is a special kind of exceptionalism here, however. For who can deny the exceptional status of the African American whose entry to America was not at Plymouth or Ellis Island but on a slave ship? And who can deny the special guilt of the Southerner and the exceptional nature of his attempted reconstruction? But these heritages are what we will call dual "exceptionalism within exceptionalism," for amid the rage of defeated peoples and the uncommon confrontation with the burden of history in America, there is as well an obsession with foundings. Du Bois and the Southern Agrarians offer their own imaginary foundings, independent and highly critical but nonetheless leaning upon the Founding as refracted from the lessons each draws from the Civil War.

America has also had its share of writers who have fought resolutely against any kind of exceptionalism, who have admitted only the delayed advent of a post-exceptionalist America. The novels of three women who write autobiographically of their attempts to create socialist experiments convey a sense of exceptionalist regret that is enormously informative. For these utopian experiments, forcefully antagonistic to American exceptionalism, are foundings as well and illustrate unanticipated efflorescences of American political culture.

All these efforts then are founding texts—failed, imaginary, or successful. But none are created in precisely the same way. Each employs the tropes of old and new but in very different arrangements. Both the utopian and ideological versions of American Exceptionalism fail to recognize the variety and ingenuity of American political thought because from one perspective everything looks possible and from another, nothing seems possible. But look, for example, at Jefferson's *Notes on the State of Virginia*. There is an exceptional newness of form here, for Jefferson offers the reader four identifiable texts in his essay—the scientific, republican, pastoral, and tourist. Each has its own evocations of the old and new that define America. Or look at Tocqueville's effort, which is exceptional in the sense that it defines America exclusively in terms of the new but manages to draw out four different conceptions of newness. Or look at the *Federalist Papers*, in which new and old are mixed in dizzying proportions. We are so constantly and expertly reminded of the sorry histories of republics. We are so warned not to ignore them that when Publius tells us to embrace the new in No. 14 we accede because he has established himself as the authority of the new.

Sometimes newness is openly rejected in favor of the old, as when Lincoln tells us to revere the "oldness" of the *Declaration* or when the Southern Agrarians complain so bitterly about the newness that is America that their embrace of the old seems to carry them right out of the nation. But newness always manages to seep back. Lincoln spoke of the *Declaration* as old/venerated but also as old/embalmed. The latter required that the *Declaration* be brought back to life. (Re)newal was given exceptional rendering in the "Gettysburg Address." The Agrarians who so loathed the new found themselves acknowledging experimentation and uniqueness in the creation of the "old" South.

Finally we confront the core question of American Exceptionalism. If America is exceptional because of its tradition of confronting the new, is America *exceptional*? Are these riffs on the new and old a source of enormous cultural vitality? Or are they sanctions of either cultural boundlessness or exclusion? Is it possible that American Exceptionalism could be theorized in terms of both attributes?

Notes

1   For examples of recent debates, see: Ian Tyrrell, "American Exceptionalism in an Age of International History," *American Historical Review* 96(1991), 1031–55; Michael McGerr, "The Price of International History," *American Historical Review* 96(1991), 1056–70; Byron E. Shaffer, ed., *Is America Different?* (New York: Oxford University Press, 1991); Michael Kammen, "The Problem of American Exceptionalism: A Reconsideration," *American Quarterly* 45(1993), 1–43; Seymour Martin Lipset, *American Exceptionalism: A Double Edged Sword* (New York: Norton, 1996).

2   Louis Hartz, *The Liberal Tradition in America* (New York: Harcourt, Brace, Jovanovich, 1955), 211–12.

3   Adams' contention that there was "no special providence for Americans" and that they were "like all other people, and shall do like other nations" was part of a general loss of confidence in the regenerative impact of the revolution for republican principles. See: Gordon Wood, *The Creation of the American Republic, 1776–1787* (Chapel Hill: University of North Carolina Press, 1969) 569–74. FDR's doubts were much more short-lived. See: Philip Abbott, *The Exemplary Presidency: Franklin D. Roosevelt and the American Political Tradition* (Amherst: University of Massachusetts Press, 1991), 56–62.

4   Daniel Bell, "The End of American Exceptionalism," *Public Interest* 4 (Fall, 1975), 193–224; Houston Baker, *Blues, Ideology and Afro-American Literature* (Chicago: University of Chicago Press, 1987); Alan Nadel, *Containment Culture: American Narratives, Post-Modernism and the Atomic Age* (Durham, NC: Duke University Press, 1995).

5   *The End of Victory Culture: Cold War America and the Disillusionment of a Generation* (New York: Basic Books, 1995), 15.

6   Daniel Boorstin, *The Genius of American Politics* (Chicago: University of Chicago Press, 1956), 3–4.

7   William F. Buckley, Jr., "Did You Ever See a Dream Walking?" in Buckley, ed., *American Conservative Thought in the Twentieth Century* (Indianapolis: Bobbs-Merill, 1970), xvi; Leon Samson, unpublished lecture (April 11, 1932), V. F. Calverton Collection, New York Public Library.

8   Leslie Fielder, "Cross the Border—Close the Gap" in *The Collected Essays of Leslie Fielder* (New York: Stein and Day, 1971), vol. II, 473.

9   David M. Potter, *People of Plenty* (Chicago: University of Chicago Press, 1954), 118–19.

10   Samuel Huntington, *American Politics: The Promise of Disharmony* (Cambridge: Harvard University Press, 1981) presents a sustained critique of this

version of critical utopianism through a conceptualization of American history in terms of "creedal passion periods." Also see J. Martin Evans, *America: The View From Europe* (New York: Norton, 1976), 21–41 and Rob Kroes, *If You've Seen One, You've Seen the Mall: Europeans and American Mass Culture* (Urbana: University of Illinois Press, 1996) for European views of America as a "fool's paradise" as well as a formulation along these lines in Jean Baudrillard's characterization of America as an "eccentric modernity" in which "hypereality" dominates. *America* (London: Verso, 1988), 75–79.

11   See: Simon Schama, *The Embarrassment of Riches: An Interpretation of Dutch Culture in the Golden Age* (New York: Fontana Press, 1987), ch. 2.

12   George L. Mosse, *Masses and Man: Nationalist and Fascist Perceptions of Reality* (New York: Grosset and Dunlop, 1980).

13   See: Ramon Eduardo Ruiz, *The Great Rebellion: Mexico 1905–1924* (New York: Norton, 1980), ch. 23.

14   See Lipset, *American Exceptionalism*, for an analysis of Japanese "Nihonron" (pp. 211–63).

15   Gordon S. Wood, *The Radicalism of the American Revolution* (New York: Knopf, 1992). But Wood notes that if one measures the radicalism of revolutions "by the degree of social misery or economic deprivation suffered, or by the number of people killed or economic deprivation suffered," then the conventional emphasis on the uniqueness of the American revolution "becomes true enough." The American revolution was thus "not unique; it was only different" (p. 7). At the close of his analysis, Wood adopts American *exceptionalism*: "there is no denying the wonder of it [the American revolution] and the real earthly benefits it brought to the hitherto neglected and despised masses of common laboring people. The American Revolution created this democracy, and we are living with its consequences still" (p. 369).

16   Sean Wilentz, *Chants Democratic: New York City and the Rise of the American Working Class, 1788–1850* (New York: 1984) and "Against American Exceptionalism: Class Consciousness and the American Labor Movement, 1790–1920," *International Labor and Working Class History* 26 (Fall, 1984), 1–24. Wilentz admits, however, that the Knights of Labor did not represent a "sharply defined proletarianism." "Against American Exceptionalism," 14.

17   Karen Orren, *Belated Feudalism: Labor, Law and Liberal Development in the United States* (Cambridge: Cambridge University Press, 1991).

18   See: Richard Hofstadter's essay later expanded in his *Progressive Historians*: "Turner and the Frontier Myth," *American Scholar* 18 (Fall, 1949), 433–43. But see David M. Wrobel's *The End of American Exceptionalism: Frontier Anxiety from the Old West to the New Deal* (Lawrence, KS: University of Kansas Press, 1993) for an attempt to rescue the frontier thesis from Hofstadter's charge that he had put too much emphasis on "real estate, and not enough on a state of mind."

19   Theda Skocpol, *Protecting Soldiers and Mothers: The Political Origins of Social Policy in the United States* (Cambridge, MA: Harvard University Press, 1992). While Skocpol rejects exceptionalism as too vague to account for national differences on welfare policy, her alternative explanation, "analysis of American political development," has all the features of the ideological version of American Exceptionalism. Her emphasis on historical contingency (the Civil War), institutional arrangements, electoral rules, and "gendered" politics all bear the marks of exceptionalist analysis.

20   See, for example: Grant Reeher, *Narratives of Justice: Legislators' Beliefs About Distributive Fairness* (Ann Arbor: University of Michigan Press, 1996). While Reeher claims to have found a wider range of political beliefs among state legislators he studies, he admits that what we call an ideological interpretation of American exceptionalism is not "entirely wrong" (p. 242).

21   Fredric Jameson, "On Habits of the Heart" in Charles H. Reynolds and Ralph V. Norman, eds., *Community in America* (Berkeley: University of California Press, 1988), 111.

22   Alexis de Tocqueville, *Democracy in America,* trans. George Lawrence (London: Fontana Press, 1969), I, 12. See Eduardo Nolla's account of Tocqueville's conception of political science which emphasizes a methodology of the new. "Democracy or the Closed Book" in Peter Augustine Lawler and Joseph Alulis, eds. *Tocqueville's Defense of Human Liberty* (New York: Garland Press, 1993), 85–95.

23   Baudrillard, *America,* 76.

24   José Martí, *The America of José Martí* (London: Farrar, Straus and Giroux, 1954), 124.

25   *The Writings of Henry David Thoreau: Journal* (Princeton: Princeton University Press, 1990), vol. 3, 186.

26   Jefferson, of course, still did artfully mix the exceptional as unprecedented with historical analogies to the Saxon migration to Great Britain. "A Summary View of the Rights of English America" in Adrienne Koch and William Peden, eds., *The Life and Selected Writings of Thomas Jefferson* (New York: Modern Library, 1944).

27   G. F. W. Hegel, *Lectures on the Philosophy of History* (New York; Colonial Press, 1900), 85

Chapter 2

Contemporary Critiques
The Exceptionalist Presence

In his critique of Robert Bellah et al., *Habits of the Heart,* Jameson complained that its assumption of American Exceptionalism is "as noxious and as deserving of ideological critique as the American individualism which is the authors' target."[1] In her presidential address before the American Political Science Association, Judith Shklar attempted to rescue American political theory from the indictment that its "obsessive and unconscious commitment to a liberal faith . . . prevents it from asking profound and critical questions." She contended that the history of American political theory is not one of "bland uniformity" with sparks of "petty intellectual squabbles."

I argue here that both analyses are incomplete and require revision because both fail to place the concept of American Exceptionalism at the center of their analyses while simultaneously employing major portions of the theory. This failure leads both Jameson and Shklar to replicate the historical pattern of American political theory since their respective redemptive projects simulate those they seek to study. In other words, both writers in rejecting the concept of American Exceptionalism, become by the enormous force of an exceptionalist political culture participants in that cultural pattern itself. By thus beginning at the present, we can gain a perspective on the nature of the presence of the exceptional in America.

American Exceptionalism, Individualism, and Community

Jameson's complaint concerning *Habits of the Heart* begins with his assertion that American Exceptionalism, as an unstated but central focus, is the "ultimate reason that genuine left alternatives play no part in a book whose thrust would seem to be a radical or at least antihegemonic one." For Jameson, *Habits of the Heart* "still leaves us locked into the confines of that familiar old idea. . . America is special, Americans are unique: therefore a boundary is drawn that automatically excludes any comparison with the experience of other peoples and nations in the world today (including their politics) and universalizes its subject matter by parochialization." If, continues Jameson, "we were forced to recognize that other parts of the world have different experiences of community or collectivity and a different history of the penetration of individualism (and forms of the therapeutic), then everything would change." Such a recognition would create "a new ballgame" in which "forms of praxis become conceivable that would render unnecessary the moralizing appeal to pious American values and ideals of 'community' for which no objective preconditions can be discovered in 'actually existing' capitalism today."[2]

By briefly unpacking this complaint with a view toward identifying his own suppositions, we can begin to see the outlines of what can be reasonably called Jameson's own version of American Exceptionalism. The absence of what Jameson calls a left wing alternative given the focus of *Habits of the Heart* is traced to the absence of a consideration of a "third language." But, according to Jameson, the reason for this absence is "inescapable": "it is that this is a book about Americans, and Marxism and socialism alike are not American. . . ."[3] Jameson's two prominent satirical tropes amplify his assumptions. That the examination of other societies would produce a "new ball game" borrows on a distinctively American expression of newness broader than the use of a national vernacular. A "new ball game" is a designation that asserts that circumstances have so significantly changed that one likely scenario is now not a likely ending and that the game, despite its "lateness" and its predictable outcome, is again unpredictable or indeterminate. Thus a team that is behind 10–0 in the fifth inning and ties the game produces a "new ball game."

To Jameson, the assumption of American Exceptionalism limits the theoretical experimentation that might occur if there were an examination of "the parts of the world which experienced different experiences of community or collectivity and a different history."[4] Ridding political analysis of the concept might tie the score and leave the winner in doubt. The expression "actually existing capitalism" is, of course, an ironic inversion of the old socialist argument that no matter what deficiencies might exist in socialist regimes they deserve the support of radicals because, after all, they represent some praxis, however distorted, of victories on the part of workers. Thus one who calls himself a socialist but who refuses to support an "actually existing" socialist society limits his credentials as a radical. The obverse of this long, intricate historical argument among the Left is that, since the principles of socialism are so conspicuously absent in "actually existing" regimes, support is counter-revolutionary. By suggesting that American Exceptionalism hides or disguises real social and political practices, Jameson is suggesting that it functions in much the same way as it did for Stalinist apologists. There are no "objective conditions" for community in "actually existing" capitalist societies, and to the extent to which the theory of American exceptionalism condones some potential relationship, its adherents are guilty of bad faith. Thus, for Jameson, American exceptionalism needs to be exposed and rejected because the focus on American conceptions of community limits the consideration of other forms of community and there are no genuine American forms of community.

Let me very briefly present three early statements of American Exceptionalism (to which I return later in this chapter), statements that have been much copied and employed in an enormous variety of ideological uses. Roughly stated, they might be called versions of religious, republican, and liberal statements of American Exceptionalism and they also roughly correspond to Bellah and his associates' "languages." In its original statement, the religious version marked the settlement of America as a new Israel. The identification with Israel reflected less an anthropological or historical reference than the deliberate construction of a providential account of world events. Especially for the first and second generation of clerics, the "meaning of America" could be found in topological extrapolations from Israeli history. So prominent were these frequent typologies that New Englanders "came to understand the history of Israel as well—perhaps better—than their parents knew the history of England."[5] The contention that the new world constituted a grand epic, separate from profane history, took various forms, including an emphasis on the "Jewish republic" as a typology as questions of independence emerged. The republican interpretation of American Exceptionalism, which ideologically animated the American Revolution, employed a wide variety of exemplary models, including Sparta and Athens, republican Rome, Calvin's Geneva, early Saxon settlements in England and republican Florence. Charles Lee once said that he "used to regret not being thrown into the world in the glorious third or fourth century of the Romans," but now his hopes were "at length bid fair for being realized."[6] The liberal version, which appears as early as Crevecoeur's exploration of "What is an American?" certainly contains as its central thrust America as a place of economic opportunity but it also emphasizes the multicultural origins of American Exceptionalism. The European, transplanted in America, is a new persona, composed of "Western pilgrims," "melted into a new race." Paine used this trope to deny the existence of a cultural bond with England. Britain was not the "parent country" of Americans but instead a place of refuge for people from "every part of Europe." "We claim the brotherhood with every European Christian," said Paine, and "triumph in the generosity of the sentiment. . . ."[7]

What is so intriguing about these statements of American Exceptionalism is that each borrows centrally from experiences of other peoples with community. In fact, American Exceptionalist assumptions of specialness and uniqueness were dependent on imitating and revising previous forms of community. In Cotton Mather's *Magnalia*, John Winthrop became a "new English Nehemiah," who in "managing the affairs of our new American Jerusalem," was an "exact parallel unto that governor of Israel." But Mather was also intent upon establishing the point that this was also a new experiment. His comparison of the Great Migration to the Flood was an attempt to illustrate the newness of the New England community: "Wherever they sat down, they were so mindful of their errand into the wilderness . . ."[8] Similarly, the republicans' identification with historically distant regimes involved the theoretical construction of composite communities. Samuel Adams, for example, spoke of a "Christian Sparta." The liberal assertion that America was peopled by the detritus of Europe certainly constituted a trope that featured the newness of America, but even in this instance America represented a potential pan-European community that could not emerge on the continent because, as was the case in France, the "flower of the country" was denied property ownership and employed as servants.[9]

Exceptionalist theorists then consciously attempted to construct "new ball game(s)" as part of an effort to distinguish themselves as a separate community from the dominant (and empirically central) fact that they were colonists on the periphery of an imperialist empire. If these statements of American Exceptionalism do employ comparisons to other peoples with community in patterns that involve theoretical tropes of both imitation and newness, is Jameson's second contention, that no form of community that is centered on the American experience, a viable position?

Jameson criticizes the conceptualization of community by the authors of *Habits of the Heart* as misplaced because it is "traditional and retrospective." Rather than conceiving of community as a static concept that "strategically foregrounds that sense of the past," the authors should have substituted the "active slogan of the 'community project.'"[10] Jameson's critique on this point is actually a layered one. On the one hand, he suggests that the search for earlier American forms of community is a hopeless enterprise because every conceivable historical reformulation is infected with the first language of individualism. On the other, he intimates that certain forms of community, to whatever extent they might be free of individualism, are inappropriate avenues of investigation because they privilege past formulations rather than anticipating future forms. Thus, Jameson charges that Bellah and his associates lack a grasp of praxis in two fundamental senses: their focus on older American forms of community is an "admission of failure" because without a "radical break" they are imprisoned in the individualistic American project, are forced to find "the deeper meanings of our individualism," and are "not at all clear" what the success of their project might mean, and *any* retrospective conception of community is "static," hence failing to reorient our thinking.

The latter critique, of course, is intimately connected to Jameson's own enterprise, in which community can only be legitimately conceptualized in terms of ruptures from existing practices. Jameson thus contends that the past "cannot be confronted without nausea" and much prefers the active slogan of the "collective project" to that of the community. As to the viability of the American past in particular, it does not require a theory of American Exceptionalism to question whether previous American communitarian efforts are less worthy of selective imitation than the Stalinist project or the "premature and abortive revolutions such as those in Kampuchea and Afghanistan," which Jameson contends do not discredit Marxist analysis.[11]

America and the Periodization Question

The general points Jameson raises in both portions of his second critique represent old queries in the history of American political culture. Are American communities viable? Are American communities headed for disintegration into ever smaller micro-communities? John Winthrop once wondered if the New England towns were not destined to "splinter . . . into a hundred earnest little Utopias, each feeding on its own special type of holiness and each breeding new types, multiplying like earthworms, by division." The nagging suspicion that new communities cannot be created from a correct amalgamate of previous communities troubled the most imaginative of the New England typologists as well as the republicans. "The love of gold grows faster than the heap of acquisition," complained Adams as he wondered whether American republicanism represented a doomed experiment. Even Paine asked how long would America's nonage last before it "let slip the opportunity" for new political formulations.[12]

Although encased in another "language," Jameson's own project is, in fact, a replication of these very same American efforts and doubts. Jameson constructs his own typological model of American history. Borrowing from Ernest Mandel's typology, which posits a "new stage" in capitalist development that extends from market to monopoly to new imperialist economies, Jameson constructs three corresponding cultural forms: realism, modernism, and postmodernism.[13] The American realist "capitalist moment" is, surprisingly, not assigned a period by Jameson, but if one relies upon his appropriation of Mandel's typology, this cultural form expired sometime in the mid-nineteenth century. Similarly, the modern period appears to have emerged in full force by World War I. Only in his topological periodization of postmodernism does Jameson commit himself to the kind of periodical specificity that he demands of theory. After a brief moment of apparent "freedom" from 1960 to 1974, which proved to be nothing more than a system massively switching gears, the "postmodern era" emerged.

Jameson is very anxious to mark off the numerous competing theories of postmodernism from his own. His matrix of postmodernists breaks down theoretical formulations into antimodernist/promodernist theorists (Wolfe and Jencks), antimodernist/anti-promodernist (Tafuri), pro-modernist/pro-postmodernist (Lyotard), and pro-modernist/anti-postmodernist (Kramer, Habermas) but he defends his own interpretation of postmodernism as less a cultural style than a stage in the development of capital. According to Jameson, all postmodernist theorists are in agreement that "some decisive break" has occurred; however it might be evaluated. Habermas might seek to rescue the critical function of modernism from a postmodernist geist; Tafuri might offer a theory of postmodernism as an extension of the reification of capital implicit in modernism, or Venturi might present a populist interpretation of postmodernism. But each of these theories fails in the sense that each fails to specify the causes of this newly perceived duality. Marxists resist the incorporation of a new stage in their analysis; other theorists parochialize the phenomenon in terms of some process of Americanization and still others collect postmodernist features as part of their critique of modernism. Only by periodizing theory and focusing upon the unique features of a new "third stage" of capital can postmodernism be truly understood.

Jameson, however, is aware that periodization entails a confrontation with the "unavoidable representational problem." Since there is no such thing as "'late capitalism in general' but only this or that specific national form," he recognizes that "non-North American readers will inevitably deplore the *Americanocentricism* of my own account."[14] He attempts to rescue his theorization from this anticipated allegation of American Exceptionalism by contending that it is "justified only to the degree that it was the brief 'American century' (1945–73) that constituted the hothouse, or forcing ground, of the new system, while the development of the cultural forms of postmodernism may be said to be the first specifically North American global style."[15] Of course, the assertion that America is first and new in creating cultural and political forms, that these forms will emanate globally (or will recede), is itself a characteristic feature of American exceptionalist theory which played itself out in different forms in the works of Mather, Jefferson, and Paine.

It is in this context of the admission of a temporary Americanocentricism that Jameson attempts to provide historical specificity to the emergence of the postmodern. His "periodizing the sixties" is thus centered upon establishing the assertion that this moment of "immense freeing or unbinding of cultural energies" can somehow be explained without recourse to an American Exceptionalist theory.[16] The essay is, in fact, an especially remarkable causerie in this respect. Jameson manages to offer a narrative of America in the 1960s without a single citation of an American radical, a single instance in which American radical thought constituted a contribution to the radical project of the period, and a single instance in which American radical movements represented an effort to redefine political power and authority.

Scores of theorists are brought forward and analyzed in terms of the roles they performed in responding to various crises. The work of Sartre and Fanon, Debray and most of all Mao (who represents the "richest of all the great revolutionary ideologies of the sixties"[17]) provides the framework for the radical critique. In fact, the Berkeley free speech movement is treated as evidence of the appreciation of a Hegelian "Other," as given contemporary valorization by Sartre; the New Left critique of bureaucracy and the insistence that the personal is political is derived from Mao's critique of Soviet bureaucracy; the women's movement constituted "building a Yenan of a new and unpredictable kind." Jameson's project of distancing American radicalism from the sixties is so complete that when American radicals do actually appropriate the symbols of Maoism, Jameson asserts that they constitute a "modern exotic or orientalist" version of the confused French 1848 revolutionaries that Marx described who "conjure up spirits . . . to their service and borrow from them the names, battle cries and costumes."[18] The American civil rights movement deserves to be dated from the Greensboro sit-ins in 1960 because this "First World political movement" was an extension of French decolonization in Africa and the Algerian struggle. The "crucial detonator—a new Year I" for North American radicalism was the Cuban revolution.

This interpretation of the sixties is, of course, ludicrous. Jameson not only ignores the American origins of radical protest as a reexamination of the postwar social contract. Irving Howe's brilliant characterization of New Leftism as "Emersonianism with shock treatment" and Staughton Lynd's definition of American radicalism as personal witness which replicated abolitionism recognized in part the periodic and unpredictable confrontations with the Other in American history.[19] A dogged pursuit of this perspective could lead to the equally ludicrous assessment that Maoism was an imitation or refraction of sixties radicalism in America with the cultural revolution posing as a replay of American counterculturalism and the attack on bureaucratic privilege as a Jeffersonian moment in the Chinese revolution. But Jameson, in his effort to avoid the critique that periodization entails diachrony, also ignores any facet of progression in American radicalism. That the self-definition of the American radical should have changed from one who regarded individuals as "infinitely precious and possessed of unfulfilled capacities for reason, freedom and life" to one who sang "the most beautiful sound I ever heard, Kim Il Sung" to the tune of "Maria" is the central puzzle for nearly every sixties-in-the-seventies and sixties-in-the-eighties commentator.[20] The perception on the part of many American radicals that American culture did not possess the elasticity for significant change and that models must be imitated from everywhere is an extremely complex process that Jameson almost completely erases from his periodization.

Jameson, however, deftly avoids an inversion of his argument (one which Debray advanced when he said that "in France, the Columbuses of political modernity thought that following Godard's *La Chinoise* they were discovering China in Paris, when in fact they were landing in California"[21]) by suggesting that the conclusion that the cause of American radicalism can be found in the Third World represents a kind of act of historical cunning which he is able to avoid. The fact is that "the conception of the Third World 60s as a moment when all over the world chains and shackles of a classical imperialist kind were thrown off in a stirring wave of 'wars of liberation' is an altogether mythical simplification."[22] For in Jameson's periodization, capital can "just as easily" be conceptualized as in a moment of "full dynamic and innovative expansion" as in global retreat. Grinding toward a new level of growth and power, capital was in the midst of a new revolution, a Green Revolution, in which all the world is brought under economic domination through the new technology of computers, the mechanization of agriculture and nuclear energy, and new political forms (neo-colonization and the multinational corporation) that govern in the latest cycle. This new globalization temporarily unleashes previously "untheorized new forces," but ultimately only represents "an immense and inflationary superstructural credit."[23] In fact, according to Jameson, the most advanced revolutionary theory of the sixties represented, in actuality, the marginalization of radicalism under the new form of domination by capital. The Cuban foco strategy, theorized by Debray, conceived of revolutionary activity without geographical space. Without a Leninist vanguard or a vision of a liberated Yenan, the new revolutionary operated from a new "nonplace" in an arena of "perpetual displacement." The fact that the "first world" bourgeoisie appropriated the sign of the "terrorist" as a new privileged form of otherness is the least of Jameson's theorization. For the foco strategy paralleled philosophical developments in which there was a "perpetual guerrilla war among the material signifiers of textual formulations."[24] As flourishing radical movements were under the illusion of liberation at the very moment when they were about to be marginalized and mutated, so too did sixties cultural producers fall into the world, in the form of postmodernism, at the very moment when they too appeared to be a victorious force.

"Periodizing the Sixties" thus offers two great detours in its attempt to avoid Americanocentricism. In the first, American radicalism is drawn as an efflorescence of Third World developments as interpreted by "first world" commentators. In the second, this very derivativeness is overlaid with a theoretical structure (Mandel's model) that places the radical critique as an (indirect) response to the newly emerging structures of late capital. Jameson does not engage in any direct specification (as did American sixties radicals who struggled to "name the system!") of the source of this new globalization of capital, but his narrative leaves no other interpretation than that it is driven by new American forces of production. Thus, not only Maoism but what turned out to be all the other "ever more devalued signifiers" of radicalism were brought forth by American developments.

Jameson's periodization is inconceivable without a theory of American Exceptionalism. For without positing America as the locus of capitalist development and the new third stage as a shift from European imperialism as a global force, his narrative on his terms sinks to incomprehensibility since it would fail to specify an "objective situation" and that "situation's structural limits."[25] The relative hiddenness in this portion of his periodization corresponds to the theoretical hiddenness uncovered in the first detour. In the first, America is theorized in terms of radical protest that emerges from and is driven by its location as a "privileged" political space in the imperialist system. In the second, America is theorized as "late capital." This bifurcated signification of radical protest/late capitalism permits Jameson to posit America as both a dependent and an independent variable.

There is, however, one final detour in Jameson's account. The second detour reveals the locus of an "as yet untheorized original space of some new 'world system.'"[26] Jameson notes that while the negative effects of this new order are obvious one cannot ignore its "progressive aspects," just as Marx appreciated the promise of a world market and Lenin the formation of "the older imperialist network." For both Marx and Lenin understood that "liberation did not entail a return to smaller forms of social organization but grasped the promise of a new and more comprehensive socialism." "Is this not the case," asks Jameson, "with the yet more global and totalizing space of the new world system, which demands the intervention and elaboration of an internationalism of a radically new type?"[27] Thus he ends his periodization of the sixties with the conclusion that "traditional" Marxism, if "untrue during this period . . . must necessarily become true again when the dreary realities of exploitation, extraction of surplus value, proletarianization, and the resistance to it in the form of class struggle, all slowly reassert themselves on a new and expanded world scale, as they seem currently in the process of doing."[28] This third, final detour, of which America as late capital is the precipitating cause, establishes the truth of the Marxist narrative and, of course, obliterates everything that is not organizable as (American) capital and in the process obliterates (transforms) America itself.

I also suggest that the actual structure of Jameson's narrative, to use his own methodological technique, is homologous to historically prior accounts of American Exceptionalism. I take as an example Cotton Mather's *Magnalia Christi Americana,* published in 1702. Like Jameson's project, Mather's is a deeply ideologically conservative one. Whereas Jameson seeks to reestablish the truth of the Marxist narrative in face of both its global waning of influence and its revisionist interpretations, Mather attempts to write his own periodization in the context of the declension, the apparent "visible shrink" and "dying Religion" of Protestantism both in New England and in the New World.[29] As in Jameson's case, America provides the basis for a complex theorization. In Mather's first detour, the Great Migration is interpreted in terms of the mistaken actions of "certain Little-Soul'd Ceremony-Mongers" in the Anglican Church. The source of sacred history rests with the "True Protestant Reforming Church of England," temporarily under the dominion of "a Romanizing Faction" and the "First Planters of New England" who called "the Church of England their Dear Mother." New Englanders, thrust "into the horrible thickets of America" await return after completion of the "errand into the wilderness."[30] In this detour, the New England Church stands on the periphery of the reformation and "humbly Petition to be a Part of it." But despite Mather's restrained employment of the exodus trope, Magnalia leans heavily upon the American churches as constituting a new Israel. Native Americans become Canaanites, England becomes Egypt and Bradford Moses.[31] In this second detour America's newness is drawn in terms of its replication of Israel. America as Israel provides Mather with the core structure for his Jeremiadic periodization. If New England were an efflorescence of the English reformation, its history was tethered to the rise and fall of Protestant politics abroad. To the extent that New England represented a typology to Israel, its errand was markedly more significant. Its "seven candles" were not a light to the English Church but a beacon that indicated an independent Providential design. In this detour, failure to complete the errand on the part of New Englanders represented "a fearful degeneracy." But the evocation of a new Israel also required a shift from America as a wilderness to "the Garden of New England." Ministries were "seedbeds" and Harvard was a "river, without the streams whereof, these regions would have been mere unwatered places for the devil."[32]

Each of these detours, however, are overlayered by a third in which America is given a meaning beyond the Reformation and even beyond a typology of ancient Israel. America was not even known to the authors of the Scriptures, contends Mather, because it had been "concealed" by the devil. "Geography must now work for a Christianography in Regions far enough beyond the Bounds wherein the Church of God had thro' all former Ages been circumscribed," and Mather posits a millennial vision in which this "New Jerusalem" becomes the location for "the mighty deeds of Christ." The American errand is a struggle with "the last conflict with anti-christ."[33]

It would be anachronistic to contend that Mather's project in *Magnalia* involved an attempt to avoid a confrontation with American Exceptionalism. Mather, in fact, is theorizing in a period in which a conception of America is contested and inchoate. But in an important sense Mather's efforts confirm Jameson's own Americanocentricism because Mather's periodization involves the same progressively more generalized conception of America. First there is the detour that theorizes American history as a privileged space opened by European developments (the Reformed Church of England/Third World anticolonial protest). Then there is the detour in which America is theoretically bifurcated (wilderness/garden; radicalism/late capital) and the dissection employed to trace a theoretically "hidden" project emanating from America (the replication of Israel; the transition to the third stage of capital). Finally there is the grand detour, millennial in both instances, in which the truly "concealed" America is revealed as the locus for the transformation of humanity (the Second Coming; a new world system) in which America itself is erased.

The homology between Jameson's and Mather's periodizations illustrates the complex struggle to define America as somehow constituting a nexus in a world system. That Jameson's periodization constitutes a series of theoretical constructs tying America's development to the global events, past and future, does not establish its independence from exceptionalism but rather confirms its replication. The charge that exceptionalism universalizes through parochialization is thus an accurate description of the exceptionalist enterprise as long as we realize that such theories also move, as do Jameson's and Mather's, in the opposite direction and that the exceptionalist project itself demands no special affective relationship between the interpreter and the subject. Attempts at periodization compute this systematic ambiguity. America as a definitional moving target, shifting from the periphery to the center of world events on the basis of a theoretical periodization until America as a category ultimately explodes, admit such a wide variety of variations, as Jameson's and Mather's efforts illustrate, that the periodization exercise itself seems to collapse from the power of its own transparadigmatic capacity.

America as Dual Narrative

Jameson seeks to erase exceptionalism by globalization while Shklar seeks to erase it by bifurcation. Shklar's project rests upon the construction of a historical narrative that sees American political theory as a series of complex debates over two experiments conducted simultaneously: one in democracy, the other in tyranny. The democratic debate produced three "diverse and complex" conceptions of political science in the works of Jefferson, Madison, and Hamilton, and a debate on the expansion of democracy in the first four decades of the last century. Coterminous with these efforts were examinations of the institution of slavery, culminating in what Louis Hartz called the emergence of the "Southern Reactionary Enlightenment" in the 1850s. Industrialism and the failure of reconstruction produced another conceptualization of the limits of democracy in the form of Social Darwinism, which Shklar characterizes as much more problematic than uniform in its insistence that democracy accede to the demands of the machine age. Shklar closes her narrative by suggesting that Charles Merriam, and later John Dewey, refashioned the democratic debate through the formation of a "new, university-based, city-wise social science" that emphasized social planning.

This narrative is, of course, necessarily a select one. Yet there is no mention of the colossal project of Abraham Lincoln. Shklar neither discusses the historical opportunity that FDR's brains trust attempted to seize in the Great Depression nor does she discuss the enormous burden that the Cold War placed upon American intellect. In addition, Shklar claims that the "social sciences are submerged biographies of the silent majority of humanity,"[34] but there is a notable absence of the spokespeople whose thought has been given voice by social historians. These omissions are not in themselves crucial. What is significant is the theoretical model from which Shklar constructs her narrative, which leads her to neglect these cultural encounters. Is the argument that American political theory is "a profound meditation upon our political experiences," conceptualized as dual experiments in democracy and tyranny and the victory of the former, the appropriate alternative to the view that American political theory is "mired in the legacy of John Locke"? While there is some plausibility in parts of Shklar's argument, it is incomplete and in need of revision since it rests upon an unwillingness to include the conceptual apparatus that is essential to her own theoretical act of redemption. I intend to challenge Shklar's assertion that the history of American political thought represents a kind of discernible process of liberation and democratization and that American political science represents a culmination of this process. On the contrary, I intend to show that Shklar's position is an identifiable form of American Exceptionalism through an alternate historical narrative, that patterns of liberation and oppression are much more complexly intertwined in American political thought than she suggests, and that American political science, in substantial ways, secludes rather than illuminates these patterns.

Despite its centrality in American culture and in American political science, Shklar bases her own redemptive project upon a repeated rejection of American Exceptionalism, although she does not specifically identify the concept with which she is actually engaging in a dialogue.[35] She rejects the charge that American political theory can be characterized by "an obsessive and unconscious commitment to a liberal faith that prevents it from asking profound and critical questions." She rejects the charge that when "lively controversies" do occur they "are mere shadowboxing compared to the real thing, the kind of ideological combat that feudalism and class war generated in Europe," and argues that there has been a great deal of theoretical sharing between "both sides of the puddle." She urges that we "finally end that endless Jeremiad about the absence of socialism and conservatism."[36] In actuality, however, Shklar is seeking to reject her interpretation of the ideological-critical formation of the concept of American exceptionalism. In fact, the unnamed protagonist in the essay is Louis Hartz. Hartz hoped that his analysis of the history of American political theory and his identification of the concept of a liberal society with its own laws of development might give Americans the "power for transcending itself in American liberalism," and thus held out the slim hope, almost universally ignored by his critics (including Shklar), that a full recognition of American Exceptionalism might bring forth utopian potential never realized in the history of American political theory.

Thus, Shklar's theory and supporting historical narrative is an example, and an exceptionally well-conceived one, of American Exceptionalism of the utopian-critical variety and of the directions to which it can lead. In fact, Shklar lists a series of phenomena that have "contributed to distinguishing American political thought from its cultural neighbors." The list includes features commonly discussed in exceptionalist theory, including the early ballot, federalism, judicial review, the American university system, and chattel slavery.[37] It is the two practices of slavery and democracy, however, that Shklar isolates as the key features that animate American political theory and political science.[38]

Slavery in a "modern constitutional state is truly unique," and America in this respect was "neither a liberal nor a democratic country" until the Civil War amendments. The history, then, of American political theory and science can be told in terms of a movement of possibility or even one in which the redemptive capacities of American culture were always imminent ("embryonic" is Shklar's term), since "at the deepest level all the social sciences are part of a process of democratization."[39] Although Shklar insists that her account allows for historical contingency and even extensive critique ("It need hardly be mentioned that this trend was in no way incompatible with a rich tradition of flailing every aspect of America's political culture"), she concludes that the outcome of this "intellectual adventure" in terms of the victory of democracy was "eventually to be expected."

If Shklar is presenting an account of American Exceptionalism, albeit unacknowledged, how might her supporting historical narrative be rewritten to match her theory? If the following brief analysis is correct, the two experiments that Shklar outlines are irretrievably intertwined in large part because America is by cultural self-definition in a perpetual state of redemption. Shklar's narrative, simplified, reads something like this: the founding produced three political sciences which, though flawed, showed the directions the march to democracy could take; the Jacksonians picked up the torch in another generation; southern political scientists represented a detour through their reconceptualization of tyranny, which was replicated in distilled form by Social Darwinists; modern political science was born in the twentieth century by scientists such as Merriam and Dewey who brought the "democratic tendencies of the social sciences generally and the overt ideology of mainstream American political science in harmony." The narrative I offer, based upon American Exceptionalism as the central structure of political discourse in America, proceeds in this manner:

the founder's political sciences were adaptations to their project of employing American Exceptionalism to advance agendas in which democratic commitments were mixed with goals of control; the Jacksonians can more profitably be assessed, less as democrats than as petit bourgeois in an American political world without aristocrats, whose role in the tyranny-democracy debate is profoundly problematic; the Southern reactionaries were incidentally defeated by Lincoln's political science which was directed against antistatist sentiment through a transformation of Whig doctrine into a formulation of American exceptionalism as creedal reaffirmation; Social Darwinism drew its cultural power not from imbibing elements of Southern fatalism but from offering a conceptualization of individual freedom under conditions of industrialization; modern political science offered a celebration of "America as-is" in the name of scientific planning.

Shklar contends that three founders (Jefferson, Hamilton, Madison) exemplified "three political sciences in America." In fact, Jefferson's "speculative and physiological" method and Madison's "institutional and historical" and Hamilton's "empirical and behavioral" ones seem to uncannily anticipate precisely the schools of American political science today. Shklar goes so far as to suggest that it was Jefferson's close friend Condorcet who applied advanced mathematics to voting in legislative bodies, Colbert who informed Hamilton about administrative science, and Montesquieu whom Madison admired as the "master of the new political science." Shklar's point in suggesting that the contemporary political science—say, of Lowi, Huntington, and Dahl— is present in these founders is to confirm her contention that American political thought has always been "diverse" and "creative" and "complex" and that there is a clear connecting link between current political science and American political thought. "We have in our bitter century learned again," she says, "to appreciate their ideals of freedom, human rights, and justice. The founders have left us not only several ways of trying to make sense of American politics but also an enduring public ethos."[40] Shklar admits that each of these founders (and their respective political sciences) failed to deal with central problems of repression in America, particularly black chattel slavery. But to her, "the truth of the matter is that it is not social science as such but the kind of inquiries we choose that are often questionable." Thus it was not the founders' political sciences that were flawed but "current psychology" and "ideology."[41]

It is certainly true that the founding produced three great distinct models of political science, but a complete account of these projects would include the central role that American Exceptionalism plays in each. It is difficult to underestimate the role that American Exceptionalism played in Jefferson's theory, as we shall outline in more detail in chapter three. Jefferson was so taken with the unique possibilities of the American experiment that in his *Notes on Virginia* he actually applied this model to natural phenomena. Even flora and fauna, in Jefferson's observations, were different (and, for the most part, superior) in America. His selection of the yeoman as the exemplary citizen and agriculture as the exemplary occupation for Americans were adaptations from classical republicanism, but they were also derived from a belief that the availability of land in America and the absence of an aristocracy would produce a new kind of farmer, an American farmer, who had none of the attributes of the European peasantry. Jefferson's belief in moral sense theory propelled him to democratic sentiments in large part because he believed that in America natural sentiment had not been warped by both riches and poverty and religious superstition. He once recommended that young men not study abroad lest they be corrupted by European society. His great foray into partisan politics in 1800 was occasioned by his belief that Federalist "monocrats" plotted the Europeanization of America. Disturbingly ambivalent on the slavery question, Jefferson is also the utopian exceptionalist par excellence.

None of the founders held a more jaded view of the American experiment of 1787 than Alexander Hamilton. Hamilton, in fact, brilliantly and covertly sought to Europeanize the American constitution through his emphasis on judicial review and the presidency as saving remnants of aristocracy. But it was Hamilton's genius to accept the premises of American Exceptionalism in his arguments. In *The Federalist,* he refuted the antifederalist assertion that the presidency was the "fetus of monarchy" (there was "no diadem sparkling" on the president's brow) by arguing that "republican jealousy" required a single executive, and republicans in the past relied too heavily on temporary dictators. Rotation in office was actually an invitation to executive dominance.[42] He argued for a strong industrialized America in "Report on Manufacturers" on the basis of the American dream of economic mobility. Manufacturing would provide employment and a basis for assimilation for future immigrants who hope to "transplant themselves" in America.

Like most of the founders, Madison had come to doubt the utopian conception of American Exceptionalism. America seemed to be traveling down the same troubled road of many other republics. But amidst this general pessimism and sense of historical tragedy is a remark Madison made in *The Federalist* that explains much about the innovative character of the second founding. "Shut your ears," urges Madison in No. 14, to the language of classical republicanism. "Is it not the glory of the people of America, that, whilst they have paid a decent regard to the opinions of former times and nations, they have not suffered a blind veneration of antiquity, for custom or for names, to overrule the suggestions of their own common sense, the knowledge of their own situation, and the lessons of their own experience?"[43]

The "glory of the people of America" has significantly different interpretations in Jefferson, Hamilton, and Madison, but their respective conceptions of political science cannot be appreciated without a consideration of their interpretations and cultural concessions to American Exceptionalism, particularly in terms of their willingness to employ American "newness" as part of their own projects to redeem America. Of course, these explorations of newness provided models of freedom, including explorations of new political and economic structures unimaginable in the "first world." But is it not possible also to contend that it was American Exceptionalism that permitted these founders to disguise repression and that their political science (itself "new" and hence American) served this effort? Jefferson's speculative anthropology permitted him to draw a framework in *Notes on the State of Virginia* that determined that what was not new was not American, conflated European Americans and Native Americans as "young" peoples and refused to analyze African Americans in terms of their original culture, insisting that "we will consider them here. . . where the facts are not apocryphal. . ."[44] Madison's new science of politics permitted him to discard the democracies of antiquity as models and argue that America "can claim the merit of making the discovery of the basis of the unmixed and extensive republic."[45] Hamilton's behaviorialism permitted him to expand on the trope of America as a refuge, in his case as an outlet for the movement of capital (manufacturers would "probably flock from Europe to the United States" under a stable government in America), and at the same time assert that with industrialization "women and children are rendered more useful and the latter more early useful by manufacturing establishments."[46]

But if Shklar's reading of the founders' political science requires a revision when American Exceptionalism is added, her reluctance to acknowledge the theory leads to a serious misreading of political thought in Jacksonian America. After arguing that the failures of her selected founders to address and resolve the problem of race in America were not the result of their respective political science, she turns to this period as revealing for the "study of democratization" since the "vocabulary of American political controversy was transformed." Actually, Shklar grants a great deal to American Exceptionalism when she portrays the Jacksonians as women and men who sought to extend the suffrage and insert the concept of rights "in every democratic sentence" through their attack on "aristocrats" as "citizens who used wealth to acquire an unfair share of political influence."[47] "The European past should be forgotten" is the premise that she uses to characterize the first four decades of the nineteenth century.

But were the Jacksonians the proponents of the democratic experiment, much less the social democrats that Shklar's narrative suggests? Whitman's ode to democracy is marred by racism; Jackson's Native American policy had genocidal proportions; the Democrats' economic policies looked very much like Reaganomics. In fact, it was the Whigs, Shklar's discussion of Choate notwithstanding, who were the party of a national idea, which included at least a debate on slavery, proposals for federal funding of prisons and asylums, and demands for recognition of the humanity of Native Americans.[48] It would be misleading to contend that the Jacksonians were on the side of tyranny in Shklar's narrative of the two American experiments, but some weight must be given to the reformist and democratic conception of Whig political science, which Shklar simply identifies as one which is only preoccupied with protecting property by "building an infrangible wall against the threat of democratic legislation."[49]

More importantly, an American exceptionalist framework would have placed antebellum politics in the context of a unique democratic struggle without an aristocracy. One of the most puzzling aspects of democratic mass movements in America is their ferocious antistatist and localist character, their mixtures of communal generosity and personal ambition, and their language of universal rights and spitefulness toward other groups. While the petit-bourgeois is, as Hartz notes, a "familiar Western type" who has "never been glamorous in Western thought," he becomes magnified almost beyond recognition in America, where his collective self-assertion has the appearance of a national will, especially when he turns to reform and seeks to capture the state in order to destroy it. In this context, it is the upper-bourgeoisie who defends the state apparatus against the immoderate and provincial vision of the shopkeeper. Thus Webster asked in his famous debate with Hayne: "Can there be nothing in government except for the exercise of mere control? Can nothing be done without corruption? What is positively beneficent, whatever is actively good, whatever opens channels of intercourse, augments population, enhances the value of property, and diffuses knowledge—must all this be rejected and reprobated as an obnoxious policy?"[50]

If Shklar had given theoretical recognition to American Exceptionalism she would have not only recognized the redemptive project entailed in Whig political thought and the exceptional character of the second party system as a grand battlefield between two enormously enlarged sections of a national bourgeoisie, but she would have been in a position to assess what is certainly the most extraordinary redemptive project in American political thought: Lincoln's reconceptualization of America as a nation.

Like many students of American political thought, Shklar is fascinated with the southern defense of slavery and, like others, pays more attention to Fitzhugh and others than did antebellum northerners. On this point as well she employs American exceptionalism in her narrative. Southern political theory was an "indigenous authoritarian ideology that was utterly unique as was the slavery it encompassed."[51] But part of the uniqueness of the Southern defense of slavery lies in the extent to which people like Fitzhugh were impelled to argue for the Europeanization of America. This forceful rejection of American Exceptionalism did create a intriguing cultural opening. Fitzhugh even offered some prescient observations on the authoritarian base of European socialism when he recommended slavery as the "oldest, the best and most common form of Socialism." It is Hartz, Shklar's theoretical opponent, who described this effort as the "Southern reactionary enlightenment" and claims that its theorists initiated "the great imaginative moment in American political thought, the moment when America almost got out of itself, as it were, and looked with some objectivity on the liberal formula it has known since birth."[52] Yet, however unique was the moment (which Shklar highlights in her Manichean narrative of the two experiments), the South achieved this strange enlightenment through a total self-marginalization in terms of American culture. Ironically, it was Calhoun who covered his racism with elaborate tropes on the threat of majority rule and respectful citations of Madison and Jefferson and argued that the concurrent majority was "truly and emphatically American, without example and parallel," who was able to elicit a Northern response.

If the South could not find the political vocabulary to "redeem" the North in its experiment to create a society that Fitzhugh characterized as one in which "virtue loses all her loveliness," Lincoln succeeded in implementing his own project. It is difficult to present adequately, even in outline, Lincoln's conception of political science. He certainly grasped the nature and significance of ambition, as had Hamilton, and he certainly grasped the cultural power of Jeffersonian natural right. He also grasped the nature of the institutional limitations on leadership advanced by Madison. But Lincoln radically transformed all these visions of political science. While he claimed "all power to Jefferson" and paid extravagant obeisance to the founders, Henry Clay was Lincoln's exemplar. Yet his vision was quite different from the Whig program for an American system of roads, canals, and tariffs because Lincoln gave the national idea a religious reconceptualization. America as a nation was engaged in a unique experiment not only in substance (it was a nation dedicated to the proposition that *all men were created equal*) but in plan (it was a nation dedicated to the *proposition* that all men were created equal). Should America depart significantly from its own creedal self-definition, it would cease to exist as an entity, and only through pursuit of a path of trial, rebirth, and dedication could it be recaptured. Magnificent in its inventiveness as a formulation that galvanized the North on a issue of cultural ambivalence and as an exemplar for Americans who confronted subsequent crises, Lincolnian political science, with its hugely amplified employment of the "charm and terror" of American Exceptionalism, nevertheless raises questions about the extent to which other policy disputes when translated into a cosmology of national redemption close or expand national debate and increase or decrease democracy.[53]

Lincoln's formulation, however, collapsed when the Civil War ended. The ideological features of a liberal society reasserted themselves in the reconstruction experiment. Although people such as Stevens and Phillips outlined the radical steps necessary to re-make the South, public opinion flinched. This failure of nerve emerged less from a selective absorption of antebellum Southern sociological fatalism, as Shklar suggests, than from a rededication to Lockean liberalism as the appropriate path for African American redemption. For example, the *Nation* argued that the black freeman must now travel on the same "dusty and ragged highway of competition" as other citizens were compelled to do. The editors, surveying reconstruction in South Carolina, concluded: "This is . . . socialism."

The remnant of Lincoln's political science that did survive the post-war period, however, was his elucidation of centrality of economic mobility in America, which he frequently charged was being challenged by the expansion of slavery. To Shklar, the theoretical systematization of economic growth and corporate consolidation was a singularly problematic enterprise in America. She notes William Graham Sumner's reluctance to embrace Social Darwinism without reservation. But this aspect of her narrative misses the extent to which theorists such as Sumner sought to "Americanize" the new ideology. American Social Darwinists were reluctant to accept Herbert Spencer's position on the dysfunctional consequences of charity and insisted upon the utility of public schooling and democratic institutions. Sumner's repeated eulogies for the "forgotten man" reached theoretical proportions in an 1889 essay in which he evoked Jacksonian sentiment to defend his Darwinism. Government regulation would only create a "plutocracy" worse than the present situation: "the contest between numbers and wealth is nothing but a contest between two sets of lawyers, one drawing acts in behalf of the state, and the other devising means of defeating those acts in behalf of their clients." To Sumner this was a "lamentable contest," for the rich would not only always win but also would in the process create new organizations "half political and half industrial."[54] But the real Americanization of Darwinism occurred at the level of popular culture. In general terms, men such as Russell Conwell, Booker T. Washington, and Horatio Alger, Jr. emphasized less the systemic constraints than the opportunities still available for Americans. One of Alger's characters reminds his readers that the difference between the "rich merchant" and the "ragged fellow" is not in natural ability but in the fact that "the one has used his ability as a stepping stone to success. . . ." To identify arguments such as these as a "sociological fatalism" which illustrates how "the South won the war of ideas," is to miss completely the charm of this celebratory form of American Exceptionalism which was totally absent from the oddly Europeanized political science of the "reactionary Enlightenment."

In Shklar's narrative the culmination of the democratic experiment rests with the birth of political science as a discipline devoted to the construction of a "meaningful democratic theory that took change for granted." But it is in this context of Social Darwinism, which gave scientific discourse a privileged character and a new corporate order that placed new obstacles and some opportunities before the American upper-middle class, that modern political science was born. Without a nationally sponsored university nor any significant professionalized civil service as existed in Europe, American political scientists searched for a base from which to study politics. Their commitment to liberalism has been nearly unanimous but so too has been their commitment to function as a scientific elite for American society. The virtual melding of these two commitments left a much more ambiguous legacy in terms of the democratic experiment than Shklar implies. For American political science has often actively defined its goals in terms of a celebratory interpretation of American Exceptionalism.

Modern political science was still in its infancy as a discipline when the Great Depression challenged this largely unstated premise. Many writers explicitly rejected American Exceptionalism and repeated George Soule's question, "Why should the Russians have all the fun?" It is very loosely within this spirit of setting new parameters for political science that FDR in 1932 spoke of the need for "bold, persistent experimentation" in public policy. Writing in the depth of the Depression, Adolph Berle assured readers that a planned society would still be an American one: "If . . . we were to adopt the Russian Soviet system entire, it would look a good deal more like the Rotary Club or the four railway brotherhoods than like the Moscow Soviet. . . ."[55] John Dewey focused his attack on America as "United States, Incorporated" in *Individualism: Old And New*, serialized in the *New Republic* in 1929 and 1930, and repeated Lincoln's warning that a "house divided" could not stand. The America of the Lynd's Middletown was dead and a only concerted effort in planning could redeem the nation. While he expressed admiration for the imagination and resourcefulness of the Soviets, Dewey's new "public" constituted an attempt to rescue the "true American individualism" that had been "obscured and crowded out" by corporate priorities, which were legitimized through "the greatest flood of mass suggestion that any people has ever experienced. . . ."[56]

Although constantly frustrated by the eclecticism of Roosevelt, American political scientists theorized from the Depression a historical opportunity to merge power with intellect and to create a new American political science in which public policy would be a rational response to the systemic inadequacies of both American culture and American institutions. The experiences of World War II and the emergence of the Cold War radically altered this brief moment of critical-utopian exceptionalism. American political scientists arrived in their theoretical adulthood in a generation that Daniel Bell called "twice-born."[57] After beginning their political lives filled with faith and hope, the Holocaust and Stalinism created in his generation a new vision of "pessimism, evil, tragedy and despair." But American political science as a discipline did not dwell so much on evil and despair. Instead, it focused on the inadequacies of democratic *theory* and presented a redefined redemptive mission of science. In the heyday of the behavioral era, there was a veritable blossoming of theories that explained both the functionality of limited political participation and the exceptional nature of the American polity. Robert Dahl spoke for a generation of political scientists when he said that "this strange hybrid, the normal American political system, is not for export to others," but it is a "relatively efficient system . . . for maintaining peace in a restless and immoderate people. . . ."[58]

There were challenges to the kinds of political science that began their investigations, as did Prothro and Griggs, with the statement that "our research design was based on the major assumption that the United States was a democracy."[59] A diverse group of political scientists in exile from Europe attempted to examine rather than simply assert American Exceptionalism. Leo Strauss argued that the positivist science of politics could erode, rather than maintain, the exceptionalist nature of the American polity. Hannah Arendt examined the exceptional character of the American Revolution and Founding as well as the lost opportunities for political freedom. Herbert Marcuse presented a horrific model of America as an exceptional "totalitarian" culture. This project of standing outside America through an examination of American Exceptionalism was pursued, of course, by Louis Hartz, who closed *The Liberal Tradition in America* with the question, "Can a people 'born equal' ever understand peoples elsewhere that have become so? Can it ever understand itself?"[60] C. Wright Mills created a ferocious reaction in American political science when he challenged its methods and argued that through the Cold War and corporate hegemony America's Jacksonian citizenry had lost its self-confidence. Antebellum America, composed of a "community of publics" with "no authoritarian center," had lost its sense of citizenship and had become a "mass."[61]

Shklar mentions the civil rights movement in her narrative, but it is impossible to connect American political science to this effort for the simple fact that the discipline did not offer a philosophy (or science) of citizenship. The re-examination of American Exceptionalism offered by both King and Malcolm X and the assertion of citizenship offered in the "Port Huron Statement" were undertaken outside the *geisteswissenschaften* of American political science. In fact, from its inception American political science has been characterized by an equivocal, if not hostile, relationship to social movements, particularly those that were seen to challenge its modernist episteme.[62]

The historical narrative offered by Shklar speaks to two distinct American experiments, one liberal and one illiberal, each competing for the American mind. Sometimes her narrative suggests that the struggle is actually animated by the conflict between the two projects. Who could better appreciate the absence of freedom than the Virginian slaveholder or the Jacksonian tradesperson who could see the chasm that separated the African American from the democratic experiment? And, by implication, who could better appreciate this dialectic than those in a position to theorize and then implement its transcendence? But if the addenda above are correct, one can see that a culture that gives voice to monumental aspirations of wealth and individual transformation historically justifies both tyranny and liberation in scores of intricate combinations. Each theoretical act of redemption on the part of American political science, from the competing conceptions of the founders to contemporary formulations, assumes that injustice is provisional and remediable either through individual rededication and/or elite reform. This pattern of redemption does not exhaust ways in which liberal society incorporates or contains both oppression and freedom in its discourse, but Shklar participates in this project by ignoring the character of resistance to, and redefinition of, elite sponsored redemptive ventures by the American demos. This is not to say that the relationship between both political theory and political science and social movements can ever be perfectly, or even roughly, synchronized. But an unacknowledged involvement in the cultural project of American Exceptionalism not only does not illuminate these antagonisms but secludes them.

Shklar ends her essay with the observation that if one were to criticize American political theory "it should not be that it is Oedipally attached to liberalism" but that "it failed to understand itself and lacked the imagination to project a plausibly better future." Yet if there is any central cultural motif to American culture it is the belief in newness and its capacity to restore or modernize itself. Since Shklar's account so reflects this disposition ("If we can learn to do better, it is because democracy is itself dynamic"), we need more than ever ask the question: Can a culture that so firmly and axiomatically believes in its own redemptive powers ever redeem itself?

Conclusion

Shklar closes her narrative by contending that the present historical moment represents a risorgimento of American political theory. "We no longer feel compelled to despise the values expressed in the language of rights, justice liberty, and consent with which American political theory began." While she insists that there is "no homogeneity and no straight line in our history at all," she believes that "our end was our beginning." Indeed, this assessment is possible because Shklar's redemption of political thought is itself a version of American Exceptionalism. In fact, her account illustrates how smoothly a critical exceptionalism slides into a celebratory one. For what could be more exceptionalist than the premise that America represents a unique experiment brought to Hegelian-like fulfillment from the "intellectual germs" of the founders and was redeemed historically through constant struggle? And what could be more American exceptionalist than the belief that the triumph of democracy is really not an American idea but a universal idea working its way through humanity with America as its world carrier? In fact, in this present historical moment when the Marxist idea is in eclipse and truly conservative criticism appears quixotic, what looks more universal, more "profound" than the American experiment, and what looks more archaic than the "endless Jeremiad about the absence of socialism and conservatism"?

Jameson's account in this regard represents an antipodal project since he hopes to seclude American Exceptionalism from his explanation by way of theorizing a "third stage" of international economic development, thus preserving his own narrative of resistance to capital that identifies a common theoretical thread to the past. Thus—like Shklar—for Jameson, America, in what may be the most hegemonic moment in its history, is reduced, erased, and (re)placed, not as an actor in a grand democratic experiment but as a temporary locus for the emergence of a new world system. Jameson acknowledges that some readers might find an *Americanocentricism* in his account, but since he places the engine of the third stage in the concept of a new stage of capital, America (or Americanocentricism) is only a contingent historical object, which is slight compared to the power of the new stage itself.

Despite the flaws in both these formulations, the accounts of Jameson and Shklar nevertheless show us a route to explore America Exceptionalism. For both writers illustrate a pattern common to all

American texts. That is, they both involve a strategy that acknowledges and secludes America in terms of newness. The Shklar/Jameson strategy is to attempt to capture America as sign—late capital/democracy—and attach newness to the sign rather than to America itself. Thus America becomes the hidden source of the new in both projects. By placing America in a narrative of the unfolding of the democratic idea or of a new stage of capital, both writers capture newness in terms broader that America itself and thus believe they have avoided the "oldness" ("parochialism" or "uniformity") of American Exceptionalism. But by doing so Shklar becomes a celebratory utopian exceptionalist and Jameson a critical ideological one and thus they continue a project that preserves and extends the exceptionalist idea in American political thought.

Yet while these two contemporary critics of American Exceptionalism illustrate the basic pattern of American exceptionalist texts, the interaction between America and the old and the new is quite varied. Thus we set out to look at a series of exceptional texts to see how in more detail we are "what we are" by how we talk.

Notes

1 "On Habits of the Heart" in Charles H. Reynolds and Ralph V. Norman, eds., *Community in America* (Berkeley: University of California Press, 1988), 111.

2 *Ibid.*, 109–11.

3 *Ibid.*, 110.

4 *Ibid.*, 111.

5 Harry S. Stout, *The New England Soul: Preaching and Religious Culture in Colonial New England* (New York: Oxford University Press, 1986), p. 71.

6 Lee to Patrick Henry, cited in Gordon Wood, *The Creation of the American Republic, 1776–1787* (Chapel Hill: University of North Carolina Press, 1969), 53.

7 "Common Sense" in *The Essential Thomas Paine*, ed. Sidney Hook (New York: New American Library, 1969), 39.

8 Cotton Mather, *Magnalia Christi Americana*, ed. Kenneth B. Murdock (Cambridge: Harvard University Press, 1977), 213.

9 Jefferson to Bishop Madison (1785) in Adrienne Koch and William Peden, eds., *The Life and Selected Writings of Thomas Jefferson* (New York: Modern Library, 1944), 389.

10 Jameson, "On Habits of the Heart," 107.

11 "On Habits of the Heart,"109; Fredric Jameson, "Interview," *Diacritics*, 12 (1982), 80, 85.

12 Edmund S. Morgan, *The Puritan Dilemma* (Boston: Little, Brown and Co., 1958), 155; John Adams, "Defence of the Constitutions," in Charles F. Adams, ed., *Works of John Adams*, IV (Boston, 1856), 392; Paine, "Common Sense," 56.

13 Fredric Jameson, *Postmodernism, or, The Cultural Logic of Late Capitalism* (Durham: Duke University Press, 1991), 35–36.

14 *Ibid.*, xx.

15 *Ibid.*

16 "Periodizing the Sixties" in Jameson, *The Ideology of Theory:Essays 1971–1986* (Minneapolis: University of Minnesota Press, 1988), 178–208.

17 *Ibid.*, 188.

18 *Ibid.*, 189.

19 Irving Howe, "New Styles in Leftism," in ed. Howe, *Beyond the New Left* (New York, 1970), 20; Staughton Lynd, *Intellectual Origins of American Radicalism* ((New York: Pantheon, 1968).

20 "Port Huron Statement" in James Miller, *"Democracy is in the Streets"* (New York: Simon and Schuster, 1987), 332; "Weatherman Songbook" in *Weatherman*, ed. Harold James (New York: Ramparts, 1970), 355.

21 Regis Debray, "A Modest Contribution," *New Literary Review* 115 (1979), 58.

22 Jameson, "Periodizing the Sixties," 185.

23 *Ibid.*, 208.

24 *Ibid.*, 194.

25 *Ibid.*, 179.

26 Jameson, *Postmodernism*, 50.

27 *Ibid.*

28 "Periodizing the Sixties," 208.

29 See: Peter Gay, *A Loss of Mastery* (New York: Vintage, 1968), 53–87 for a focus on the *Magnalia* as the "rages of a defeated man."

30 Mather, *Magnalia*, 90–92.

31 *Ibid.*, 165, 207.

32 *Ibid.*, 55, 56.

33 *Ibid.*, 116–23. In Mather's periodization God did not challenge the sovereignty of Satan over America until three conditions were met: the "resurrection of literature" in the fifteenth century, the "opening of America" by explorers, and the "Reformation of Religion." (117–18).

34 *Ibid.*, 4.

35 In *American Citizenship* (Cambridge: Harvard University Press, 1991) Shklar defines her position as one that rejects the notion that America has marched down a "straight liberal highway" and emphasizes the extent to which "antiliberal dispositions" have successfully asserted themselves (p.13) as if the characterization of America as a liberal society constitutes the only definitional boundary of American Exceptionalism.

36 Shklar, "Redeeming Political Theory," 3–4.

37 *Ibid.*, 4.

38 Jon Roper, *Democracy and Its Critics: Anglo-American Democratic Thought in the Nineteenth Century* (London: Unwin Hyman, 1989), argues that, in addition to the slavery question, the arguments over democratization were

different in England, where culture was regarded as a defense against democracy, and liberty contained strong aristocratic resonances rather than individualistic or republican ones.

39 Shklar, "Redeeming Political Theory," 4.

40 Ibid., 8.

41 Ibid., 6.

42 *The Federalist Papers*, ed. Clinton Rossiter (New York: New American Library, 1961), 407, 423, 437–38.

43 Ibid., 104.

44 Thomas Jefferson, *Notes on the State of Virginia*, ed., William Peden (New
York: Norton, 1972), 139.

45 *Federalist Papers*, 101.

46 *Selected Writings of Alexander Hamilton*, ed., Morton J. Frisch (Washington, DC: American Enterprise Institute, 1985), 290–91.

47 Shklar, "Redeeming American Political Theory," 9.

48 The evacuation of the Cherokees was attacked by Edward Everett as a "gigan-
tic crime." See Daniel Walker Howe, *The Political Culture of the American
Whigs* (Chicago: University of Chicago Press, 1979) who discusses the Whig
agenda in redemptive terms and emphasizes the "modernist" aspects of their
project.

49 Shklar, "Redeeming American Political Theory," 10.

50 Daniel Webster, "Speeches in the Senate of the United States on the Resolution of Mr. Foote" in *Speeches and Forensic Arguments*, ed. Daniel Webster,
vol. I (Boston: Perkins, Marvin and Co., 1835), 366–67.

51 Shklar, "Redeeming American Political Theory," 11.

52 Hartz, *The Liberal Tradition in America*, 176.

53 See, for example, Philip Abbott, *The Exemplary Presidency* (Amherst: University of Massachusetts Press, 1990), ch. 8 on the policy implications of
FDR's use of Lincolnian political science.

54 William Graham Sumner, "The Conflict of Plutocracy and Democracy" in *The
Essays of William Graham Sumner*, eds. Albert Galloway Keller and Maurice
R. Davis (New Haven: Yale University Press, 1934), vol. II, 230.

55 Adolph Berle, "The Social Economics of the New Deal," *New York Times
Magazine*, October 29, 1933, 19.

56 John Dewey, *Individualism Old and New* (New York: Capricorn, 1962), 42.

57 Daniel Bell, *The End of Ideology* (Glencoe: Free Press, 1960), 28.

58   Robert A. Dahl, *A Preface to Democratic Theory* (Chicago: University of Chicago Press, 1956), 151.

59   James W. Prothro and Charles H. Grigg, "Fundamental Principles of Democracy: Bases of Agreement and Disagreement," *Journal of Politics* 22 (1960), 282.

60   Hartz, *The Liberal Tradition in America*, 309.

61   Mills' classic statement appeared in *The Power Elite* (New York: Oxford University Press, 1956), but his conclusion was in large part premised upon his belief that the Jacksonian middle class had lost its property, its community, and political independence as outlined in *White Collar* (New York: Oxford University Press, 1951).

62   See especially: Dorothy Ross, *The Origins of American Social Science* (Cambridge: Cambridge University Press, 1991), 3–21; Christopher Lasch, *The True and Only Heaven* (New York: Norton, 1991), 455–75.

Chapter 3

The Beloved Text
America's Multiple Newness in Jefferson's *Notes on the State of Virginia*

The two contemporary critics we have just analyzed attempt to deny exceptionalism through complex invocations of newness. Jefferson's project is a perfect opposite. Admittedly, there is a sense of the old—quaint might be a better word—in Thomas Jefferson's *Notes on the State of Virginia*. But this is an oldness (quaintness) that looks backward to the 1780s. Large portions of Jefferson's science are certainly flawed. He refused to accept the principle of species extinction and advanced the theory that fossil shells were "mineral simulacra."[1] The very scope of his interests and his willingness to examine and theorize on matters of geography, paleontology, anatomy, and mineralogy cast him in the role of the amateur in our age of corporate science. This volume on America begins with a provincialist introduction ("Virginia is bounded on the East by the Atlantic . . .") that has always infuriated his later nationalist detractors. His agrarian warnings about industry appear to make his usefulness limited in a nation that has fitfully accepted the Hamiltonian vision of America. And, of course, there is his racism. Passages in Query XIV on racial aesthetics make even the historically sophisticated wince.

Yet even these archaic features of the *Notes* are overwhelmed by Jefferson's central object: the portrayal of America in all its facets—natural, cultural, political, and economic—in terms of newness. That America was exceptional in both the senses of "different" and "extraordinary" because it was new involved a degree of creativity that is hidden from us in large part because we still see America in this respect through Jefferson's eyes. The axiomatic character of Jefferson's projection of America leads us to focus so readily upon its quaintness and, more importantly, secludes from us his strategy of using newness as a tactic of enclosure. For, to Jefferson, what was not new was not American.

The complexity of America as new is also submerged by the *Notes* as a text itself. There is a sense in which the *Notes* appears to be a work already "deconstructed." It is composed of a set of "queries" by Marbois and only slightly revised by Jefferson. Some of them continue for many pages and others (like Query XIX) only for a few words. There is no introduction and no conclusion. Thus what has become a recognized American tradition of determining a "politically correct" Jeffersonian position by citing passages from some letters and excising others, is not in the least challenged by any reference to the *Notes* as a central text.[2] In fact, the *Notes* is eminently suited to this same enterprise. Buried in Query VI on "Productions, Mineral, Vegetable and Animal," with its list of "Birds of Virginia" and discussion of shell formation, is the Enlightenment inspired proverb, "Ignorance is preferable to error; and he is less remote from the truth who believes nothing, than he who believes what is wrong." Need an agrarian quote? Take "Those who labour in the earth are the chosen people of God." A substantiation of religious freedom? There is: "it does me no injury for my neighbor to say there are twenty gods, or no god." Need evidence of racism among the founders? See Query XIV. Need evidence of the negative consequences of racism? See Query XVII.

This is not to say that there have not been those who have not reconstructed this deconstructed text. Henry Steele Commager has argued that despite those first lines that begin "almost artlessly," the *Notes* is more than "a guide book, even an encyclopedia," but is "an agenda of the American Enlightenment." Commager notes the fascination with the classical world of Rome and Greece, but contends that this too was part of the Enlightenment project.[3] For Garrett Sheldon the "center" of Jefferson's "classical republican theory" was his devotion to the ward system, which makes its appearance in the *Notes* in Query XIV as Jefferson discusses his plans for education in the new republic.[4] The republican perspective, while it certainly admits a variety of emphases, contains at least a tinge of Enlightenment critique, focusing as it does on the perils of progress and reliance on homogeneity, which are both apparent in Query VIII. And it is in this "text" that Jefferson, the religious skeptic, speaks of the probability of "supernatural interference." For Leo Marx, the core of the *Notes* is

Jefferson's application of the classical pastoral to America: "The symbolic setting favored by Jefferson . . . resembles the Virgilian landscape of reconciliation . . ."[5] The republican ethos placed an enormous moral weight upon the primacy of public space. The pastoral tradition, however, while it was no less committed to rural life, conceptualized the ideal into a dialogue about the relative merits of the public and private in a highly stylized utopian discourse. For Edward Dumbald, the unifying feature of the *Notes* is the persona of Jefferson as "a sightseer."[6] Although Jefferson frequently complained about the burdens and temptations of travel, it was his role of "tourist" that animates his responses to the inquiries of Marbois, and the question arises as to what is the relationship of this persona to the other foci of the *Notes*.

Jacques Derrida has argued that a genre always is in the process of deconstruction.[7] But in the case of the *Notes*, the question that constantly arises is what is the genre within which Jefferson is writing? If the *Notes* is a text of scientific enlightenment, why is there the "highly figurative, mythopoetic language"[8] that not only appears in Query XIX but in the midst of the description of the Natural Bridge in Query V? Or to put the question inversely, if the *Notes* is a pastoral, why is this form so thickly encased with a description of the Virginia landscape in terms of scientific inquiry? If the *Notes* is a commentary on postrevolutionary republicanism, why does Jefferson write so rarely in the passionate language of the patriot as he does at the close of Query XII ("Our situation is indeed perilous")? If the *Notes* is a tour guide, why does Jefferson depart so frequently from the voice of the local and why does he so recommend a place given his fear that immigration will produce a "heterogeneous, incoherent, distracted mass"?

What if, given both the credibility of each of these reconstructions and the difficulty in assigning any one of them exclusive status in which other genres are fully absorbed or synthesized, we proceeded from the premise that the *Notes on the State of Virginia* is not one text but four: an exercise in Enlightenment science; a statement of postrevolutionary republicanism; a pastoral; a tour guide? It is certainly not inconceivable that a text combines genres. The great works of Western political thought contain competing and contradictory genres ground into new syntheses that often separate in varying degrees under criticism. What appears remarkable about the *Notes*, however, is how these genres seem to coexist. It is also certainly possible that the *Notes* as a complete text is incoherent, a product of

Jefferson's haste or eclecticism. But if this is the case, we need to ask why Jefferson and the *Notes* have held such fascination for subsequent generations of Americans. Perhaps the answer lies in the fact that Jefferson employed the concept of newness to transform these four genres in a fashion that permitted him to leave each of them intact and that this perspective can illuminate Jefferson's project in a way that none of these uniform genre interpretations do.

The Scientific Text

Commager argues that the *Notes* as genre is a "typical Enlightenment inquiry" which "takes its place, effortlessly, in the mainstream of Enlightenment literature . . . that addressed itself to the exploration of Climate, or the interaction of Nature and Man, and the literature that embraced Civilization, or the social, political, and moral institutions of Man." Thus Jefferson the philosophe had no need to revise or alter the queries of Marbois, the philosophe. The unpretentiousness of so many of the queries was itself part of the Enlightenment genre. "Every philosophe, on both sides of the water, knew how to deal with this sort of thing; after all just consider what the philosophe did with the innocuous subjects assigned them in the great Encyclopedie!"[9] Yet if we separate the queries which are primarily "a guide book," and reserve them as a separate genre of the tourist text, Jefferson's Enlightenment project is evident in portions of only nine of the twenty-three queries.

In his persona as scientist, Jefferson gathered data systematically, engaged in his own experiments, reported on those of others, and undertook theoretical speculation. These activities appear most prominently in Query VI, "Productions Animal, Vegetable and Mineral," in which Jefferson challenges the arguments of Buffon. Buffon's argument that animal life in America was "inferior" was actually itself a version of American Exceptionalism. Animals common to both continents were smaller in the New World; those peculiar to America were small; domesticated animals degenerated in the American environment; there were fewer species in America. Jefferson patiently unpacked Buffon's hypotheses, pointing out that Buffon was contradictory in stating that growth was dependent upon heat and the absence of moisture. He offered tables comparing relative weight of quadrupeds in both continents which disputed Buffon. He engaged in a complicated quest to determine the nature and size of the American mammoth and then reported his queries to Native Americans; he also examined skeletal remains and speculated upon its apparent extinction. Jefferson concluded: "But to whatever animal we ascribe these remains, it is certain such a one existed in America, and that it has been the largest of all terrestrial beings."[10]

Jefferson's refutations of Buffon thrilled his American contemporaries.[11] But there was more import to Jefferson's scientific success than a vindication of an incipient nation's pride. For by challenging the Enlightenment philosophes on their own terms, Jefferson embarked upon a project that split the Enlightenment in two. Many philosophes saw Jefferson's project as a confirmation of their own efforts. But if we compare Jefferson's position to a European schism that was to occur over one hundred years later, itself another act in the Enlightenment project, we can gain some appreciation for Jefferson's achievement. After the October revolution, the Communists of the new Soviet Union portrayed their experiment as more advanced and more deserving of support than those of the Socialists. They were creating a new Soviet man while others were engaged only in speculation and reform. So too Jefferson, the American philosophe, was claiming that the Enlightenment experiment was being played out in the New World.[12] So too Jefferson spoke alternately hopefully about Europe's progress (in catching up to America in regard to politics) and disdainfully about European obstacles.

If it seems as if too much weight is being placed upon the refutation of the more quaint aspects of Enlightenment natural science, one has only to review the lengths to which Jefferson carried his argument. His successful refutation showed that he, the American, was the better scientist, who was more theoretically rigorous (how could the great Buffon so confuse the identification of dependent and independent variables?) and who accepted only reliable data ("it does not appear" that Buffon had "measured, or seen" animals in America or inquired into the scientific methods of the travelers he cited). In the slash and burn style of scientific competition, Jefferson "praised" his foe in regard to a "single" sentence: "I love as much a person who corrects me in error as another who teaches me truth . . ."[13]

If it was American science that uncovered faulty European speculation in regard to animal size and weight, had Buffon and others also been misled in their views of "man in America, whether aboriginal or transplanted"? In answering this question, Jefferson engaged in a strategy that was at once enormously bold and monumentally significant for American history. He proposed a project of racial science, employing the same methods he used in regard to quadrupeds, to refute the European philosophes. Simply put, Jefferson identified two groups as "new" and hence American, the Native American and the European white, and relegated African Americans to the status of un-American.

Commentators have, of course, long noted Jefferson's pained discussions of race in America. Without fully excusing Jefferson's remarks, some degree of exculpation is often granted on the basis of two points: his firm contention that all races are merely varieties of the same species and his equally firm contention that the potential of African Americans is an empirical question. Thus, so one assessment goes, Jefferson's adoption of a monogenetic account of humanity and his Baconian commitment to assessing racial capacities empirically and with "great diffidence" is an illustration of the power of the Enlightenment Jefferson over Jefferson the Southern planter. For example, Daniel Boorstin concludes that Jefferson, who "had been reared in a society where there seemed little to confirm the equal talents of the Negro," nevertheless stuck to the Linnaean system despite temptations to introduce some category between humans as a single species and varieties introduced by environment. He concludes: "He was not sure enough of the irrelevance of the Negro's color to assign him the same ancient parents as the white man; yet he was too much of an equalitarian to suggest that the Negro might have been created a distinct species."[14]

On the other hand, some readers find a lack of good will in Jefferson's notes on race. There is a willingness to consider environmental factors in regard to moral behavior on Jefferson's part ("That disposition to theft with which they have been branded, must be ascribed to their situation, and not to any depravity of the moral sense") but reluctance to give much weight to such factors in regard to cultural achievement. Thus Jefferson attempts to make the African American slave morally responsible but raises great doubts about his intellectual capacities.[15]

Both of these assessments miss an even more daring maneuver on Jefferson's part. Marbois had not asked a question about slavery in Virginia. While it is unlikely that one could ignore any treatment of an institution so central to the state's economy, Jefferson still had the freedom to include his analysis in any number of Marbois' queries and to determine the relative length he would devote to the subject. Slavery is a prominent theme of the *Notes* but discussion occurs in Query

XIII and Query XVIII. Query VI, on minerals, vegetables, and animals, which contains his response to Buffon and Raynal on the effect of the American environment on human animals, includes no mention of slavery and very little discussion of African Americans, despite Jefferson's stated intention that his observations are based upon "man, white, red, black."[16] It does, however, include an extensive defense of the biological fitness and the cultural potential of both Native Americans and white European settlers. To Jefferson, the Native American is brave, "affectionate to his children, careful of them, and indulgent in the extreme," and faithful in friendship, the exact opposite of Buffon's conclusions. Those characteristics which Jefferson recognizes as critique, both biological and cultural, are dismissed as environmentally caused. Thus the alleged lack of sexual "ardor" and relative physical smallness is traced to the harshness of primitive life. Jefferson admits the servile status of women but contends that this "unjust drudgery" is "the case with every barbarous people."[17] He positively exults in the status of Buffon's observations as comparable to the "fables of Aesop" when he reports that the French philosophe's notes on lack of body hair is the result of cultural practice. (Native Americans plucked their hair, Jefferson informs us.) As to the "genius" of the Native American, Jefferson proudly points to Chief Logan's address to Lord Dunmore, which he compares to the speeches of Demosthenes and Cicero.

Having dismissed biological causation in terms of Buffon's theory of heat and moisture and having asserted that cultural correlations of the Native American in terms of the European are possible, Jefferson proceeds to compare native peoples to the Europeans north of the Alps at the time of the Roman invasions, carefully noting that the greater population of the latter would "multiply the chances of improvement." "How many good poets, how many able mathematicians, how many great inventors in the arts and sciences, had Europe North of the Alps then produced?" asks Jefferson as he reminds his readers that even under more favorable conditions it still took sixteen centuries to produce a Newton.[18]

Buffon's charge that Native Americans were a cultureless people was replicated by Raynal who contended that European Americans had "not yet produced one good poet, one able mathematician, one man of genius in a single art or a single science." Jefferson responds with the names of Washington, Franklin, and Rittenhouse as rebuttals that "this reproach is unjust as it is unkind." In challenging the European Enlightenment assessment of America, Jefferson had conflated the categories of Native American and European American. Biologically, the former was "on the same module with the 'Homo sapiens Euopeanaeus.'" Native Americans were a preliterate society but from Jefferson's perspective both groups were compared culturally with early northern European culture. European-Americans, like Native American peoples, were "but a child of yesterday."[19]

It certainly would have been plausible for Jefferson to group European Americans and African Americans as transplanted peoples, comparing their relative achievements and biological aspects under the very different conditions of their New World environment. That Jefferson undertook a quite different strategy, grouping Native Americans and European Americans as dual examples in exploring the question of "whether nature has enlisted herself as a Cis or Trans-Atlantic partisan," was especially significant since this bracketing of red-white/black placed African Americans beyond his defense of America and, in fact, placed them beyond his definition of America itself as a subject of scientific discourse.

The absence of African Americans in Query VI is especially noteworthy when one considers their inclusion in Query XIV ("Laws"). Jefferson still treats race in scientific terms in this discussion and includes the same standards he offered in Query VI on biological features and cultural achievement. But the mixture of empirical evidence and speculation has been secluded from his definition of America and its scientific defense against the French philosophes, and now becomes a legal problem. The query begins in Jefferson's tourist mode. He describes the Virginia legal system, including a discussion of poor laws, asserting in terms of the latter that he had "never yet saw a Native American begging in the streets and highways."[20] The discussion next shifts to the republican text as Jefferson notes that "many of the laws which were in force during the monarchy being relative to that government, or inculcating principles inconsistent with republicanism" required revision. The first subject of the plan of revisal which Jefferson takes up is slavery. He notes that the bill did not include a plan for slave emancipation but reports that an amendment has been prepared to be offered to the legislature. The plan includes the education of slaves and a plan for colonization in which an equal number of free whites were to arrive to take their place.

Jefferson poses the question, "Why not retain and incorporate blacks into the state, and thus save the expense of supplying, by importation of white settlers, the vacancies they will leave?"[21] He lists "deep rooted prejudices" on the part of whites and "ten thousand recollections" of injuries on the part of African Americans as part of his justification and also includes a biological assertion concerning the "the real distinctions which nature has made."[22] Defenders of Jefferson often remark that he ends his discussion with the conclusion that racial inferiority "must be hazarded with great diffidence" and his insistence upon a monogenetic account of race, but only if one insists that Jefferson's commitment to deportation rests with racial antagonisms caused by slavery and not upon biological racism ("the real distinctions which nature has made") can one find some kind of escape hatch.

The entire thrust of the material between the presentation of the revisal plan of deportation and the conclusion works to separate Native Americans and European Americans from African Americans. Jefferson's focus upon color itself is not technically related to biological differences since he is not sure about its origins in nature. Yet he is not only convinced of its significance ("And is this difference of no importance?") but draws a graded account of color among red and white ("fine mixtures" and "greater or less suffusions"), which he counterpoints to the "eternal monotony" of black. He had insisted upon comparing Native Americans to early northern Europeans in Query VI. Here he not only refuses to make the same comparison but argues that the evaluation of culture must not be based upon the African experience but in Virginian slavery "where the facts are not apocryphal." When Jefferson does engage in transcultural comparisons it is with Roman slavery and here he insists that the ancient institution was more brutal. His critique of African American culture thus becomes a virtual replication of Raynal's assessment of the white settlers: there are no poets, no orators, no scientists, no inventors, no artists.

Query XIV, thus, is a continuation of the scientific text of the *Notes* that proceeds in whole or in part of Queries V through VIII, XI, XV, XVII, and XX. It is in Queries VI and XIV, however, that Jefferson defines America in scientific terms. The Jeffersonian landscapes and animal and vegetable life are defended as equal to those of Europe. Both Native Americans and European settlers represent "new" cultures whose early achievements are valorized. The African American is scientifically defined out of America, and he takes on the characteristics of the European philosophe critique. Jefferson likewise continued to discuss slavery and race in the other "texts" of the *Notes*, most notably in the republican context, but here too the African American is a problem for *Americans*.

The Republican Text

Jefferson's de-Americanization of the slave takes place in the course of the Query on laws in which he had continued his discussion of the Virginian revisals begun in the previous query. Thus, reading from Query XII and XIV to Query XVIII ("Manners") one can see how slavery and race are treated in the republican text. Jefferson had ignored African Americans in his scientific defense and inserted his scientific doubts about racial equality in the midst of the discussion of his deportation plan in which he reviewed the republican revisals. He returns to the question of slavery as the sole response to Marbois' query on manners ("The particular customs and manners that may happen to be received in that state?"). Here he offers an impassioned critique of slavery from a republican perspective that was later employed by Lincoln in his appropriation of Jefferson.[23]

At the close of Query XIV Jefferson spoke of the corruption that inevitably arises when a significant portion of a population is not enfranchised. "Every government degenerates when trusted to the rulers of the people alone," concluded Jefferson after he noted that "in every government on earth is some trace of human weakness, some germ of corruption and degeneracy, which cunning will discover and wickedness insensibly open, cultivate, and improve."[24] Query XVIII continues, as if no succeeding chapters intervened, with these observations as applied to slavery. The master-slave relationship is one of "unremitting despotism" and "degrading submissions," which children imitate and the statesman, who "permitting one half the citizens thus to trample on the rights of the other," condones.[25]

Slavery is thus described as a major, indeed a central, cause of corruption. The republican morals of the masters are destroyed, as well as their industry (for who, asks Jefferson, would labor in a warm climate "who can make another labor for him"?). Only deportation can resolve this process of corruption for as the morals and industry of the master disintegrate so too does the "amor patriae" of the slave. "For if a slave can have a country, it must be any other in preference to that in which he is born to live and labor."[26] Thus in the republican text, the African-American, albeit a victim, is the source of corruption that must be excised for the republic to survive, and Jefferson describes another kind of American newness in terms of republican theory. Corruption, the mechanism by which time is ideologically recorded in republican thought, had been traced to a variety of sources, and Jefferson repeated limited enfranchisement as one in Query IV. Jefferson now connects it to the institution of slavery and thus defines another form of American Exceptionalism as newness.[27]

The republican text of the *Notes* is not, of course, concerned exclusively with slavery, but the America described is one that is dependent upon the newness of the future. Query XIII begins with a republican history of Virginia (which corresponds to the natural history offered in Query VI), beginning with Elizabeth's letters-patent to Sir Walter Raleigh to "search for remote heathen lands, not inhabited by Christian people" and closing with the "appeal to arms" by which colonies "declared themselves independent states" and established "separately a new form of government."[28] In his republican history Jefferson does not frame his comments in terms of political counterparts to Buffon. The focus of his delineation of political newness is the Virginia constitution of 1776 and the 1779 report of the Committee of Revisals, of which Jefferson was a member. The first constitution was, according to Jefferson, formed when "we were new and inexperienced in the science of government." Thus Jefferson pairs his discussion of the "very capital defects" in the constitution to the remedies offered in the revisals. Unlike the authors of the *Federalist Papers*, however, Jefferson does not focus upon defects in republicanism in the original constitution but rather argues that the faults of "inexperience" rest with its failure to fully embrace republicanism. Too many men "who pay and fight for its support" are not enfranchised; representation is unequal ("nineteen thousand men, living below the falls of the rivers, possess half the senate"); the House and Senate are too "homogeneous"; branches of government are too consolidated; the constitution was not submitted to the people. The faults in the Constitution are faults that have bedeviled regimes throughout history and Jefferson admits, in one of his few departures from American Exceptionalism, that "human nature is the same on every side of the Atlantic. . . ."[29] The task at hand is, however, to promote liberty under conditions of relative newness: "The time to guard against corruption and tyranny, is before they have gotten hold of us. It is better to keep the wolf out of the fold, than to trust to drawing his teeth and talons after he shall have entered."[30] Newness as "inexperience" produced these defects; the newness of republican America will cure them.

Nowhere in the *Notes* does Jefferson discuss his own political situation in 1781, but the fact remains that he was a tainted political figure when he composed these responses to the Marbois' queries. A bill had been proposed that called for an inquiry "into the Conduct of the Executive for the last twelve months." The inquiry raised questions about Jefferson's actions as governor during the British invasion of the state. Although completely absolved of any wrongdoing or poor judgment, he was forced to delay a planned trip to Europe while the legislature met to consider the matter. The incident plagued Jefferson throughout his entire career, and in 1781 he was particularly hurt and angry from injuries that "inflicted a wound on my spirit which will only be cured by the all-healing grave," swearing to retire from public life at forty-one. This forced withdrawal not only accentuated Jefferson's declared opposition to existing constitutional arrangements but also created a new voice for his pronouncements. At least according to his stated intentions, he was a founder in the Rousseauean sense of the lawgiver who proposed and withdrew. His eloquent warning at the close of Query XIII in regard to proposed legislation calling for a temporary dictatorship is meant to convey the alternative that faces America if his revisals are not implemented.

Marbois' queries about Virginia's constitution and laws are thus particularly instructive in this context because Jefferson's focus in both queries is less on the present than on the future. The legislature "should look forward to a time, and not a distant one, when corruption in this, as in the country from which we derive our origin, will have seized the heads of government, and be spread by them through the body of the people . . ." and Jefferson himself describes Virginia as a political entity foremost in "as-if" futuristic terms: a state with a new constitution, without slavery, and with a new system of education. The other queries in the republican text carry on this notion of the newness of the American future; indeed Jefferson describes America/Virginia in terms of the future. Jefferson describes an economy without tobacco but one that is based upon wheat, which is "the reverse in every circumstance." Wheat preserves "fertility, it feeds the laborers plentifully, requires from them only a moderate toil . . . raises great numbers of animals for food and diffuses plenty and happiness among the whole."[31] He describes a polity without "religious slavery" and criticizes the 1776 convention for not providing implementation of Article 16 of the "Declaration of Rights." In fact, the "enclosures" in which Jefferson marks off his descriptions of the American future (limited immigration and manufacturing) are based in large part upon his projections of a Virginia composed of enfranchised, educated wheat farmers rather than the present arrangements of Virginian society, a constitution which is controlled by a group of slaveholding, tobacco growing "aristocrats." The "quaint" Jefferson who protects America from the threat of immigrants who would "render it a heterogeneous, incoherent, distracted mass" and from the "canker" of industry reflects republican antipathies to cultural complexity and luxury. These enclosures are, however, framed in terms of an America projected as a new experiment. That Jefferson is willing to undertake measures to project a society that "would-be," provides him (and later generations) with a rationale for defending an American newness that exists as a possibility for the enclosures only make sense in those terms. The threat from without (the introduction of immigrants and those "wanting in husbandry") is a threat because America can so radically transform itself into an exceptional entity.

The Pastoral Text

The authority of the republican text thus rests upon Jefferson's ingenuity in describing a republican future as present or imminent in America. This flight from existing arrangements also seems to occur from a different direction in Query XIX on manufacture, as well as in several other queries. Query XIX is generally taken as evidence of Jefferson's agrarianism, the preferred political economy of republicanism. But as Leo Marx has observed, there is a marked shift in style that occurs midway through this query. The passage begins with Jefferson speaking "in the spare, dispassionate idiom of political economy" as he reviews the argument that "every state should manufacture for itself" and questions its applicability to America, where the "immensity of land" avoids the necessity of finding support for surplus populations. Then the narrative alters abruptly after he asks the question "Is it best then that all our citizens should be employed in its improvement, or that one half should be called off from that to exercise manufactures and handicraft arts for the other?"[32] Here, so argues Marx, Jefferson "suddenly changes voices" as he speaks of those who "labour in the earth" as "the chosen people of God." What follows is a passionate description of the yeoman farmer as a man of independence and incorruptibility. Jefferson contends that it is in this figure in which God "keeps alive that sacred fire, which otherwise might escape from the face of the earth."[33]

The Virgilian farmer stood as a "mythical cult-figure" in pastoral writing, and Jefferson relocates him in America. In the *Ecologues* he is threatened with the dispossession of his farm by military veterans. In Jefferson's narrative the threat comes from imitating industrializing

Europe, where all "the lands are either cultivated, or locked up against the cultivator."[34] Thus America could avoid the fate of Meliboeus if it imported manufactured goods. "The loss by the transportation of commodities across the Atlantic will be made up in happiness and permanence of government."[35]

The fragility of the pastoral environment as expressed in classical terms includes not only the external threat of dispossession by the forces of "civilization" (in Jefferson's case read as European political economy) but also by the counterforce of nature untamed. In its classical form, the pastoral offered a reconciliation by scripting the herdsman as a figure of considerable philosophical reflection. To William Empson, the simplicity of the shepherd's life is also paired with his sophistication. (He is, after all, also a poet.) This "trick" permits the pastoralist to avoid the questions of class conflict in their brute form.[36] Jefferson, by insisting upon the nobility of the Native American and the "as-if" educated yeoman, disarms the critique of the pastoral as some sort of reversion to the savagery of primitive life ("no communion, no commonwealth, no state of society" according to Buffon) or the savagery of the "mobs of great cities."[37] Thus the classical pastoral is revised as a "new" form less as a mediation between rich and poor than as one that is the result of a revision of the philosophe critique of America and a rejection of its political economy. Thus Jefferson's pastoral text takes an "old" form of European literature, transposes it upon the American environment at a time when the pastoral was in the process of reexamination in Europe as a lost ideal, and establishes its "newness" among these uncorrupted "chosen people."

There is a sense, of course, in which Jefferson's pastoral revision contains its own "trick." The pastoral cult-figure is one in a state of perfect repose (except as he considers the imminence of his dispossession, which can be said to heighten the sweetness of pastoral serenity). In the republican text Jefferson provided his own critique when he spoke of the fact that none would "labour for himself who can make another labor for him" in the Virginian climate. Does the repose of the American Titrus rest upon the practice of slavery? Jefferson's great-granddaughter nonchalantly provided the answer after studying the Jefferson family records: "This is, perhaps, a fair picture of the ease and leisure of the life of an old Virginian, and to the causes which produced this style of life was due, also, the great hospitality for which Virginians have ever been so renowned. The process of farming was then so simple that the labor and cultivation of an estate were easily and most profitably carried on by an overseer and the slaves, the master only riding occasionally over his plantation to see that his orders were executed."[38]

Granting the enormous contradiction of slavery, which is secluded in this text of the *Notes*, the pastoral figure of the yeoman generally leans upon the republican text comfortably, even when Jefferson pauses to introduce another element of the form, the poetic landscape, when he describes American geography in the Arcadian terms of "placid and delightful," "sublime," and "beautiful" in Queries II, IV, and V. Yet there are contradictions between the republican text and the pastoral one that cannot be avoided. Republicanism, as both its adherents and critics noted, not only requires the politically vigilant citizenry that Jefferson described in Query XIV but also a polity given over to public activity as the highest good. The good life in the pastoral text, however, involves a clear retreat from public concerns. Jefferson's advocation of rural life for its opportunity for leisure and his frequent expression of weariness from "the sublime delights of riding in the storm" and his desire to return to the "bosom of my family, my farm and my books," correspond to the pastoral tradition's emphasis upon the life of "ease under the awning of a spreading beech" and the "happy leisure" of the farm removed from the disorder of political life.[39]

The poetic force of the pastoral, with its fundamental commitment to the elevation of being rather than doing, struggles against the republican text in another way as well. As Annette Kolodny has observed, "Jefferson's *Notes on Virginia* continually hints at, but steadfastly refuses to make explicit, the essence of the pastoral paradox: man might, indeed, win mastery over the landscape, but only at the cost of emotional and psychological separation from it." Jefferson's republican yeoman who struggles to master nature as a way to become master of himself, threatens the purity of the pastoral landscape. Jefferson recognized this possibility when he spoke so eloquently of the advantages of wheat farming, which clothe the "earth with herbage . . . preserving its fertility," in contrast to growing tobacco, which leaves the earth "impoverished." But the question of the extent to which farming necessarily alters the landscape remained.[40]

The Tourist Text

The tourist text is the most neglected genre of the *Notes*. Most commentators veer from ignoring the lengthy descriptions of Virginia, which take up most of the *Notes*, to folding them into their own projects of reconstruction. Thus, Commager acknowledges the "guide book" character of much of the *Notes* before contending that it is "a typical Enlightenment inquiry." Leo Marx too admits Jefferson, "not being an artist . . . he never had to get all his feelings down in a single piece," but contends that the "matter-of-fact" narrative and "the wealth and specificity of geographical detail . . . conditions our response to what comes later, much as the whaling lore in *Moby-Dick* affects our feelings about metaphysical quest."[41]

Reconstructions such as these, however, fail to capture the independence of the large portions of the *Notes* as a separate genre. Certainly, sections of Jefferson's descriptions can be folded into the scientific text, which tends to be gathered in Query VI and certainly, Jefferson, often abruptly, leaves his role as scientist to give the Virginia terrain a pastoral cast. But there is as much an alteration of voice in many of the queries from both these genres as there are in the other cases we have discussed.

Take, for example, Query IV ("Mountains"), which is preceded by a largely matter-of-fact description of Virginia's rivers. The Blue Ridge provides Jefferson the occasion to remark upon geographical creation (mountains were formed first and "rivers began to flow afterwards") and the possibility of ancient volcanoes as well as the opportunity to introduce Arcadian description ("a small catch of smooth blue horizon . . . inviting you . . . to pass through the breach and participate in the calm below . . ."). Interspersed, however, between these scientific and pastoral genres is a different kind of text. "European geographers" have failed to see the range of the mountains, and Jefferson notes that "our mountains are not solitary and scattered confusedly over the face of the country."[42] Jefferson then focuses on the sights missed by both Europeans and locals. The sight of the mountains as one crosses the Potomac includes "terrible precipices hanging over you" and the "fine country around that." He concludes: "This scene is worth a voyage across the Atlantic." It is also a sight which those "who have passed their lives within half a dozen miles" have also missed.[43]

In many of the queries Jefferson thus takes on the persona of the tourist. He was not the world traveler that he would soon become after the *Notes* were concluded and who later computed that a full year of his life was spent en route to various destinations.[44] In fact, his resentment of the Virginia legislature's charges against him was aggravated by the fact that his defense required him to delay his first trip to Europe. But Jefferson in the early 1780s was an *American* traveler who had visited Philadelphia as a member of the Continental Congress, toured New England and ironically, saw much of the Virginia country-side as he avoided invading British forces.

It is thus the tourist text that gives the *Notes* its sense of place. Writing as scientist, Jefferson's geography spans the known continent. In the republican text, the institution of slavery and his discussion of the revisals anchors the text in Virginia, but the genre permits him to engage in comparisons to the sister states to the North and across time to Rome. The pastoral certainly relies on the Virginia landscape for its formulation, but it is glazed with poetic meaning. Thus the *Notes* circles Virginia as a place in these genres and Jefferson himself referred to the book as "Notes on our country" as well as one that addressed the "Natural and Political State of Virginia."[45] A focus on the tourist text, however, leads one to conclude that "the book sometimes reads as though it should be titled 'Notes on the Vicinity of Monticello.'"[46]

The beginning of the *Notes* forthrightly introduces the tourist genre: "Virginia is bounded on the East by the Atlantic: on the North by a line of latitude, crossing the Eastern Shore, through Watkin's Point, being about 37. 57'. . . .". Jefferson tells his European readers literally where Virginia is located and how large it is ("one third larger than the islands of Great Britain and Ireland. . . .").[47] It is not really accurate to conclude, as Marx does, that what we call the tourist text ends at Query VII, not only because the first seven queries contain other texts (scientific and pastoral) but because Jefferson extends his discussion to other concerns of the would-be traveler (such as an explanation of tavern rates in Query XV and money in Query XXI).

It is true, however, that nature is Jefferson's preoccupation as a tourist guide ("the only public buildings worthy of mention are the capitol, the palace, and the hospital for lunatics, all of them in Williamsburg"[48]). His contribution to newness in this text rests upon conveying the novelty of natural sights that the prospective tourist has never seen. If the Natural Bridge was worth the trip across the Atlantic, so too was the Ohio, "the most beautiful river on earth." At Monticello there is the effect of "looming," in which "distant objects appear larger, in opposition to the general law of vision." Madison's cave is composed of limestone which, as it trickles down the sides, forms "an elegant drapery."[49]

The novelties that Jefferson describes produce all the range of effects that a sightseer can be expected to experience—from awe to serenity. In the case of Native American mounds, Jefferson also introduces curiosity. Jefferson too is not adverse to reporting the discomforts that face the American traveler. American springs produce an "unfortunate fluctuation between heat and cold," and Europeans will also find that their stone or brick homes are warmer in the winter and cooler in the summer than the wood abodes that Americans prefer out of "prejudice."[50]

The distinctiveness of Jefferson's voice in this genre derives not just from the fact that he speaks not as a paradigm-buster in these passages, but that his American boosterism in this case is based upon the experience of sight and feeling rather than measurement. Thus Jefferson himself is the sightseer, and the reader sees Virginia through his eyes. The authenticity of his reportage rests upon his personal vision as Jefferson, the local, sees Virginia nature as new because he has committed himself to convey it to others, a fact that other locals have never undertaken despite their proximity to the same landscapes. If it is Jefferson's status as a local that gives the guide text its veracity (a tactic he would never pursue in his refutation of Buffon in the scientific text since his status here is one of the more thorough empiricist) and his status as tourist himself that provides the insights for the objects he selects as "worth the voyage across the Atlantic," both these personas lean upon and conflict with the other texts. The republican text requires the seclusion of America from immigration, as does the pastoral genre by requiring isolation in a different way. Indeed, Jefferson himself discouraged youth from European tourism, citing the threat of moral contamination.[51] On the other hand, the tourist guide provides Jefferson not only with another opportunity to evoke newness in yet another form but also to express his own appreciation of the local. By the early 1780s Jefferson has already actively been constructing stories of his home and household on a Virginia mountaintop that he alternatively named "Rowanty," "Hermitage," and finally "Monticello." He was, in other words, making a sense of place as domicile as he was describing its environs to Marbois.[52]

Jeffersonian Newness

In a recent reflection upon the Jeffersonian legacy, Joyce Appleby has discovered a new quaintness to Jefferson: "We live in a world of 'posts.' The buildings going up around us are postmodern; our literary criticism is poststructural; our sociology postpositivist; our legal scholarship postrealist; our political science postbehaviorial; the whole era postindustrial." She wonders if it is not "time to ask, are we post-Jeffersonian?"[53] Her query is, of course, based upon the assumption that Jefferson's "images and tropes," such as is given in the *Notes,* are based upon an obsolete comprehensive Enlightenment project. "A telling sign of our postmodernity," she concludes, "is that we have difficulty accepting Jefferson's arguments with their scientific gloss of universal truths, first principles, and immutable norms. The words that fill our public debates—pluralism, diversity, multiculturalism, relativism—point to different truths about human experience."[54]

If, however, our previous analysis is correct, we are led to return to an examination of the *Notes* that rejects this quaintness of Jefferson as an author devoid of "posts" yet still acknowledges the relevance and significance of the *Notes* as an enterprise in the formulation of multiple texts. While there have been important criticisms, no figure in American history has been more beloved than Jefferson. The *Notes* provides, I think, the key to this affection for it expresses the very multivocality that Appleby insists is absent in Jefferson's discourse. In the scientific text, Jefferson embarks upon the new project of "nationalizing" the Enlightenment, conflating Native and European Americans as "new" peoples. In the republican text, America is described in "as-if" terms; in the pastoral, "reappearance" is the motif with the yeoman as the poet; "first sight" is the form of newness when Jefferson writes as tourist guide. As we have suggested, these four recognizable genres not only each employ a different "voice" and structure but complex elisions among them. Sometimes one leans upon and then collides against another (the republican and pastoral texts, for example), sometimes one informs another (the scientific and republican texts), and sometimes they exist as parallel statements of America (the scientific and tourist texts).

In fact, as we have shown in our analysis of the scientific text, Jefferson used the narrative of American emancipation as a way to separate the African American as part of this project. Slavery and its legacy is the American crime against humanity and Jefferson's scientific Enlightenment grand narrative perpetuated the evil. Yet it is also important to note that it was in republican text, with all its suspicion about the naturalness of a modernist historical trajectory and its focus on the inevitability of corruption, that Jefferson offered his critique of racism. That the republican text also actually provided Jefferson with his own solution to this massive crime in the form of deportation suggests that either the grand narrative was capable of employing critiques to further "hide" its crimes or that, in the American case at least, the appropriation of premodern narratives offered a jaggedness to the grand narrative. It was in regard to the latter, after all, that the project of the American "reactionary Enlightenment" emerged so ferociously in the antebellum period to excise the republican text from Jefferson while retaining his scientific racism.[55] There is as well the question the status of the pastoral and tourist texts in relation to the grand narrative of which Jefferson is alleged to epitomize. The "emancipation" of the pastoral requires a retreat from reform. In fact, the pastoralist in his rejection of the great projects of change writes of a life without movement "sprawling in the shade." So too the tourist text, which celebrates the local as a source of distinctiveness.

It is this presentation of America enclosed in terms of multiple newness that makes Jefferson so central a figure since failure (as the incapacity to realize newness) is dependent upon no single genre. Racism is justified, then hidden, and then condemned, depending upon what texts are shuffled and read. Is agrarianism dead? Which form—republican or pastoral? Has the republican experiment failed? It still exists as imminence in its "as-if" form, and there is the retreat to the pastoral and the local in any case.

Jefferson is not the only guide to the new in American political thought, for we now turn to Madison's advice in Federalist No.14. But he does exemplify "multiple newness" as a source of American Exceptionalism with the American political theorist as the authority of the new.

Notes

1   For assessments of Jefferson as scientist, see Silvio A. Bedini, *Thomas Jefferson: Statesman of Science* (New York: Macmillan, 1990); Edwin T. Martin, *Thomas Jefferson: Scientist* (New York: Schuman, 1952).

2   Merrill D. Peterson's classic history of the enormous "political usefulness" of Jefferson for subsequent generations is premised upon the "dangling and disarrayed" character of his thought, caused in large part by his failure "to work out a systematic statement of his philosophy." *The Jeffersonian Image in the American Mind* (New York: Oxford University Press, 1960), p. 444.

3   Henry Steele Commager, *Jefferson, Nationalism, and the Enlightenment* (New York: George Braziller, 1975), pp. 36, 130–31. Also see: Charles A. Miller, *Jefferson and Nature: An Interpretation* (Baltimore: Johns Hopkins University Press, 1988), 12ff and George Alan Davy who contends that the framework of the *Notes* corresponds to Duncan's *Elements of Logick* and Locke's *Essay*. "Argumentation and the Unified Structure in *Notes on the State of Virginia*," *Eighteenth-Century Studies* 26 (Summer, 1993), 581–93.

4   Garrett Sheldon, *The Political Philosophy of Thomas Jefferson* (Baltimore: Johns Hopkins University Press, 1991). Also see: Ralph Lerner, *The Thinking Revolutionary* (Ithaca: Cornell University Press, 1987), ch. 2.

5   Leo Marx, *The Machine in the Garden* (New York: Oxford University Press, 1964), p. 122. Richard K. Matthews also accepts Marx's reading. *The Radical Politics of Thomas Jefferson* (Lawrence, KS.: University Press of Kansas, 1984), 43–52.

6   Edward Dumbauld, *Thomas Jefferson: American Tourist* (Norman: University of Oklahoma Press, 1946).

7   Jacques Derrida, "The Law of Genre," in *On Narrative*, W. J. T. Mitchell (Chicago: University of Chicago Press, 1980), 51–77. In this essay I leave aside the general question of the relationship of text to genre asserting only that in the case of the *Notes* each text constitutes a genre.

8   Marx, *The Machine in the Garden*, 126.

9   Commager, *Jefferson, Nationalism, and the Enlightenment*, 37.

10   Thomas Jefferson, *Notes on the State of Virginia*, William Peden, ed. (New York: Norton, 1954), 46–47.

11   See: Martin, *Thomas Jefferson: Scientist*, ch. 7.

12   See Gilbert Chinard's classic, *Thomas Jefferson: Apostle of Americanism* (Boston: Little, Brown, 1929). For an insightful analysis of the debate among philosophes over America, particularly after independence, see: Germain

Arciniegas, *America in Europe* (New York: Harcourt, Brace and Jovanovich, 1986), pp. 115–65.

13   *Ibid.*, 49, 54, 58.

14   Daniel Boorstin, *The Lost World of Thomas Jefferson* (New York, 1948), 93. Also see Dumas Malone's defense: Jefferson's "comments on race were those of a scientific mind, softened by humanitarianism. Or to put it more precisely, they represented the tentative judgment of a kindly and scientifically minded man who deplored the absence of sufficient data and adequate criteria." *Jefferson the Virginian* (Boston: Little, Brown, 1948), 267.

15   On this point, see especially, Winthrop Jordan, *The White Man's Burden* (New York, 1974). John Chester Miller argues that the tentativeness of his assertions regarding race was less important historically than the "gloss of pseudoscientific verification" he "helped to inaugurate." *The Wolf by the Ears: Thomas Jefferson and Slavery* (New York: Macmillan, 1977), 58.

16   The exception is his discussion of albino African Americans. *Notes*, 70–71.

17   *Notes*, 60.

18   *Ibid.*, 63.

19   *Ibid.*, 64, 65.

20   *Ibid.*, 133.

21   *Ibid.*, 138.

22   *Ibid.*

23   See, for example, Lincoln's Peoria Address in which he asserts that the relation between master and slave is "pro tanto a total violation" of "our ancient faith" of the principle of consent. Lincoln too in the same speech denied African Americans political and social equality and recommended deportation. *The Life and Writings of Abraham Lincoln*, ed., Philip Van Doren Stern (New York: Modern Library, 1940), 349, 363.

24   *Ibid.*, 148.

25   *Ibid.*, 162.

26   *Ibid.*, 163.

27   Jean Yarbough argues that when Jefferson writes within the republican tradition he supports (at least implicitly) racial equality while his "scientific" writings lead to racism. This argument, which bifurcates the *Declaration of Independence* and the *Notes* as republican and scientific texts, misses the point that it is when Jefferson proceeds from republican perspectives that he arrives at his program of deportation. "Race and the Moral Foundation of the American Republic: Another Look at the *Declaration* and the *Notes on Virginia*," *Journal of Politics* 53 (February, 1991), 90–105.

28 *Ibid.*, 118.

29 *Ibid.*, 121.

30 *Ibid.*

31 *Ibid.*, 168.

32 *Ibid.*, 124.

33 *Ibid.*, 165.

34 *Ibid.*, 164.

35 Ibid., 169.

36 William Empson, *Some Versions of the Pastoral* (London, 1950), 11.

37 Omitted also from Jefferson's pastoral is any semblance of its Christian revisions, so popular among the New England ministry, with the shepherd as religious figure.

38 Sarah N. Randolph, *The Domestic Life of Thomas Jefferson* (New York: Harper, 1871), 24.

39 For a review of Jefferson's repeated defense of farming as an alternative to political life, see: Barbara McEwan, *Thomas Jefferson: Farmer* (Jefferson, NC: McFarland and Co., 1991).

40 Annette Kolodny, *The Lay of the Land* (Chapel Hill: University of North Carolina Press, 1975), 28. Jefferson recognizes environmental problems in Query VI. The nitre in the caves at Rich creek had been extracted by settlers who in their pursuits never bothered to consider once the deposit was "exhausted, to see how far or soon it receives another impregnation." *Notes*, 34.

41 Marx, *The Machine in the Garden*, 119.

42 *Notes*, 18.

43 *Notes*, 19–20.

44 Edward Dumwald, *Thomas Jefferson: American Tourist*, 3.

45 *The Papers of Thomas Jefferson*, ed, Julian P. Boyd (Princeton, 1950–), vol. VIII, X, pp. 17, 243.

46 Miller, *Jefferson and Nature*, 18.

47 *Notes*, 3,4.

48 *Ibid.*, 152.

49 *Ibid.*, 10, 22, 80.

50 *Ibid.*, 80, 154.

51   *The Writings of Thomas Jefferson*, eds. Andrew A. Lipscomb and A. Ellery Bergh (Washington, 1903), V, 186–88.

52   See Rhys Issac's innovative construction of Jefferson's "story–telling" and sense of place. "The First Monticello" in *Jeffersonian Legacies*, Peter S. Onof, ed. (Charlottesville: University of Virgina Press, 1993), 77–108.

53   Joyce Appleby, "Introduction: Jefferson and His Complex Legacy" in *Jeffersonian Legacies*, 14–15.

54   *Ibid.*, 15.

55   See especially Louis Hartz on this point. *The Liberal Tradition in America* (New York: Harcourt, Brace, Jovanovich, 1955), ch. 6, 7. Hartz notes the paradox of the Southern "sociologist" who set out to "slay Jefferson only to embrace him with a passion in the end" but from this perspective, he was attempting to extract one of the "texts" from the *Notes* just as Andrew Nelson Lytle, generations later, evoked the scene of the "sacred fire" in the *Notes*. Twelve Southerners, *I'll Take My Stand* (New York, 1930), p. 219. Thus Rogers M. Smith's assertion that the arguments of the Southern reactionaries were "non-liberal" misses the multiple sources of racism within the tradition inaugurated by Jefferson. "Beyond Tocqueville, Myrdal, and Hartz: The Multiple Traditions in America," *American Political Science Review* 87 (September, 1993), 554.

Chapter 4

The Sacred Text
What's New in the *Federalist Papers*

The centrality of the *Federalist Papers* in American political thought is indisputable. Even the most severe critics of Publius grant its monumental importance as a "new explanation of politics, of whose beauty and symmetry the Federalists themselves only gradually became aware" and as a "masterly statement" in support of a literal or at least ideological coup d'état. For others, the *Federalist Papers* is a sacred text, a text that captured the "thought and intention of those few men who fully grasped what the 'assembly of demi-gods' was doing" and to which Americans return to recapture "a level of thoughtfulness about fundamental political alternatives."[1] The uniqueness then of the *Federalist Papers* is thus tethered to an act, the act of founding. The act certainly produced some important incoherencies in interpretation (multiple authorship; inability to pursue lengthy philosophical argument; repetition; the frequent use of "quick kill" in argumentation), but it is foremost the source of its power and authority. For without a narrative that places the *Federalist Papers* closely, if not causally, to the constitutional convention and the successful ratification, the text would lose much of its capacity to dominate American political discourse. Its arguments would be ones based upon a rejected and archaic document, and its predictions and explanations could never be tested (much as is the status of the arguments of the antifederalists).

The American founding is thus the *Federalist Papers'* central claim to newness defined as uniqueness. Reading the *Federalist Papers* *after* the founding always reopens this newness since no student can fail to appreciate the exceptional opportunity that Publius confronted.

"You are called upon to deliberate on a new Constitution for the United States of America" was Hamilton's initial line in No.1.[2] Yet this founding moment is an ancient event by American standards, and the modern reader is at the same time forced to consider the distance between the founding moment of Publius and is at once driven to treat the text as an "old" one. Its continuing "essential hegemonic function"[3] in accounting for the present contours of American politics may be judged benevolent or negative, but its capacity to determine events gives the text a venerable status even if it might be a begrudging one. This conjunction of new/old, including various definitions of the terms, has been the driving force in interpretations of the *Federalist Papers* as reader's emphases involve considerations of Publius' "practicality" and "realism" (that is, his appreciation for the old) and the novelty ("newness") of his solutions to the perennial problems of republics and governments in general as well as assessments as to whether Publius forged a major break between republicanism ("old") in his support of a "new" liberal ideology. [4]

It is this fascination with what is old and new in the *Federalist Papers* that, I think, is the key to interpreting this exceptional text for it is on precisely these terms that Publius himself framed his arguments, as did those who opposed the second founding. In the broadest of terms, the antifederalists argued that the Constitution was new in various negative senses as untested, exotic, and unknown while Publius contended that the Constitution must be seen as the result of "oldness" since it reflected long historical experience, and he constantly criticized the utopianism of its detractors. Yet the antifederalists still insisted upon the novelty of the American revolution and the American experience and criticized the Constitution as a work that oozed a lack of faith in republican government and hence was "old"; so suspicious, in fact, of the people's capacity to govern that the convention created a system which "squints towards monarchy."[5] Moreover, Publius frequently emphasized the newness of his "science of politics," which was unavailable in important respects to the ancients and castigated those who preached "gloomy doctrines, which predict the impracticability of a national system."[6] Even the pseudonym "Publius" epitomizes old/new in the *Federalist Papers*. The authors wrote under the "old" name of the founder of the Roman Republic but did so "as a rather proud, and radical, innovator within that tradition."[7] In fact, a passage that illustrates the deftness and complexity of Publius' employment of the terms "new" and "old" can be found in No.14 in which he recasts the debate by dividing newness into experimentation required to meet new conditions and the rashness entailed in refusal to change:

> Harken not to the voice which petulantly tells you that the form of government recommended for your adoption is a novelty in the political world; that it has never yet had a place in the theories of the wildest projectors; that it rashly attempts what is impossible to accomplish. No my countrymen, shut your ears against this unhallowed language. Shut your hearts against the poison which it conveys; the kindred blood which flows in the veins of American citizens, the mingled blood which they have shed in defence of their sacred rights, consecrate their union, and excite horror at the idea of becoming aliens, rivals, enemies. And if novelties are to be shunned, believe me, the most alarming of all novelties, the most wild of all projects, the most rash of all attempts, is that of rending us in pieces, in order to preserve our liberties and promote our happiness. But why is the experiment of an extended republic to be rejected merely because it may comprise what is new? Is it not the glory of the people of America, that whilst they have paid decent regard to the opinions of former times and other nations, they have not suffered a blind veneration for antiquity, for custom, or for names, to overrule the suggestions of their own good sense, the knowledge of their own situation, and the lessons of their own experience?

It is the theme of this chapter that these defenses and critiques of things both old and new in the *Federalist Papers* are explored in a set of "stories" or narratives about America. Thus Publius' success in winning the debate over oldness/newness can be seen in his excellence as a storyteller of the new. His stories are a mixture of history— ancient and modern, scripts of the convention and the ratification (in which he assigns himself a leading role), and futuristic scenarios. When we read the *Federalist Papers* we participate in his acts of storytelling, appreciating and replicating the pairings of old and new he created as we attempt to add chapters to his narratives. Since as Americans we must all begin with Publius' stories, because of his authority as founder, he forces us to conceive America as an exceptional ("new") narrative of old and new.

What are the stories that Publius uses to encase his arguments of oldness/newness? First there is the account of the founding and its relationship to those in the past. Then there are what can be called "disaster scenarios" should the founding not materialize. The disaster scenario is paired against a different story of the American future, America as a "rising nation," if only the Constitution were ratified. Finally there is the story of how in detail the Constitution will function in the future, which includes Publius' reversions of critics' disaster scenarios. Taken as a whole, they can be conceived as a genre of basic narratives that were distilled from republican political thought. The fascination with beginnings, the tragic history of republics, and the efforts to assure their continuity across time constituted the core of the republican project. Overlayered with the adoption of these narratives was also a liberal one as well, one which told a story of escape from history by a commercial people blessed with exceptional historical circumstances. Thus Publius' adeptness in merging republican and liberal themes, which has so confounded his critics and charmed his supporters, is reflected in this new mixture of narratives he tells or retells.

Founding Stories

The *Federalist Papers* abounds with stories of historical foundings in the ancient republics—in Crete, Athens, Sparta, Rome. It was Publius' task to connect these narratives with his immediate situation in order to present a story of the American founding. Three elements were interlocked to form such a grand narrative of the convention. The first involved the assertion that the Articles of Confederation did not constitute a founding at all or one so flawed that it did not deserve to be included in any American founding narrative. Thus Hamilton in his introductory number, when he poses the exceptional moment that faces the American people, does not emphasize that this is a second chance. Jay follows by asserting that America was already one nation (Providence had granted Americans "one connected country . . . a united people, a people descended from the same ancestors, speaking the same language, professing the same religion, attached to the same principles of government, very similar in manner and customs") but not one state. The time was "inauspicious" during the revolution for such a creation and hence "found to be greatly deficient and inadequate."[8]

Publius argues with vivid examples in what we call the disaster scenario that the Confederation is for all practical purposes simply a way station for thirteen states or several confederations and hence the proposed Constitution represents *the* founding of America. Moreover, since the Confederation had never been approved by the people as a whole it was fundamentally unsound: "The fabric of the American Empire ought to rest on the solid basis of THE CONSENT OF THE

PEOPLE" and hence the challenge that confronted Americans as to whether foundings could be based upon "reflection or choice" and not accident or force still had not been met.[9]

This constant push toward a narrative that placed the Constitution as the only real founding moment is supported by Publius' contention that its opponents were unwilling to conceive of America in terms of "any general system" and that the "great and radical vice" of the Confederation was its reliance upon states in their "corporate or collective capacities" for legislation.[10] Hence there was drawn a newness to the Constitution in respect to the founding of other republics. Madison even goes so far as to suggest that the foundings of all the ancient republics were flawed because they failed to found stable arrangements among themselves. The ancient and modern examples of confederation—the Lycian and Achaean Leagues, the Laecedemonian Confederacy and Germany, Switzerland, and the Netherlands—each experimented with different arrangements among members but each collapsed into "anarchy among its members" or "tyranny in the head."[11] At best then the Confederation was an "old" political structure and its striking resemblances to its predecessors confirmed that such arrangements characterized by a "sovereignty over sovereigns, a government over government" were "a solecism in theory" and "in practice . . . subversive of the order and ends of civil polity. . . ."[12]

There is thus in Publius' narrative a division of the founding of collections of republics between those old forms—confederations—which were numerous and uniform failures, and the founding proposed by the constitutional convention, which was unique and capable of breaking this long string of ruinous experimentation. Hamilton thus begs Americans: "Let us at last break the fatal charm which has too long seduced us from the paths of felicity and prosperity."[13]

Adding to the narrative that placed America in a position that other republics had also faced, Publius also creates a script for the ratification debate itself. Foundings are exceptional moments in the history of nations, Hamilton tells readers in No. 1. The massive political changes that are imminent loosen "a torrent of angry and malignant passions."[14] There are classes of citizens who resist change for fear that under a new constitution their power will be diminished. There are others who quickly perceive there is extraordinary political opportunity opened up to them. They hope to prey upon the uncertainty of the moment to force political projects which will provide outlets for their drive for power. Add to this, says Publius, personal animosities, party rivalry, and "the honest errors of minds led astray by preconceived jealousies and fears."[15]

Foundings in republics present even more problems. Publius predicts that the "noble enthusiasm for liberty" in republics will make citizens especially suspicious of the "enlightened zeal for the energy and efficiency of government" and warns that during this exceptional moment the love of liberty will "apt to be infected with the spirit of narrow and illiberal distrust." Moreover, "history will teach us" that those who lead the people in these suspicions will use them as a "mask" for their ambition. "Those men who have overturned the liberties of republics, the greatest number have begun their career, by paying an obsequious court to the people. . . ."[16] Thus Publius warns us in this narrative of the immediate future that complaints about the Constitution based upon "republican jealousy" are "old" ones, which reappear in each founding moment. They are either natural suspicions (such as those regarding the status of state militias, a bill of rights or rotation in office discussed later in the *Federalist Papers*) or they are expected concerns fueled and magnified by ambitious and untrustworthy leaders. Publius can be alternately patient (if patronizing) in regard to the former. For example, concerning the fear that "some favourite class of men in exclusion of others" might be the object of the provision of federal control of regulating elections, Hamilton replies: "Of all chimeral suppositions, this seems to be the most chimeral."[17] As to the latter, Publius is always poised to attack as "wanton" and "malignant" any assertion that the proposed Constitution constituted a "conspiracy against the liberties of the people."[18]

The effect of following this script, in which complaints about liberty are predicted and defined as misguided apprehensions on the part of citizens or the result of fishing in troubled waters on the part of elites, places Publius in a "new" role in this founding. Having grasped the "accumulated experience of the ages," he speaks in a voice new to the founding moment. "I frankly acknowledge to you my convictions, and I will freely lay before you the reasons on which they are founded," say Publius in the introductory essay. He concludes in No. 85 that while he might have been guilty of occasional "intemperances of expression," he had addressed himself "purely to your judgments, and have studiously avoided those asperities which are apt to disgrace disputants of all parties, and which have not been a little provoked by the language and conduct of the opponents of the constitution."[19] Publius thus offers himself as a new guide to the founding new in history as he presents arguments as calmly and fairly as he can.[20]

The danger of the founding moment in history and in America in the present is repeated throughout the *Federalist Papers*. In No. 49, for example, Publius offers a critique of Jefferson's proposal in his *Notes on the State of Virginia* that suggests that whenever two of three branches of government agree by a two-thirds vote that a new constitution is warranted, a convention be called. Madison admits that "like every thing from the same pen," Jefferson's plan "marks a turn of thinking original" and that the proposal "seems strictly consonant" with republican theory which reserves the right of the people to "new-model the powers of government."[21] But Publius worries first about the plan itself (Would the legislative branch overwhelm the others? Would an executive-judicial coalition be thwarted by men at the convention who would likely come from the ranks of the legislature "whose conduct was arraigned"?) and then about the likelihood and consequences of "frequent appeals" for ever more foundings. Governments would be deprived "of that veneration, which time bestows on everything, without which perhaps the wisest and freest governments would not possess requisite stability." Only in a nation of philosophers should his caution be discarded, an occurrence "as little to be expected as the philosophical race of kings wished for by Plato." And then there are the passions awakened in every founding moment. Such "experiments are of too ticklish a nature to be unnecessarily multiplied."[22] Even a more limited and "periodic" mechanism for constitutional revision like the "novel experiment" with the Council of Censors in Pennsylvania is rejected as a practice that excites passions to a dangerous level. Publius, who embraces the new in several important respects, is anxious to enclose this moment as quickly as possible. Any amendments would "prolong the precarious state of our national affairs, and expose the union to the jeopardy of successive experiments."[23] He cites the repeated failures of the United Netherlands to effect a founding beyond confederacy and urges readers to note the "melancholy and monitory history" of "this unhappy people."[24]

Foundings are dangerous. Their outcomes are unpredictable; flawed constitutions eventually bring down republics and republican confederations. Thus Publius supports this founding moment only because he firmly believes in its uniqueness among rare events. In No. 37 he contends that the Convention was a great "exception" to the "dark and degrading pictures" of other foundings. The Founders' burdens were magnified by the special task of combining energy in government "with the inviolable attention due to liberty, and to the Republican form."[25] Locating a reasonable line of demarcation between the relationship between state and national governments, between large and small states, and among branches of government within these constraints challenged the limits of human understanding. Moreover, the Convention enjoyed to "a very great degree, an exemption from the pestilential influence of party animosities" and a "deep conviction of the necessity of sacrificing private opinions and partial interests to the public good."[26]

The newness of the American founding was thus "astonishing." The Convention had reached the limits of human understanding in matters even more difficult to fathom than those of natural science and had done so without the usual motivations of party and self-interest. So certain is Madison of the perfection of the work of the Convention, if one were only to ignore outcomes "planned" in a philosopher's "closet" or "Imagination," that he cautiously suggests divine intervention: "It is impossible for the man of pious reflection not to perceive in it, a finger of that Almighty hand which has so frequently and signally extended to our relief in the critical stages of revolution."[27] Publius' role as "new guide" provided him with a role safely distant from one that asserted that he (in conjunction with the other members of the Convention or even himself in his position as prime theoretical expositor) deserved these accolades but the connection could be unveiled after its success.

Madison was well aware of the fact that the secrecy of the Convention's deliberations was a subject of extreme suspicion on the part of the antifederalists (that "dark conclave"), and his narrative of the Convention's newness is thus based upon the assertion that the outcome of the convention, given the extraordinary obstacles, "must have enjoyed" an "exemption" from party animosity. It is noteworthy that Madison reviews none of the various proposals offered during the Convention but rather simply challenges its opponents to imagine what kind of agreements they would be able to produce at a second convention. In fact, in No.38 he further emphasizes the newness of the founding by noting that the Convention was a group undertaking, rather than the usual route of a founding by "some individual citizen of preeminent wisdom and approved integrity." Indeed founders such as Minos, Theseus, Draco, Solon, Lycurgus, Romulus, and Numa also employed violence and myth to effect their results rather than submit their recommendations to the people.

The founding narrative that Publius thus constructs teems with the newness of "American improvements": the Constitution was a new kind of founding in the history of republics since it "new modelled" a "general system"; Publius is a "new" guide to the founding, free of commentaries derived from the "angry and malignant passions" he predicts will emerge; the Convention surmounted "the infirmities and depravities of the human character" that have afflicted previous efforts at founding and relied upon ratification "by the people themselves." These evocations of newness assume striking proportions because Publius speaks from a decidedly conservative perspective. He recognizes the "dark and degrading pictures" of foundings and the passions that founding moments unleash. Publius is very reluctant to recommend newness other than at this precise historical moment. He argues that a reverence for laws requires the rarity of foundings, the success of the Convention participants themselves was the result of the fact that they were animated by a "despair" of any "new experiments," the consequence of amendment would "expose the union to the jeopardy of successive experiments."

Disaster and Rising Nation Scenarios

Publius' account of the founding is centrally tied to what he sees as its alternative. Disaster scenarios, which occupy most of the first fourteen numbers and are repeated throughout the *Federalist Papers*, constitute a story of what would happen to America without the proposed founding. The Rising Nation scenario, which appears more intermittently and is related in detail in No.11, is a narrative of the American future if the Constitution were ratified. In the former, America's "oldness" is exposed. The nation, both citizens and leaders, will replicate the animosities of past republics and finally lose their republican character altogether as they would become "Europeanized." Moreover, "new" factors in America will actually accelerate this "old" process. On the other hand, should the Constitution be ratified, a "new" history is possible in which America not only retains its youth but is rejuvenated by constitutional arrangements.

The scenario of an America "wholly disunited, or united in partial confederacies" appears early in the *Federalist Papers*. It is introduced in No.2 by Jay, who argues that the Constitution's opponents are contesting ratification because they are actually promoting "a division of the States into distinct confederacies or sovereignties." Jay thus provides confirmation of Hamilton's warning that the founding moment will provide opportunities for the "perverted ambition" of a "class of men" who seek "fairer prospects of elevation from the subdivision of the empire into several partial confederacies." He assigns a new-ness to these alleged motives of the Constitution's opponents by con-tending that Americans prefer to "be one nation, under one federal government" and that it is designing politicians who have now offered this "new doctrine" and "these new political tenets" that call for "safety and happiness" in a division of the States into distinct "confederacies or sovereignties."[28]

The disaster scenario uses interchangeably the predictions of thir-teen separate republics or several confederacies as two versions of a "disunited America." In No.5 Jay reminds his readers that England had missed its opportunity at union and suffered "for ages divided into three, and those three were almost constantly embroiled in quarrels and wars with one another." He asks, "should the People of America divide themselves into three of four nations, would not the same thing happen" and draws an image of "a period not very distant" in which several American confederacies would become "distinct nations" of unequal power.[29] Of the "proposed Confederacies" the Northern one would be the strongest, and he describes it as the "Northern Hive." It is not "rash conjecture" to predict that its "young swarms might be tempted to gather honey in the more blooming fields and milder air of their luxurious and more delicate neighbors." Jay adds to his narrative the vulnerability of a divided America to foreign aggression: "Leave America divided into thirteen, or if you please into three or four inde-pendent confederacies, what armies could they raise and pay, what fleets could they ever hope to have?" He asks if one confederacy/state would really "spend their blood and money" in defence of another or if "flattery" or "jealousy" would lead them to neutrality.[30]

Hamilton pursues the prediction of separate republics ("indepen-dent unconnected sovereignties" formed "out of the wreck of the gen-eral confederacy") in Nos.6 to 8 and tells stories that are based upon the experience of ancient republics and recent events in America of "frequent and violent contests" with one another and internally. The "celebrated" Pericles initiated four wars on the basis of resentment, pique, and immediate political gain and was the "primitive author" of "that famous and fatal war" (the Peloponnesian war), which "termi-nated in the ruin of the Athenian commonwealth." Carthage was the "aggressor in the very war that ended in her destruction." The "haughty" republic of Venice engaged in constant war and was an "object of terror" to other city-states. And then there are the American examples of "revolt," "menacing disturbances," and "insurrection": Shay's rebellion and secessionist movements in North Carolina and Wyoming Valley, Pennsylvania.[31]

He denies that the "genius of republics" is "pacific," even those commercial republics like America are no exception. No.8 in particular draws a vivid picture of the American future. States would "with little difficulty overrun their less populous neighbors. Conquests would be easy to be made, as difficult to be retained. War therefore would be desultory and predatory. Plunder and devastation ever march in a train of irregulars. The calamities of individuals would make the principal figure in the events, which would characterize our military exploits."[32] Constant warfare would elevate the executive at the expense of legislative authority; armies would come to be regarded as the citizens, not just as their protectors but as their superiors. Republics' constitutions would acquire a progressive direction toward monarchy, and "we should see in a little time established in every part of this country, the same engines of despotism, which have been the scourge of the old world."[33]

Readers of the *Federalist Papers* often note what we would call arguments from oldness in these disaster scenarios.[34] Publius insists his predictions are based upon "the uniform course of human events" and the "accumulated experience of the ages," which tells us that republics are as "addicted to war" as monarchies, that the spirit of commerce only provides "new incentives" for aggression, and that America would not be exempt from the same feelings of "horror and disgust" that arise when we read the histories of republics. Those who do not accept this narrative live in "the deceitful dream of a golden age" for they fail to recognize that America is "remote from the happy empire of perfect wisdom and perfect virtue."[35] But even in this context Publius adds "new" elements in his disaster scenarios that form a kind of negative American Exceptionalism. Fortifications and large standing armies in Europe served to make war costly and defensive. Not so in America where their absence would encourage blitzkrieg strategies. The American frontier would provide "an ample theatre for hostile pretensions, without any umpire or judge," the number and vulnerability of American ports of entry would provide "easy" access to foreign fleets, and the public debt from the revolution would be an additional pretext for "external invasion and internal contention."

It is, in fact, these exceptional sources of discord, added to those derived from knowledge gleaned from the "accumulated experience of the ages," which would rapidly lead to the replication of European

politics in America in several senses. America would replicate the con-
vulsions of ancient republics like Athens and Carthage; America would
then come to resemble Europe with its national divisions (Jay) and its
political structures of despotism (Hamilton); America would become
an extension of European rivalries "gradually entangled in all the per-
nicious labyrinths of European politics and wars."

Publius, however, tells another story as well, one which will come
about if the founding is successful. The two most common horrors in
the disaster scenarios involve war and economic dislocation, events
which are avoided in the Rising Nation stories.[36] The refrain of the
Rising Nation scenario is "if we mean to be a commercial people
. . ."[37] Publius presents the prediction that America cannot become a
Rising Nation without the new Constitution, which would open up the
"veins of commerce" and permit "a free circulation of commodities of
every part" and once it becomes a highly successful commercial nation "it must form part of our policy, to be able one day to defend that
commerce," which only the new constitutional arrangements can provide.[38] Thus he carries forward his admonition in the disaster scenario
that commercial republics are not exempt from aggressiveness but now
contends that the American commercial republic "new modelled" as a
"general system" can defend itself against internal discord and the
designs of other nations, which Publius argues "would not be difficult
to trace by facts . . . to the cabinets of Ministers" at the present
moment. [39]

Economic activity under condition of disunion in the disaster scenario is "fettered," "interrupted," "stifled," and subject to "obstruc-
tion, or stagnation" while under a united system the "means of grati-
fication" . . . serves to vivify and invigorate the "channels of industry."[40]
Thus Publius connects the unity that provides the "energy" in government, of which he so frequently speaks with the vigor of commercial
activity. Newness as energy is thus the central trope of the Rising
Nation scenario, and Publius gives special weight to the exceptional
nature of American enterprise when he speaks of the "unequalled spirit
of enterprise, which signalizes the genius of American Merchants and
Navigators," the "adventurous spirit, which characterizes the commercial character of America" and the "active" American mechanic, the
"industrious" American manufacturer, and the "laborous" American
husbandman.

Publius tells a story of the results of this youthful commercial energy as land values rise, the federal government has increasing rev-

enues, and export markets begin to emerge. European nations already are aware of the Rising Nation scenario. They see "what this country is becoming, with painful solicitude" and plan to foster divisions in America as a political project aimed at "clipping our wings, by which we might soar to a dangerous greatness."[41] Thus the Rising Nation must start the "great national object of a NAVY" from the "nursery of seamen it now is" to protect American commerce. "Different portions of confederated America" can contribute to this "essential establishement." The South can provide wood, the Middle Atlantic iron, and the "Northern hive" seamen.

In the disaster scenario America was absorbed in the "oldness" of Europe by imitating the conflicts of petty states and by becoming an extension of European conflicts. In the Rising Nation scenario America can "aim at the ascendant," rejecting the European view that she is the "Mistress of the World" who is entitled to carve up and dominate the other three parts of the globe. Hamilton depicts America the Rising Nation as the force that can "vindicate the honor of the human race" and "teach the assuming brother moderation." Publius, who prides himself on his reasoned arguments lets restraint fall aside as he concludes: "Union will enable us to do it. Disunion will add another victim to his triumphs. Let Americans disdain to be the instruments of European greatness! Let the thirteen states, bound together in a strict and indissoluble union, concur in erecting one great American system, superior to the control of all trans-atlantic force or influence, and able to dictate the terms of the connection between the old and new world!"[42]

Constitutional Vistas

Publius is quite willing to embrace the newness of the founding moment and explore sharply drawn scenarios of the future with and without ratification. He is much more cautious in his discussion of the consequences of specific constitutional arrangements. About the newness of the federal plan in general he exults in regard to its source in the discovery of a new science of politics and its capacity to alter the natural history of republics. Montesquieu is confidently corrected, and Madison tells readers that while Europeans were meritorious in discovering the principle of representation, "America can claim the merit of making the discovery the basis of unmixed and extensive republics."[43] He is proud of the "manly spirit" that has led to the "numerous innovations displayed on the American theatre" to which, he predicts, posterity will be indebted. About the exact nature of federalism and its future trajectory, however, Publius resorts to strategies of evasive reassurance. The Convention aimed "only at a partial Union or consolidation," exact boundaries are always difficult to determine, the Constitution was "in strictness" neither unitary nor federal but a combination of both, and only implementation and practice can fully reveal "the meaning of all the parts."

Publius' caution here is understandable since he is now confronted with the inverse of the situation when he was attacking the Confederation as a flawed founding and responded with his disaster stories and a narrative of a Rising Nation. In defending specific constitutional arrangements, Publius must confront the disaster scenarios of the antifederalists. While his founding stories demonstrated the sorrowful histories of previous republics, which he linked to his stories of an America disunited in thirteen or three or four parts, an article by article examination of the Constitution itself introduced the notion of newness as the untestedness/unknown, even the curious/exotic. Publius had appropriated newness as rare/exceptional (the Convention; even his own persona of a speaker of candor), as novel/innovative/experimental (the extended, compound republic), as youthful/energetic (the Rising Nation). Yet this definition of newness as untested/unknown remained his most significant challenge for he could not completely retreat from his various claims of newness nor could he ignore the fundamental newness as untestedness of the founding he so ardently supported.

Publius had offered warnings in his ratification script of the likely criticisms that would arise in this new moment, and he returns frequently to these prophesies. Regarding suspicions that the Senate will become a "tyrannical aristocracy," he replies in part: "However useful jealousy may be in republics, yet when, like Bile in the natural, it abounds too much in the body politic; the eyes of both become very liable to be deceived by the delusive appearances which that malady casts surrounding objects."[44] Certainly, he concludes, it is this disease of perception that prompts the fear that the president and senate will act in collusion against the interests of the states and that there are no safeguards against senatorial corruption. Concerns about the power of the president come from critics who manipulate the people's aversion to monarchy. After defending against charges that members of the House will not be sufficiently attached to their electors, Publius questions the motives of his critics: "What then are we to understand by the objection which this paper has combated? What are we to say to the men who profess the most flaming zeal for Republican Government, yet boldly impeach the fundamental principle of it; who pretend to be champions for the right and capacity of the people to choose their own rulers, yet maintain that they will prefer those only who will immediately and infallibly betray the trust committed to them?"[45]

While Publius scripts criticism as a predictable response to newness emanating from ambition and self-interest, he also emphasizes the continuity of the founding with past American practice and even republicanism in general. Here then is a form of storytelling that is itself new to Publius, and he must be especially careful in pursuing this narrative for if the Constitution in its specific parts is a mere extension of the Confederation, the need for the founding is itself called into question. Madison faced this very dilemma in No.40 when he confronted the exceptionally delicate question of the legality of the convention. While he insisted upon the absolute necessity of a new Constitution, he concluded that "the truth is, that the great principles of the Constitution proposed by the Convention, may be considered less as absolutely new, than as the expansion of principles which are found in the articles of Confederation." No sooner than he makes the claim of continuity, he adds that the principles of the present system were "so feeble and confined" that "a degree of enlargement" was required which gives to the "new system, the aspect of an entire transformation of the old."[46]

The usual adeptness of Publius in manipulating old/new thus nearly disintegrates in this discussion but in regard to defending specific constitutional provisions he manages a more successful narrative in large part through the presentation of moving targets. He insists that every part of the Constitution is "strictly republican" and that no other government would be "defensible." While acknowledgment is made that the Constitution consists of "political experiments," its republican character is defended because the Constitution is consistent with the "fundamental principles of the revolution" and the more general claim that it is based upon the "the capacity of mankind for self-government." These claims to continuity are partially assured because Madison has already captured the theoretical ground of newness, telling readers what is really novel and what is really not. He thus contends that the definition of a republic is itself a variable one and capable of revision, and the criticism that some "bold and radical innovation" had been undertaken in regard to consolidation is unfounded because the Constitution is "neither wholly national, nor wholly federal."

Publius' claim then that any experimentation that exists in constitutional arrangements is firmly within the republican tradition nicely reframes the old/new debate from one which read tested/untested to one which read failure/success in terms of innovation. The Convention had only adopted provisions that already had been adopted by the "genius of the American people" and removed or reformed those that were acknowledged failures. Thus Madison notes the "errors" which the "founders of our republics" had admitted (and corrected) in their failure to recognize the likelihood of legislative usurpation in his defense of the separation of powers in the Constitution, and Hamilton contends that the practice of most of the states in regard to standing armies was the same as that provided for by the Constitution. The size of the House of Representatives was within the mean of ratios in existing state legislatures. The Presidency represented no retreat to monarchy but was an office quite like the Governor of New York, and the Supreme Court was not a "novel and unprecedented" institution but a "copy of several state constitutions."[47]

The story that Publius tells when he reviews the Constitution piece by piece is thus one of "oldness" as a continuation of the ongoing experimentation on the part of the "founders of our republics" at the state level. The acknowledged experiment of the Constitution is hence not "new" as untested since it is largely a continuation of revisals of recognized errors. Publius had again undercut a nefarious definition of newness by his constant citation of existing state practices and their own recent innovations.

Critics of the Constitution, of course, did not fail to point out that the Constitution had engaged in a qualitatively new project by introducing new institutional structures at the national level and altering the confederal structure, and then they offered their own disaster scenarios of the future should the Constitution be ratified. To this, Publius responded with narratives of what can be called reverse disaster scenarios. His strategy is this: he repeats the disaster scenario of the Constitution's critics, indicates under what circumstances must hold for the narrative to take place, and then subjects it to ridicule, alleging that upon examination it is "in reality a phantom" (judicial hegemony), "chimeral supposition" (control of the House by "some favorite class of men"), a collection of "extravagant surmises" (the federal authority to call elections as a source of usurpation), and a "visionary supposition" (the "downfall of State Governments").[48]

Publius uses a wide variety of arguments to establish his reverse disaster scenarios. He is, of course, justly celebrated for his proposition that "ambition must be made to counteract ambition" as a remedy for constitutional corruption that avoids the need for frequent constitutional conventions. In No.55, after rejecting numerous antifederalist disaster scenarios that would result from the alleged smallness of the House of Representatives, he concludes with an uncharacteristic reliance upon "qualities in human nature, which justify a certain portion of esteem and confidence."[49] He also argues that some provisions are really a matter of indifference within a certain range. Thus in regard to the Convention's decision to provide for biennial rather than annual elections in the House, he replies: "No man will subject himself to the ridicule of pretending that any natural connection subsists between the sun or the seasons, and the period within which human virtue can bear the temptations of power."[50] He argues that it is "superfluous to try by the standards of theory" the principle of equal representation in the Senate since this was a provision that was the "result of compromise."[51]

Sometimes Publius offers counter-disaster scenarios of his own. Defending the constitutional provision guaranteeing republican governments to the states, he warns that units of ancient confederations became dictatorships, and asks: "who can say what experiments may be produced by the caprice of particular states, by the ambition of enterprizing leaders, or by the intrigues and influence of foreign powers?"[52] Defending Congressional authority over elections, he warns that the absence of such a provision would place the federal government at the mercy of state legislatures who might refuse to hold elections since the "scheme of separate confederacies . . . will be a never failing bait" to "influential characters" in state administrations.[53]

The most frequent response to the disaster scenarios, however, is a narrative that relies upon American Exceptionalism. In the earlier numbers Publius is anxious to reject the argument that America was an exception to the history of republican discord. When he discusses constitutional provisions, however, he is willing to support exceptionalism, at least in particular circumstances. The antifederalist disaster scenario that the Senate would "gradually acquire a dangerous preeminence in the government, and finally transform it into a tyrannical aristocracy," is based upon the axiom that liberty is endangered by abuses of power, which while correct, must also be supplemented by the axiom that liberty can be endangered by abuses of liberty. It is the latter concern, argues Publius, who draws an elaborate scenario of the numerous obstacles facing a Senate that attempted to act upon such "lawless ambition," which most applies to the United States. Confronted with skepticism that the House too will form a separate class in society, Publius reviews all sorts of restraints—ranging from self-interest to frequent elections—but relies on "above all, the vigilant and manly spirit which actuates the people of America." Critics had questioned the absence of a retirement age for judges. Publius responded that in America "fortunes are not affluent" and thus judges should not be cast out after long service to the republic.[54]

The most vivid disaster scenario of the antifederalists centered upon the absence of a prohibition against standing armies and the right of Congress to call out state militias. Standing armies were not only a theoretical specter for the antifederalist. The occupation by British forces was a fresh personal memory for many Americans who were extremely reluctant even to create a professional military force during the revolution.[55] Professional armies, especially in times of peace, represented monarchical power in its most brute form as well as a favorite occupation for young aristocrats. Thus the antifederalists presented the president as a military figure (the "president-general" was Philadelphiensis' constant appellation and "captain-general" Montezuma's) with a huge army at his command that was staffed by "young gentlemen" who would act as the federal government's tax collectors and, with the authority of Section 8 of Article 1, drag young men on penalty of death from their "families and homes to any part of the continent for any length of time."[56]

In No.8 Hamilton actually reversed the disaster scenario with his own by arguing that without ratification states would certainly be forced to raise large standing armies for their protection. In No.24 Hamilton dismissed the concern about standing armies by contending that the power to raise armies rested with Congress, not the president, and that states, when they addressed the subject in their constitutions, cautioned against their formation rather than forbade it. He carefully defended the need for a navy and "small garrisons on our frontier."[57]

It is Madison, however, who takes on the antifederalist disaster scenario head-on in No.46. The general subject of the number is itself a general constitutional prediction about which level of government will grow in the future. Madison repeats the assertion that the "first and most natural attachment of the people will be to the governments of their respective states."[58] In order to establish his proposition, he creates his own vivid scenario of federal usurpation. Read carefully, the narrative actually consists of several parts: encroachments upon a single state and resistance by the people, the governor, and the legislature; "signals of general alarm" that would go out to other states, thereby establishing correspondence and "plans of resistance"; open military conflict between the states and the federal government. This narrative of political opposition, resistance, and finally civil war is remarkably close to the antifederalist scenario, and Madison thus uses this reconstruction to establish its lack of plausibility at each stage he has narrated. Legal opposition would be "powerful and at hand" and "would present obstructions which the Federal Government would hardly be willing to encounter." Should, however, federal officials continue to pursue the "projected innovations," the opposition of the states would be similar to those of a people who "dread a foreign yoke." Madison, at this point, cannot quite imagine how Step 2 would occur: "what would be the contest in the case we are supposing?" "Who would be the parties?" By the time he proceeds to evaluating Step 3, open civil war, he continues the scenario with open incredulity. "The only refuge left for those who prophecy the downfall of state governments," he concludes, "is the visionary supposition that the Federal Government may previously accumulate a military force for the projects of ambition."[59] For such a standing army to even realistically participate in such a scenario, the people and the state would have to have elected an "uninterrupted succession" of "traitors." The traitors would have had to have pursued "uniformly and systematically" a fixed plan for a military establishment, while the people and the states waited in silence, continuing to supply materials, until the "gathering storm" burst upon them. Grant even these "incoherent dreams," says Madison, and "let a regular army, fully equal to the resources of the country be formed; and let it be entirely at the devotion of the Federal Government." Still a national army of 25,000 to 30,000 (Madison's outside estimate) would be outmatched by combined state militias of nearly half a million citizens "officered by men chosen from among themselves, fighting for their common liberties, and united and conducted by governments possessing their affections and confidence."[60]

This disaster scenario is thus reversed, first with a narrative that casts doubt upon its political, then its military plausibility. Madison clinches his argument by reversion by introducing American Exceptionalism to his own narrative. An armed citizenry and elected local governments are practices unknown in Europe where governments are "afraid to trust the people." If subjects in European nations possessed armed militias "the throne of every tyranny in Europe would be speedily overturned, in spite of the legions which surround it."

Madison had ridiculed the disaster scenario as he retold it. Now, with the "newness" derived from "the advantage of being armed, which Americans possess over the people of almost every other nation" added to his own narrative, the implausibility of the disaster scenario fades as his own reverse takes over.[61] For Madison now proudly recalls the triumphs of the American militias during the revolution and contends that it would be an "insult" to the "free and gallant citizens of America" to argue that they would be less able to defend their rights than the "debased subjects of arbitrary power" would be to rescue theirs. The specter of a rapacious standing army recedes almost completely as Madison's retelling focuses upon the bravery of the armed American citizenry.

The eclecticism of Publius' reverse disaster scenarios is impressive. He brings forth arguments that include attacks on the republican credentials of the storytelling of his critics, he waves away some stories as much more plausibly told through narratives of theoretical and practical difference or compromise, defends others as innovations tested by the postrevolutionary experiences of the states, offers his own counter-disaster narratives, and appeals to the exceptionalism of the American experience as validation of the improbability of others. Taken together, however, the reverse disaster scenarios represent a single narrative in regard to the newness of constitutional provisions as the untested and unknown. For while all of these arguments concede newness they do so only on terms Publius will grant. He will accept only narratives that are derived from his own "candor" and commitment to use "reason to condemn suspicion," those which acknowledge that many provisions are harmless changes or inevitable compromises, those which are new but already tested in the American theater, and those which recognize the exceptional nature of the American people on certain questions.

Publius as the Authority on the New

We began this chapter by contending that the authority of Publius rested with his excellence as a storyteller of the new, acknowledging that his status as storyteller is dependent upon the success of the founding itself. Certainly Publius deserves the attention he has received for his theoretical achievements in No.10 and No.51. But perhaps it might be worthwhile to consider that his authority, both during the ratification controversy and for subsequent generations, rests primarily with the stories he told. For it is his account of the convention as an "astonishing" achievement compared to other efforts in history, as well as his narratives of the perennial failures of republics ancient and modern, his reluctance to support a founding moment, and his own script for the ratification controversy, that disposes us to question the motives of critics, and which thus invites us to consider so carefully his arguments in No.10 and elsewhere. Publius' vivid disaster scenarios and his futuristic accounts of a new Rising Nation provide both negative and positive grounds for receptivity to the founding which in turn receive reassurances when he speaks of the Constitution in its specifics.

But the excellence of Publius' storytelling extends even further than its function as a kind of artillery for surrender to his theoretical innovations. For Publius' willingness to accommodate and appropriate the "new" makes him its authority. When he tells us that his positions reflect the "tried course of human affairs" and that he has consulted experience whenever it can be found, we listen. We listen, not because of the inherent reasonableness of Publius' arguments nor because we are overwhelmed by his philosophy or science, though reasonableness and philosophy and science do make their mark, but because he establishes himself as one who knows when newness is rashness and when it is prudent innovation, when it is exceptional and when it is tragic, when the new is vigorous, young, and fresh, and when it is raw, untested, and unsophisticated. It is thus not Publius' conservatism that triumphs in his account of the founding and the Constitution, at least in a direct way. For Publius can be as reformist or radical as any writer, celebrating innovation and calling upon his readers to shut their hearts to doubts about novelty. Rather it is in Publius' status as authority on the new that makes him so exceptional a storyteller of the American founding, and perhaps it is No.14 of the *Federalist Papers*, not No.10 and No.51, which represents the acme of his achievement. For by acknowledging the "newness" of the American founding, as critic or supporter, we thus acknowledge as well Publius' authority and set off again a debate that he will always win. For if it is the "glory of the American people" to support a culture that prides itself on its capacity for innovation, how could it fail not to be drawn back to the most successful of its experiments?

Notes

1 Charles Beard, *An Economic Interpretation of the Constitution* (New York: Macmillan, 1913); Gordon S. Wood, *The Creation of the American Republic* (New York: Norton, 1969), 524; Martin Diamond, "The Federalist" in Morton J. Frisch and Richard G. Stevens, eds., *American Political Thought* (Itasca, IL.: Peacock, 1983), 88.

2 *The Federalist*, Jacob E. Cooke, ed. (Middletown, CT.: Wesleyan University Press, 1961), 3.

3 Robert A. Ferguson, "'We Hold These Truths': Strategies of Control in the Literature of the Founders" in Sacvan Bercovitch, ed., *Reconstructing American Literary History* (Cambridge, MA.: Harvard University Press, 1986), 25.

4 Martin Diamond, Douglas Adair, Richard Hofstadter, and John P. Roche emphasized the practicality and experiential reasoning of Publius, although Diamond detected a prescience that Roche questioned while Adair acknowledged his novelty in appropriating Hume's concept of the commercial republic. Diamond, "The Federalist," in *American Political Thought*, 86–87; Douglas Adair, "Experience Must Be Our Only Guide" in *Fame and the Founding Fathers*, Trevor Colbourn, ed. (New York: Norton, 1974), 107–23; John P. Roche, "The Founding Fathers: A Reform Caucus in Action," *American Political Science Review* 55 (December, 1961), 799–816; Richard Hofstadter, *The American Political Tradition* (New York: Vintage, 1948). Robert Dahl's influential *A Preface to Democratic Theory* (Chicago: University of Chicago Press, 1956) granted to Publius the novelty of producing a text that was primarily composed of scientific theorems. The debate over Publius' republican/liberal anchors has had many participants including Joyce Appleby, Thomas Pangle, Isaac Kramnick, Gordon Wood, Sheldon Wolin. Joyce Appleby, "Republicanism in Old and New Contexts," *William and Mary Quarterly*, third series 43 (January, 1986), 20–34; Thomas Pangle, *The Spirit of Modern Republicanism* (Chicago: University of Chicago Press, 1988); Isaac Kramnick, "Republican Revisionism Revisted," *American Historical Review* 87 (June, 1982), 629–64; Gordon Wood, *The Creation of the American Republic*; Sheldon Wolin, *The Presence of the Past* (Baltimore: Johns Hopkins University Press, 1989). Treatments which emphasize the eclecticism of Publius in regard to old/new include: Michael Lienesch, *New Order of the Ages* (Princeton: Princeton University Press, 1988); James Farr, "Conceptual Change and Constitutional Innovation" in Terence Ball and J. G. A. Pocock, eds., *Conceptual Change and the Constitution* (Lawrence, KS: University of Kansas Press, 1988), 13–34.

5 Patrick Henry, "Debates in the Virginia Convention" in *The Antifederalists*, ed. Cecilia Kenyon (Boston: Northeastern University Press, 1985), 257.

6   *The Federalist*, No.23, 151.

7   Thomas L. Pangle, "The FEDERALIST PAPERS' Vision of Civic Health and
     the Tradition Out of Which That Vision Emerges," *Western Political Quar-
     terly* , 582.

8   *Ibid.*, No.2, 10.

9   *Ibid.*, No.22, 146. There is a strong argument for newness here and one with
     not a little irony since, including the Constitution itself, which was ratified by
     state convention, only five of the twenty-eight constitutions adopted between
     1776 and 1800 were popularly approved. See: Donald S. Lutz, *Popular Con-
     sent and Popular Control* (Baton Rouge: Louisiana State University Press,
     1980), 83; Joshua Miller, *The Rise and Fall of Democracy in Early America*
     (University Park: Pennsylvania State Press, 1991), 60–64.

10   Ibid., No.1, 7; No.15, 93.

11   Ibid., No.18, 117.

12   Ibid., No.20, 128–29.

13   Ibid., No.15, 92.

14   Ibid., No.1, 5.

15   Ibid., 4.

16   Ibid., 6.

17   Ibid., No.60, 404.

18   Ibid., No.85, 589.

19   Ibid., No.1, 6; No.85, 589.

20   Although Albert Furtwangler challenges the centrality of the *Federalist Pa-
     pers* as a decisive force in the ratification campaign, he argues that the essays
     are notable for a tone of "high, privileged civility" that was extracted and
     perfected from eighteenth century political discourse. *The Authority of Publius*
     (Ithaca: Cornell University Press, 1984), 94.

21   *The Federalist*, No.49, 338–39.

22   Ibid., 34–41.

23   Ibid., No.85, 591.

24   Ibid., No.20, 128.

25   Ibid., No.37, 233.

26   Ibid., 239.

27   Ibid., 238.

28   Ibid., No.2, 4, 8.

29   Ibid., No.5, 24.

30   Ibid., No.5, 26.

31   Ibid., No.6, 34–35.

32   Ibid., No.8, 45.

33   Ibid., 46.

34   See, for example: Vincent Ostrom, *The Political Theory of the Compound Republic* (Lincoln:University of Nebraska Press, 1987), 48–56; Michael Lienesch, *New Order of the Ages*, 121–126. Ostrom identifies them as the "logic of mutually destructuve relationships" and Lienesch as a "cautionary form of history."

35   Ibid., No.6, 36.

36   There is certainly a tension evident in the depictions of the actual features of America as a Rising Nation which has led some readers to suggest the existence of two stories told by Publius' much discussed "split personality" in regard to federalism. Yet Publius does manage to submerge conflictual storytelling in the *Federalist Papers*. Hamilton and Madison recognize the antagonism between manufacturing and landowning interests without taking sides in Nos.10, 35. Alan Gibson argues that Madison did not advance an argument for a commercial republic in the *Federalist Papers*. "The Commercial Republic and the Pluralist Critique of Marxism: An Analysis of Martin Diamond's Interpretation of Federalist 10," *Polity* 25 (Summer, 1993), 497–528. As an popular ideological motif, the "Rising Nation" trope emerges in the pre-revolutionary period with Freneau's "A Poem, on the Rising Glory of America." It is this more general nationalist expression (America's mission will not be fulfilled "till foreign crowns have vanish'd from our view") that Publius relies upon.

37   *The Federalist*, No.34, 211.

38   Ibid., No.11, 71; No.34, 211.

39   Ibid., 66.

40   Ibid., 66, 70–71, 73.

41   Ibid., 66.

42   Ibid., 73.

43   Ibid., No.14, 84.

44   Ibid., No.64, 437.

45   Ibid., No.57, 387.

46   Ibid., No.40, 262–63.

47   Ibid., No.69, 464–70; No.81, 544. In Nos.70 and 72, Publius, in one of his few departures from caution in regard to specific constitutional arrangements, challenges republican convention in regard to the plural executive and rotation in office.

48   Ibid., 81, 545; No.60, 404; No.59, 399; No.46, 320.

49   Ibid., No.55, 378.

50   Ibid., 360.

51   Ibid., No.62, 416.

52   Ibid., No.43, 292.

53   Ibid., No.59, 402.

54   Ibid., No.63, 428; No.57 387; No.79, 533.

55   See the following for examinations of the centrality of the standing army controversy in colonial American culture: John Phillip Reid, *In Defiance of the Law: The Standing Army Controversy, the Two Constitutions, and the Coming of the American Revolution* (Chapel Hill: University of North Carolina Press, 1981); Royster, *A Revolutionary People at War* (Chapel Hill: University of North Carolina Press, 1979), ch. 1; John Todd White, "Standing Armies in Time of War: Republican Theory and Military Practice during the American Revolution," Ph.D. dissertation, George Washington University, 1978.

56   *The Antifederalists*, 72, 64, 22.

57   *The Federalist*, No.24, 153–56.

58   Ibid., No.46, 316.

59   Ibid., 320–21.

60   Ibid., 321.

61   Ibid., 320–21.

Chapter 5

The Outside Text
Tocqueville and the NEW

Unlike Publius, Tocqueville's authority derives not from the creative (new) juxtaposition of old and new. For Tocqueville everything about America is new. Yet unlike Jefferson's, Tocqueville's exploration of newness does not "deconstruct" into various interacting forms. There is, of course, a bifurcation of newness in *Democracy in America* (not unnoticed and even a bit belabored in the so-called two-democracy interpretation of Tocqueville's analysis[1]), but as significant as these constructs are, they pale before Tocqueville's confrontation with America as the *new*. Everywhere Tocqueville looks, he finds new laws and new mores and more significantly this confrontation constantly challenges him to search for new methods, new words, and new theories to explain and, we shall argue, to contain, this newness. Thus while Jefferson pursues his own projects through a quadrification of the new that relies upon both their separateness and interaction to relieve theoretical stress, Tocqueville's categories are always near envelopment as he attempts to meet his own self-imposed goal to discover a "new political science . . . for a world itself quite new."[2]

Is it this aspect of Tocqueville's American Exceptionalism in *Democracy in America* then that explains its privileged status as foreign text? More than one writer has discovered a befuddledness in Tocqueville's analysis, and his notes, even before his struggles with the second volume, support this observation.[3] If so, the American fascination with Tocqueville reproduces this process, that is, Tocqueville is re-read for solace (even when he is most critical) because his work *contains* the new in acceptable categories and he is re-read for his appreciation of the *new* as a source of renewal. This chapter attempts to retrieve the complexity of Toqueville's confrontation in order to grasp the central teaching of his account of American Exceptionalism.

Tocqueville's notes of his journeys to America reveal a constant confrontation, and indeed receptivity, to America as *new*. His mission, of course, was to report upon the new institution of the American penitentiary, but Tocqueville's fascination with the new immediately broadened. Aboard ship, he systematically questioned the voluble Peter Schermerhorn. The New York merchant seemed to whet Tocqueville's appetite for the new to even greater proportions. He learned that there were no political parties in America, that the desire for riches was immense and unceasing, and that Schermerhorn was sanguine about the potential problem of secession. Arriving in Newport, Tocqueville offers a cascade of observations on the new: "we wandered about the town. It has 16,000 inhabitants, a magnificent harbor, newly fortified, tiny houses modelled one would say on the kitchen of Beaumont-la-Chartre, but so clean they resemble opera scenery. They are all painted. There is also a church whose bell tower is a rather remarkable architectural style. I sketched it on Jules' album. We had been told that the women of Newport were noteworthy for their beauty; we found them extraordinarily ugly. This new race of people we saw bears no clear mark of its origin; it's neither English, nor French, nor German; it's a mixture of all nations. This race is entirely commercial. In the small city of Newport there are 4 or 5 banks; the same is true in all cities in the Union . . ."[4] This sense of surprise at newness continues throughout his notes. Americans seem very well educated; they seem excessively patriotic; they seem excessively friendly. He is surprised by the vitality of local government and law abidedness amid the apparent absence of sovereignty, by American "restlessness"; he is shocked by the condition of Native Americans and by the institution of slavery.[5]

By the time Tocqueville wrote *Democracy in America* there was already a tradition of the outside text as a source of national inspiration and even national identity, as well as national critique. Crevecour's *Letters* had already celebrated the existence of a new American man and Trollope criticized him for his vulgarity. These, and many others, of course, participated in the genre of the foreign traveloque. The sight of the stranger becomes authenticated as insight (much as Jefferson, the quintessential American, had inventively employed in one of his tropes in the *Notes*). This insight is especially valued in America because in a culture that is centered upon newness, who can see the new better than the foreign traveler? Once extended, this advantage is transferred, for who can have better insight than one who relies upon the sight of the stranger?

What so privileges *Democracy in America*, however, as the exemplary foreign text is that Tocqueville keeps this insight into newness so alive in his analysis. Yet this constant confrontation with newness is secluded by his equally constant attempts to find "new" explanations for this newness. There are no less than four such attempts in *Democracy in America,* which themselves are derived from Tocqueville's confrontation. If the reputation of *Democracy in America* as the foremost foreign text rests with its persistent preoccupation with newness, it does so because Tocqueville's insight itself enables him to react anew. Like Crevecour, Tocqueville can see newness in a positive light, confirming American Exceptionalism as celebration. Surveying the New England townships, he concluded that a "democracy more perfect than antiquity had dared to dream of issued in full size . . ." At the same time and like Trollope, Tocqueville offers his insights in terms of newness as critique, indeed as newness as nightmare, as shown by his famous description of "democratic despotism." Thus even as Tocqueville sets out in Volume 2 to offer his most systematic reproach of America, he reminds his readers that he is "no enemy of democracy" and that he offers his assessments in the context of the friendly critic. Indeed his insights are partially authenticated through his critique. Neither enemies nor friends usually tell the truth, and since Tocqueville is not precisely either, both his commendations and condemnations of newness deserve consideration. But America as utopia/dystopia does not exhaust Tocqueville's confrontation with newness. If America is to be understood in terms of newness in both a positive and negative sense according to Tocqueville, then is this newness confined to America, exceptional as "rare" or even "unique," or is it replicable, new as in the first instance? Tocqueville always sets his sights on American replicability. "I admit that I saw in America more than America" haunts the observations of America throughout both volumes, but Toqueville too found newness as uniqueness in America as well, particularly in its exceptional revolutionary heritage. Thus *Democracy in America* pursues each of these combinations of newness: newness as a distinctiveness to be admired but not capable of replication; newness as distinctiveness as an *American* problem; newness as first instance to be imitated; newness as first instance as warning.

The Positive Unique

The first volume of *Democracy in America* begins with a theory of American newness as first instance. Tocqueville contends that the movement to democracy has been steadily and irreversibly progressing for seven hundred years. The same forces that Tocqueville saw in Europe were "advancing more rapidly in America," and he promised thus to examine the future by examining America. At the same time, however, Tocqueville noted that he was "very far from believing" that Americans "have found the only form possible for democratic government . . . "[6] and he promised to also examine American distinctiveness.

In his journeys to America Tocqueville sought frantically to discover this distinctiveness in American geography, in its frontier, in its national character, in its laws. In *Democracy* he finally arrived at a tripartite ordering of mores, laws, and geographical setting. Yet the division and prioritization of these assessments actually sequester the sheer volume of newness that Tocqueville saw. For look at the newness that Tocqueville confronted by simply providing a list at a lower level of theorization.[7] First in terms of absences:

(1) no aristocracy
(2) no peasants
(3) no great generals
(4) no large army
(5) no foreign enemies
(6) no heavy taxes
(7) no capital
(8) no primogeniture
(9) no political parties
(10) no centralized administration
Second, in terms of presence:
(11) recent colonial founding
(12) distinctiveness of first settlers
(13) revolution in property
(14) power and authority of local governments
(15) a "vast wilderness" on its borders
(16) the sobriety of the American revolution
(17) universal suffrage
(18) moderation of voluntary associations
(19) an extraordinary Constitutional founding
(20) high level of religious sects

(21) high level of economic prosperity

(22) equality of condition

(23) reinvention of the office of Justice of the Peace

(24) judicial review

(25) sovereignty of the people

A central task of the first volume of *Democracy in America* involved theorizing the new (did these absences and presences add up to a broader notion of newness?) in order to settle upon a ranking. Tocqueville was first inclined to trace many aspects of America's absences and presences to its "vast wilderness." Particularly after his trip to Canada, however, he came to reject this notion of a positive unique. French Canadians clustered along settlements already "crowded into a space too narrow for them, although the same wilderness lay close at hand," driving up land prices and promoting inequality. Nor did the Spanish treat the frontier in the same way as the "Anglo-Americans": "Geography gave the Spaniards equal isolation, and that isolation has not prevented them from maintaining great armies."[8] Thus the presence of a wilderness could not explain, by itself, the absences Tocqueville noted.

Another focus on the positive unique appears in *Democracy in America*, what Tocqueville called the "Ango-American race," only to be subsumed within the broader category of the positive in the first instance, under the theorization of *moeurs*. Frontier origins often begin under conditions of equality of condition and while Tocqueville noted that the American settlements had neither "commoners nor nobles," these arrangements rapidly disintegrated among the French and Spanish. "The foundation of New England was something new in the world, all attendant circumstances being both peculiar and original," concluded Tocqueville.[9] Here were not speculators or pirates but the well-educated who brought whole families. But "what distinguished them from all the others was the very aim of their enterprise": "they hoped for the triumph of an idea." It was these "pious adventurers" who stamped America "not with the aristocratic freedom of the motherland, but a middle class and democratic freedom of which the world's history had not previously provided a concrete example." Thus Tocqueville credited the positive unique of the New England settlers, whose world view emitted a "sort of Biblical fragrance," for creating a "land given over to the fantasy of dreamers, where innovators should be allowed to try out experiments in freedom," theorized as a "marvelous combination" of the "spirit of religion and the spirit of freedom."[10]

Nevertheless, while Tocqueville complained that European observers tended to grant too much weight to geography as an explanation for American newness, *Democracy in America* teems with Tocqueville's fascination with the frontier as a distinctive positive. "Where," he asked, "among all that man can remember, can we find anything like what is taking place before our eyes in North America?"[11] The great civilizations of antiquity were founded upon conquest, but here was a civilization that had only to push back a few wandering tribes to begin anew. For not only were Americans blessed with beginning without the original sin of conquest (civilization still "blushes" at the triumphs of ancient societies), but these settlements were undertaken after the Great Enlightenment. In a version of the Cotton Mather thesis, Tocqueville wondered if God had not reserved America to enable a new beginning not when men were "weak and ignorant" but "by the time that they had learned to take advantage of the treasures it contained . . ."[12] Tocqueville marveled thus at the ease with which the wilderness was conquered in America and was less astonished by what he called the "double movement of migration," which "never halts." There was thus the newness of the original settlements and then the constant newness replicated as settlers moved westward. "Nothing in history is comparable to this continuous movement of mankind except perhaps that which followed the fall of the Roman Empire."[13] Thus while Tocqueville's own political project pushed him to search for newness as the positive in the first instance so that he might reform the great global advance of democracy and led him to subsume the frontier as newness under "habits of the heart," he could as well have emphasized the American frontier as itself a "new frontier," distinctly positive in the character of its settlers and the historical moment of its opening.

Still as the final version of *Democracy in America* stands, this new frontier accounts for several aspects of American newness, which Tocqueville attributed to the positive unique or "accidental or providential causes" of American democracy: its "peculiar and unique" settlement by "pious adventurers" (12); the newness of American origins (11), which permits the observer to gain unique insight into this new society ("America shows in broad daylight things elsewhere hidden from our gaze by the ignorance or barbarism of the earliest times") and also provided the settlers with the "treasures" of civilization as the first frontier broken under the influence of the Enlightenment; the absence of original sin in its founding (5); a permanent frontier ("the double movement of immigration"), which increased the American sense of restlessness but reversed historical example (previous immigrations, such as those at the collapse of the Roman Empire, brought to the "newcomer . . . death and destruction in its train, but is now the seed of life and of prosperity that he bears")[14] (13, 21, 22).

Having rejected, however, the frontier or even the new frontier, as the central source of American newness, Tocqueville focused on factors more capable of interpretation of newness as positive in the first instance. For the newness that dazzles Tocqueville so in the first chapters of *Democracy in America* is its administrative statelessness.[15] Chapter 5 begins with the observation that any study of American government must begin with the fact that there are "two completely separate and almost independent governments" in America, one is "ordinary and undefined which provides for the daily needs of society" and the other is "exceptional and circumscribed and only concerned with certain general interests." Even by focusing upon the states, Tocqueville insisted that understanding the new required examination of the American township as the "only association so well rooted in nature that wherever men assemble it forms itself."[16] Here, wrote Tocqueville, is where Americans had been most politically inventive. These "lively republics" engaged in decision-making by its own citizens and elected selectmen who provided for the poor, maintained roads, supervised property arrangements, and guaranteed public order. In a fundamental sense the citizens at large performed the function of police, and the Justice of the Peace was "deprived of the aristocratic character" it enjoyed in England.

Tocqueville saw some major remarkable aspects in the newness in these townships. The severe alienation of the European villager was replaced by the happy, patriotic, and public-regarding New Englander. Moreover, the universal desires for self-esteem and ambition, tendencies that Tocqueville found to be "troublesome" features of all societies, "take on a different character when exercised so close to home and, in a sense, within the family circle."[17] In addition, this administrative decentralization in which armies, tax collection, and welfare were local responsibilities, even though coupled with what Tocqueville regarded as generally unchecked power in the hands of state legislatures and the doctrine of popular sovereignty, preserved freedom in a way that neither the great monarchical or revolutionary governments in Europe were able to capture.

Thus for Tocqueville, America's lack of a state in this crucial administrative sense, although "unknown" or "scorned" by Europeans, was "unprecedented." As he proceeded to examine other aspects of

American government, Tocqueville found more examples of newness in the positive sense. Relying heavily upon *The Federalist Papers*, he celebrated the Constitution as a set of laws that made America unique as one that was "free and happy like a small nation and glorious and strong like a great one."[18] Unlike Publius, however, Tocqueville did not describe the Constitution as a judicious mixture of old and new but rather in terms of newness alone. As did Publius, Tocqueville supported the notion of a new kind of founding in America. Revolutionary struggles were not in themselves new "but that which is new in the history of societies is to see a great people, warned by its lawgivers that the wheels of government are stopping, turn its attention on itself without haste or fear, sound the depth of the ill, and then wait for two years to find a remedy at leisure, and then finally, when the remedy has been indicated, submit to it voluntarily without its costing humanity a single tear or drop of blood."[19] Indeed, not only did Tocqueville ignore the arguments of the anti-federalists that the Constitution threatened the local liberty he had himself just exalted, but he extracted from *The Federalist Papers* all its arguments regarding newness. Tocqueville argued that its conception of federalism was different from all other similar efforts and took Madison's contention that the constitution was neither federal nor unitary one step further. The government might be called federal but the "human mind invents things more easily than words" and he preferred the description "incomplete national government" for "this new thing."[20] Like Madison, he supported the Great Compromise as necessary and prudent but also suggested that the system of representation by both population and state was appropriate in a young nation where the states were relatively homogenous in mores and still had no tradition of seditious alliances. And like Madison and Hamilton, he supported the concept of the extended republic as a new solution to the instability of small republics. In fact, Tocqueville's discussion of the judiciary and particularly the Supreme Court, rather than focusing upon its status as the least dangerous branch, centered upon its unique and indispensable role as national tribunal that no other nation had ever created.[21]

The Positive in the First Instance

Tocqueville had certainly captured multiple cases of newness in his first effort to report on America and was able to cluster and order them, but were they destined to be "positive unique"? Despite his efforts to see more in America than America itself, Tocqueville's success in the first volume of *Democracy* to discover positives in the first instance were vague and elusive. His work had, of course, brilliantly established how in America one could see with exceptional clarity the past as well as the future, but was not even this newness the exceptionalism of the unique? The whole raison d'etre of the volume pushed toward a consideration of the positive in the first instance since he had announced that it was in Europe that the movement toward equality had gained irresistible momentum and that in America the future of Europe could be seen. Yet the conclusion of *Democracy I* is a prophesy devoted almost entirely to the *American* future. Thus when Tocqueville writes as a "traveler who has gone beyond the walls of some vast city and gone up a neighboring hill," what he sees is an exclusively American future of vastly increased population and wealth. The image of such a great nation with common point of departure, language, religion, and mores "is something entirely new in the world, something, moreover, the significance of which the imagination cannot grasp."[22]

Yet by insisting that American newness be theorized in terms of mores, Tocqueville hoped to show that American newness could be seen as one of first instance. European states might not enjoy a frontier nor might they enjoy the new one that Tocqueville described, but if the newness of America rested in its mores, the new democracy in America might be imitated, especially if modeled in conjunction with America's new legal system. Yet newness as positive in first instance is reviewed much earlier (chapter 9) and in a much more tentative way than the "positive unique." Tocqueville asks the question: "If other peoples, borrowing from this general and creative idea from the Americans, but without wishing to imitate the particular way in which they have applied it, should try to adapt it to the social state which Providence has imposed on the men of our time and should seek by this means to escape the despotism of anarchy threatening them, what reasons have we to believe that they are bound to fail in their first endeavor?"[23] Insisting that it was this question that animated the fact that he had "devoted such time" in his analysis, Tocqueville contended that what was new in America was of "interest, not to the United States only, but to the whole world; not to one nation, but to all mankind."[24]

Tocqueville is quite clear as to the consequences for Europe if positive newness in the first instance is ignored. Should absolute power reestablish itself under the advancing conditions of democracy, the form it would take would be horrific since aristocratic restraint would be largely absent. In this sense the newness of democracy that Tocqueville described in the beginning of his book is linked to the European future. The choice for the European is either slavery or freedom, "should we not, then consider the gradual development of democratic institutions and mores not as the best but as the only means remaining to us in order to remain free?"[25] But how might Europeans capture the "American example" aside from Tocqueville's suggestion that it be introduced gradually and through an imitation of some combination of American mores and laws? Previously, Tocqueville had noted that if his beloved New Englanders, with their love of liberty and religion, had been transplanted to Europe not "even the Anglo-Americans . . . could live there without considerably modifying their mores."[26] Nor could the new American federal system be copied in any obvious way. Federalism was a dangerous form of governance when surrounded by hostile powers, and states within the system favor stability in America because they are homogeneous and small ones are without traditions of collective defense against large states. Tocqueville is thus left to derive "newness positive" in the first instance from the assertion that there are other mores and laws than the new American ones yet undiscovered but capable of implementation. He clearly believes that a reformed Catholic church was capable of supporting democratic mores, that some form of administrative decentralization was possible for European nations, and perhaps that some moderating and unanticipated structures such as the role of American lawyers functioning as aristocratic substitutes were conceivable.

There is no question about the sincerity and intensity of Tocqueville's pursuit of the "positive in the first instance." Yet there are precious few examples beyond his assertion that American newness proves that one ought not to despair about replicating a democracy like the American one and that some alternative to radical democratic tendencies in Europe must be found. No doubt part of Tocqueville's vagueness about newness as "positive" in the first instance can be traced to his own critique of American democracy (newness as "negative in the first instance"), which reached new and different proportions in Volume 2. Had he had a choice of laws if he were to live among a democratic people, he would live in a monarchical regime. In any case, America as "positive in the first instance" is more accurately seen not so much in terms of its specific laws and mores, which contain democratic excess, but rather through the idea that if America constituted a new form of democracy then other nations might do so as well.

In a sense Tocqueville reserves a real form of newness to the Europeans themselves since American democracy had emerged through a fortuitous set of circumstances and its imitators would be in the position of consciously creating new forms based on the American experience. They could afford fewer mistakes than the Americans and they would be forced to proceed incrementally, but, on the other hand, without the same favorable point of departure they would be engaged in a more heroic project. Thus Tocqueville's relative vagueness about American "newness" in the first instance reserves a certain kind of newness for Europeans. America the new enables Europe the old to capture a "new" newness from the irresistible movement of democracy it has been powerless to resist for centuries. In a draft for his 1835 work, Tocqueville reveals the founding aspect of his task: "Democratie. Don't you see them advance unceasingly by a slow and irresistible effort; already they cover the field and the cities; they roll over the ruined battlements, of castles and even wash against the steps of thrones . . . Instead of wishing to raise impotent dikes, let us rather seek to build the holy guardian task which must carry the human species on this boundless ocean."[27]

Negative in the First Instance

The conventional wisdom that has emerged from readings of both volumes of *Democracy* tells us that Tocqueville's analysis of America shifted noticeably in volume 2. Although there are numerous versions of the two democracy thesis, their common focus emphasizes the change in the dominant mood of the second essay. Pessimism replaced hope in Tocqueville's analysis of America. Moreover, substantive assessments differ. The problem of centralization, apparently solved by the American example in volume 1, emerges as the central problem for democracies in volume 2. In volume 1, Tocqueville praises the elan of American democracy; volume 2 presents the famous distinction between individualism and egoism. The alienation of the European villager reappears in new form as the American citizen isolates himself from all but family and friends. "Lumpers" rather than "splitters," on the other hand, contend that critique is clearly evident in the first volume as well and that the themes of volume 2 are anticipated in

volume 1.[28] If, however, we read Tocqueville's volumes as an exploration of American Exceptionalism in terms of newness, the question of
"the two Democracies" is reconstituted. Volume 2 involves the same
confrontation with newness as volume 1 but now in the context of the
"negative in the first instance" as its driving force. This is not to say,
however, that volume 2 does not continue to explore the positive in
the first instance nor even the positive unique and the negative unique.
Tocqueville's confrontation with newness still defines his project as a
whole.

Tocqueville, as in the first volume, never forces his perspective on
newness in extremis. For example, he rejects the argument that a
democratic people have no aptitude for the arts and sciences on the
basis of the American example. We should "give up looking at all
democratic peoples through American spectacles" he tells his readers
and contends that "Americans are in an exceptional situation" and an
unlikely one in which "any other democratic people will be similarly
placed."[29] Puritan origins and commercial habits coupled with a reliance upon European culture account for the relative dearth of progress
in these areas. Thus Tocqueville preserves American newness as "negative unique" in the context of an extended argument about its newness in terms of a negative in the first instance. There is also, of
course, Tocqueville's famous account of the role of voluntary associations in America and the doctrine of self-interest that supports their
profusion in volume 2 as an example of the positive in the first instance, although here this kind of political activity is recommended as
a remedy for individualism rather than majority tyranny.

So too does the positive unique with which Tocqueville struggled in
volume 1, still emerge in his second. Tocqueville notes the relative
absence of political theories among the English and their "ill-consid-
ered scorn" of general ideas, which he traces to the dominance of the
aristocracy. The French, on the other hand, have shown a "blind faith
in the virtue and absolute truth of any theory." To Americans, however, due to their democratic heritage, theory and experience "naturally and constantly balance each other."[30]

What though are the implications of the centering of America as
the negative in the first instance in Tocqueville's analysis? We noted
that in volume 1 he struggled to make room for the positive in the first
instance by insisting upon the conceptualization of American newness in terms of mores and laws that could be partially replicated. In
volume 2 a similar tension emerges as Tocqueville forces his account

of the "new" beyond America to the category of democratic nations or peoples. As America as the "new unique" faded in his effort to consider America in terms of a different aspect of newness, America as the positive in the first instance is forced even more out of focus to make room for the negative in the first instance. As a rough indication of this movement, look at how the designation of "America" fades in the chapter headings of volume 1 from 13 out of 21, with most of the rest devoted to democratic people or nations (itself a major alteration from volume 1) to 11 of 20, in Part II, to 9 of 26 in Part III, to 0 of 8 in Part IV. Even the questions Tocqueville takes up in Part III are relatively remote from American experience in the nineteenth century: war, national defense and military organization.

This more pronounced blurring of America as the question of the negative in the first instance is approached is sometimes explained in terms of Tocqueville's alleged shift toward France as the nation best positioned to illustrate newness and/or his own political experience.[31] If this is so, however, Tocqueville's position is covert. France and French political traditions are mentioned less than in volume 1. An explanation of this phenomenon can tell us much about Tocqueville's analysis of newness. For the depiction of democratic despotism described in Part IV, which Tocqueville described as so new that it is "different from anything there is or has never been before," may not have been derived from the American experience Tocqueville observed (for what was the Jacksonian agenda if not a systematic effort to dismantle the state?) but was connected to Tocqueville's careful examination of American newness. That is, Tocqueville was disposed to examining America in terms of newness and, as he continued to look for trends that democracies were inclined to take, he focused upon patterns which were, to use his own words, with "no prototype."[32]

One can see this penchant for new explanations in Tocqueville's own critique of democracy in volume 1. For all the innovation in his analysis, and especially in his account of America as "positive new," Tocqueville had borrowed upon a complaint as old as Plato's criticism in *The Republic*. Democracies, with their equalitarian norms, lacked social discipline and were especially prone to a dictatorship by those who intuited this absence of restraint and promised salvation through more and more grants of power. Tocqueville had found these tendencies in America but concluded that they were restrained by its "excellent point of departure" in a tradition of local liberty and a prudent constitutional founding. Interestingly, the Whig prophecy of Jackson as a *Napoleon des bois* did not faze Tocqueville as he pursued the "positive new." That America could become despotic even without a revolutionary tradition and its good start in general, was a conclusion that Tocqueville could not have made without a willingness to look for new sources of despotism and also a new form of despotism itself. Not only had Tocqueville defined a new kind of despotism sans the demagogue but he also defined a new conceptual distinction in political thought—individualism and egoism. To do so required a certain obliviousness to American politics as it existed—hence the blurring—in an effort to pursue newness as a category. Thus the difference between the two volumes can be seen, with a certain irony of course, in terms of Tocqueville's further immersion into America the new. There is a sense in which volume 2, despite its apparent discarding of things American, is the more American of the two essays. To the extent to which Tocqueville has been proven correct in his analysis of alienation in America, this head-on confrontation with newness was a successful strategy.

The Negative Unique

As we noted, Tocqueville was willing to consider the "negative unique" in volume 2 in regard to both American contributions to the arts and sciences and to the theatre ("The Puritan founders of the American republics were not only hostile to all pleasures but professed a special abhorrence for the stage").[33] None of these asides, however, match the major detour he makes in his argument in volume 1 in regard to race relations. Tocqueville, who was no stranger to the institution of slavery in the French West Indies and who struggled for its abolition, was shocked by the condition of African Americans. His analysis is so extended and so direct in its examination of the impact on American democracy that it constitutes an alternate scenario of America. However much Tocqueville confronted newness in America he seemed unprepared for what he saw in regard to the "three races that inhabited America." He was prepared to accept the elimination of Native Americans as a people and a culture. While his analysis stands as a corrective to his assertion that America stood vacant before English settlers, his conclusion that the alternatives that faced indigenous peoples as equally pessimistic (physical extinction in the wilds and cultural death in white civilization) was presented with a certain equanimity. In fact, Tocqueville concluded his discussion with an ironic

exceptionalism of the "negative unique": "The Spaniards, by unparal-
leled atrocities which brand them with indelible shame, did not succeed in exterminating the Indian race and could not even prevent them
from sharing their rights; the United States Americans have attained
these results with wonderful ease, quietly, legally and philanthropi-
cally, without spilling blood and without violating a single one of the
great principles of morality in the eyes of the world. It is impossible to
destroy men with more respect to the laws of humanity."[34]

Thus while Tocqueville is prepared to confront the newness of the
domination and elimination of Native Americans, he does not conclude that this monumental tragedy appreciably affects America's excellent point of departure in either the "positive unique" or positive in
the first instance. This is not so in the case of the treatment of African
Americans. For here the institution of slavery brings into question the
future of democracy in America in a way that the revolution did so in
France. For Tocqueville the French revolution seemed to create a perpetual absence of consensus and at the same time thrust the nation
into a permanent series of crises that were animated by the revolutionary spirit. Racial slavery and its aftermath (for Tocqueville believed
that its termination was inevitable) would produce the same instability
in America.

Tocqueville explores this newness as "negative unique" in terms of
a series of dichotomies that seem to explode the advantages that he
has catalogued. In place of the absent feudalism and the prevalent
equality of condition is the distinction between ancient and modern
slavery. The latter is racially determined: "Memories of slavery disgrace the race, and race perpetuates memories of slavery. . . . The
law can abolish servitude, but only god can obliterate the races. . . .
The modern slave differs from his master not only in lacking freedom
but also in his origin. You can make the Negro free, but you cannot
prevent him facing the European as stranger."[35] This chasm is also
marked by a strange unity: "The two races are bound one to the other
without mingling; it is equally difficult for them to separate completely
or to unite."[36]

The most striking image of the consequences of this racial dualism
is Tocqueville's description of the banks of the Ohio River:

> The stream that the Indians had named the Ohio, or Beautiful River par ex-
> cellence waters one of the most magnificent valleys in which man has ever
> lived. On both banks of the Ohio stretched undulating ground with soil con-
> tinually offering the cultivator inexhaustible treasures; on both banks the air

is equally healthy and the climate temperate; they both form the frontier of a vast state; that which follows the innumerable windings of the Ohio on the left bank is called Kentucky; the other takes its name from the river itself. There is only one difference between the two states: Kentucky allows slaves, Ohio refuses to have them.

So the traveler who lets the current carry him down the Ohio till it joins the Mississippi sails, so to say, between freedom and slavery; and he has only to glance around him to see instantly which is best for mankind.[37]

Tocqueville packs much into this description. There is the bountifulness of the frontier which he hailed as "newness unique" juxtaposed to the unmistakable grimness of free and slave societies. On the right bank is confirmation of the new frontier, settlements peopled by descendants of the New Englanders, those commercial people who mixed the spirit of liberty with the spirit of freedom. But on the right bank is a frontier abused and unused, not unlike in a general sense the French and Spanish settlements. But most exceptional and most new of all for Tocqueville is the juxtaposition of the two banks themselves, for here were freedom and slavery standing side by side corresponding to two of the American republics and not tethered by a mother country and an empire. It is this brutal fact, the existence of racial slavery within an enlightenment nation, that represented America as the "negative unique."

Tocqueville contended that the two banks of the Ohio were "the final demonstration" of the "fatal" impact of slavery upon the master, and his following analysis shows its fatal impact upon the nation as a whole. Slavery has always demeaned the status of work, and Tocqueville notes that in the ancient world there was only a "very imperfect understanding of this effect . . . on the production of wealth."[38] American slavery so constituted in the modern world, and in the American form of race, has made a connection between racial pride and idleness. Beginning with the impact of the elimination of primogeniture and then with the inevitable end of slavery, the racial aristocracy of the South would crumble, but not so pride of race. Pointing to current Northern practice as the "new" future, Tocqueville predicted that discrimination against African Americans would only increase with the end of slavery, thus leading to massive deaths as competition for free labor increased. "The rest crowd into towns, where they perform the roughest work, leading a precarious and wretched existence."[39] It was perhaps possible, noted Tocqueville, that secession would give African Americans a majority in the South, in which case the fate of whites would be as precarious. Of other scenarios, Tocqueville was equally pessimistic. He regarded forced emigration as impracticable; miscegenation as unlikely. The races would rather continue to "face each other like two foreign peoples" until one eliminated the other.

Modern Tocquevillians

Tocqueville never made a systematic effort to correlate his categorizations of newness. Unlike Jefferson's study of America, however, his studies of newness do not seem to deconstruct and interact with one another. There are certainly alternative scenarios of the American future as well as different assessments of their replicability and worthiness, for the effort to explain the newness is always at the forefront of Tocqueville's analysis. One cannot say that this is the result of any direct effort on Tocqueville's part, for his efforts are focused upon defining what is new in America, how it was new, why it was new, and how and why it might be (or should be or not be) replicated. Thus his categorizations serve to encase the new. What is the result then if we allow ourselves to re-dissolve them? The answer must be that what is reformed is America as the "new-in-itself."

As a text with privileged status, *Democracy in America* reproduces itself in unique ways. *The Federalist Papers,* which, with its ingenious mixture of the old and the new and its status as performative document, stands as a text that is so exceptional that its study recapitulates its grand genesis. To read and to adopt Tocqueville's conception of American exceptionalism, however, involves a process of reaffirming newness and at the same time assessing its causes and consequences. But, as we shall briefly review, the followers of Tocqueville almost invariably encase the new more securely than he himself did, thus hiding the great contribution of *Democracy in America* to American Exceptionalism, while nevertheless securing its privileged status. There need not be any mystery to this "newness-in-itself", for the impact of Tocquevillian newness involves several related and sometimes simultaneous processes: the confirmation of one or more of his categories often rediscovered in "new" forms; the alteration of one or more of his categories into new format(s); the rediscovery of a Tocquevillian method that emphasizes the need for new departures in political analysis. It is thus only through a focus on the Tocquevillian legacy as a whole that we see that this text demands consideration and reconsideration of America as new.

Take, if only as an example, the question of American mores that so fascinated Tocqueville in volume 1 and take just a recent portion of analyses that borrow from *Democracy in America*: David Reisman's *The Lonely Crowd*; Charles Reich's *The Greening of America*; Christopher Lasch's *The Culture of Narcissism*; Bellah et al., *Habits of the Heart*.

Reisman's exploration of the new is the most explicitly reliant upon Tocqueville, and in his famous distinction between inner and other-directed character types he acknowledged Tocqueville's observations about the origins of the newness of the American. The existence of the frontier, the absence of a feudal heritage and the distinctive "recruitment" of the first settlers made a new personality type "most at home" in America. And like Tocqueville, Reisman searched for newness as the first instance: "I am also inclined to put more weight on capitalism, industrialism, and urbanization—these being international tendencies—than on any character forming peculiarities of the American scene."[40] But for Reisman, the emergence of the American other-directed personality, while bearing important similarities to Tocqueville's conformist American, which led to concerns about the tyranny of the majority of volume 1 and democratic despotism in volume 2 of *Democracy*, was fundamentally a "new" phenomenon. The other-directed American whose character and values were derived from his peers and society at large emerged after Tocqueville's visit, and Reisman was reticent to judge exactly what Tocqueville "foresaw." But the most serious revision of Tocqueville was not connected so much to Reisman's insistence on the newness of a personality type but on his evaluation of its newness. For while the other-directed American possessed many of the same characteristics that led to Tocqueville's newness as negative in the first instance—a sense of unbounded conformity and diffuse anxiety—Reisman instead searched for a positive in the first instance that might emerge as the next phase of American newness. Perhaps, argued Reisman, a new autonomy might be created as the other-directed person "through the seemingly 'idle' and countless practice of taste exchanging" began "to realize that he is actually a good deal more competent than he gets or gives himself credit for being."[41] A new American who finds autonomy through play and leisure would be consistent with the nature of American newness itself: "America is not only big and rich, it is mysterious; and its capacity for the humorous and ironical concealment of its interests matches that of the legendary Chinese."[42]

Charles Reich's *The Greening of America* captured the newness that Reisman had cautiously suggested was an imminent possibility for the other-directed American in his category "Consciousness III." Postulating earlier forms of mores that corresponded roughly to Reisman's categories, Reich contended that a new form of individualism, one that would replace the Consciousness I belief in "morality, hard work and self-denial" and the Consciousness II belief in collective planning, "sprouted up, astonishingly and miraculously, out of the stony soil of the American Corporate State." Although he was vague about its origins, Reich was certain that this form possessed a "new knowledge" of the world that grasped human potential in a noncompetitive and nonmaterialistic manner. This "desire for innocence, for the ability to be in a state of wonder or awe" was characteristic of a "new generation . . . constantly eager to experiment."[43] Reich was oblivious to the criticism that Consciousness III was a fulfillment of the Tocquevillian prophesy of the negative new in the first instance. In fact, it was in his description of Consciousness II that his negative new most paralleled Tocqueville's. What is less revisionist, however, about Reich's analysis, was not only his effort to describe a "new" set of mores but his Tocquevillian insistence that America must be understood in terms of new kinds of knowledge.

The Tocquevillian inspired studies of American mores that followed Reich's leaned much more heavily on the Tocquevillian negative. Christopher Lasch's American narcissistic personality, with his expansive yet fragile sense of self, projected as gregariousness and veiled hostility, had analogs in Tocqueville's observations on American individualism but needed to be "restated to take account of the differences between nineteenth century" forms and the "narcissism of our time." Unlike Tocqueville, Lasch located the origins of modern American individualism in capitalism rather than democratization. But, like Tocqueville, he argued that large bureaucratic structures had a major corrosive impact on all aspects of independent life. Lasch insisted that narcissism was a false newness that could be replaced with a newness that was derivative from the American past: "The will to build a new society, however, survives, along with traditions of localism, self-help, and community action that only need the vision of a new society, a decent society, to give them new vigor. . . ." Such "discipline," he concluded, "endures most of all in those who knew the old order only as a broken promise, yet who took the promise more seriously than those who merely took it for granted."[44]

Bellah and his associates reached for Tocquevillian newness in a different way. The authors were impressed with the ways in which Tocqueville's mores still found voice in their interviewees. Some seemed to "confirm Tocqueville's fears of privatism," while in others they found the "public passions" nurtured by the associational activity that he had praised. Thus Bellah and his associates' analysis capture both the negative and positive newness of Tocqueville and, given their emphasis on American sources of political consciousness and expression, imply that these features are part of an American unique. America was exceptional in the predominance of a "first language" of individualism, but other languages remained a feature of political discourse. They were capable of expansion through the employment of a "new" political science (derivable from Tocquevillian precedent) conceived as "public philosophy."[45]

It is impossible to say that these current accounts of American mores could not have been written without what Bellah has called the "towering influence" of Tocqueville. What *Democracy in America* does contribute, however, to the tradition of American exceptionalism is a ready means of identifying and confirming newness. Tocqueville defined America as the central, if not the exclusive, category for examining a historical process that was "irresistible," and he explored this exceptionalism in a variety of ways in terms of uniqueness and replicability and in terms of its negative and positive consequences. Modern Tocquevillians accept these designations (America as the center of world history and as the primary source of the new) as a premise. Tocqueville further identified the sources of these aspects of newness, which current analysts rely upon as the basis for both confirming their observations and establishing their trajectory for the identification of "new" forms. And finally, each writer calls for, as did Tocqueville, a political science that is new in that it directs attention to new developments in American political culture. For all this, American observers can thank Tocqueville. What they miss in this tradition of replicating and extending Tocqueville's insights is his project as a whole. For it is here, in his effort to describe and explain America exclusively in terms of the new, that one finds his most creative contribution. Does a culture that insists upon interpreting itself as not only the center of world history but as one, since it is self-defined as new, which is thus permanently so, miss not only the import of Tocqueville's negatives (which in some instances can involve no other response than a resignation to the new)? Does it also miss the opportunity to examine itself in any other way and to seek remedies other than in the new? Does, in other words, this friendly criticism of the outsider breed a tradition of analysis that has all the apparent features of national self-reflection but none of its real advantages?

Ralph Lerner, as part of his own study of Tocqueville, has remarked that "the more impressive a work of historical analysis, the greater the likelihood it will deceive."[46] In his confrontation with the new in *Democracy in America*, Tocqueville managed to gaze unflinchingly upon its forms and consequences with a sentiment that permitted him to see "newness as promise" that was both replicable and unique and "newness as loss" that was both irretrievable and recoverable. Writing from the perspective of a French patriot, he studied American Exceptionalism with the hope of discovering how America could save his own country and how his own country might also be saved from America. When Americans employ Tocqueville they certainly write from no less a patriotic vantage point. What dissolves, however, is the sense of "newness as condition" and what remains is "newness as salvation." Thus the delicate balances among the forms of newness Tocqueville struggled to encapsulate from his confrontation, which sometimes led him to confusions, are blurred as efforts are made to utilize his insights. Without a firm commitment to Tocqueville's teaching, *Democracy* becomes a text of national deception.

Notes

1   See James A. Schleifer's review, "The Problem of the Two Democracies" in Eduardo Nolla, ed., *Liberty, Equality, Democracy* (New York: New York University Press, 1992), 193–205.

2   Alexis de Tocqueville, *Democracy in America,* trans. George Lawrence (London: Fontana Press, 1969), I, 12. See Eduardo Nolla's account of Tocqueville's conception of political science, which emphasizes a methodology of the new. "Democracy or the Closed Book" in Peter Augustine Lawler and Joseph Alulis, eds., *Tocqueville's Defense of Human Liberty* (New York: Garland Press, 1993), 85–95.

3   See: James T. Schleifer, *The Making of Tocqueville's Democracy in America* (Chapel Hill: University of North Carolina Press, 1980), 263–74; George Wilson Pierson, *Tocqueville in America* (Garden City, NY: Anchor Books, 1959), 104; Marvin Zetterbaum, *Tocqueville and the Problem of Democracy* (Stanford: Stanford University Press, 1967); Jack Lively, *The Social and Political Thought of Alexis de Tocqueville* (Oxford: Oxford University Press, 1961), 49–50.

4   Pierson, *Tocqueville in America,* 33.

5   *Ibid.,* 43–44, 45, 77–78, 106, 146–47, 293, 364.

6   Tocqueville, *Democracy in America,* I, 18.

7   I adapt the following list from Tocqueville's own in his notes. Pierson, *Tocqueville in America,* pp. 294–95

8   Tocqueville, *Democracy in America,* I, 306.

9   *Ibid.,* 35

10   *Ibid.,* 36, 34, 39.

11   *Ibid.,* 280.

12   Ibid., 280. See: Cotton Mather, *Magnalia Christi Americana,* ed., Kenneth B. Murdock (Cambridge: Harvard University Press, 1977), 117–18.

13   Tocqueville, *Democracy in America,* I, 281.

14   *Ibid.*

15   Larry Sientop regards Tocqueville's discovery of American statelessness and the theoretical significance he attached to it as a weapon in his attack on European notions of the state as the greatest, though most unappreciated, contribution of his political thought. *Tocqueville* (Oxford: Oxford University Press, 1994), 41–68.

16 Tocqueville, *Democracy in America*, I, 61, 62.

17 *Ibid.*, 69.

18 *Ibid.*, 163.

19 *Ibid.*, 113.

20 *Ibid.*, 157.

21 *Ibid.*, 149. Despite the genius of the founding, Tocqueville believed that the continuance of the union was unlikely. See Schleifer, *The Making of Tocqueville's Democracy in America*, 102–11 who describes this conclusion as one of the "prophet in error." Schleifer contends that this pessimism was connected to his reliance upon Federalist texts. Ralph C. Hancock, however, argues that Tocqueville actually posited two scenarios. "Tocqueville on the Good of American Federalism" in Peter Augustine Lawler, ed. *Tocqueville's Political Science: Classic Essays* (New York: Garland, 1992), 133–55.

22 *Ibid.*, 412.

23 *Ibid.*, 311.

24 *Ibid.*

25 *Ibid.*, 314.

26 *Ibid.*, 309.

27 Schleifer, *The Making of Democracy in America*, 264.

28 See: Schleifer, "How Many Democracies?" 193–205 for evidence supporting the single democracy thesis. For "splitters": Seymour Drescher, "Tocqueville's Two *Democracies*," *Journal of the History of Ideas* 25 (April–June, 1964), 201–16; Robert Nisbet, "Many Tocquevilles," *American Scholar* 46 (Winter, 1977), 59–75. Jean-Claude Lamberti supports the two democracy thesis but contends that the split occurs at Part IV in the second volume. *Tocqueville and the Two Democracies* (Cambridge, MA.: Harvard University Press, 1989). The terms "lumpers" and "splitters" are offered by Drescher in "More than America: Comparison and Synthesis in Democracy in America" in Abraham S. Eisenstadt, ed., *Reconsidering Tocqueville's Democracy in America* (New Brunswick, NJ: Rutgers University Press, 1988).

29 Tocqueville, *Democracy in America*, II, 455.

30 Ibid., 441.

31 See: Drescher, "More than America," 88–89; Lamberti, *Tocqueville and the Two Democracies*, 151 ff.

32 Tocqueville, *Democracy in America*, II, 691.

33 *Ibid.*, 492.

34 *Ibid.*, I, 339.

35 *Ibid.*, 341.

36 *Ibid.*, 340.

37 *Ibid.*, 346.

38 *Ibid.*, 348.

39 *Ibid.*, 351.

40 David Riesman, *The Lonely Crowd: A Study of the Changing American Character* (New Haven: Yale University Press, 1950), 20.

41 *Ibid.*, 373.

42 *Ibid.*

43 Charles Reich, *The Greening of America* (New York: Bantam, 1970).

44 Christopher Lasch, *The Culture of Narcissism* (New York: Warner, 1979), 396–37.

45 Robert N. Bellah et al., *Habits of the Heart* (New York: Harper and Row, 1985), 297. For a critique of Bellah's use of Tocqueville, which argues that Bellah fails to acknowledge the negative in the first instance, see: Bruce Frohnen, "Materialism and Self Deification" in Lawler and Aluis, eds., *Tocqueville's Defense of Human Liberty*, 135–56.

46 Ralph Lerner, *Revolutions Revisited* (Chapel Hill: University of North Carolina Press, 1994), 112.

Chapter 6

The Merged Text
The *Declaration of Independence* from Philadelphia to Gettysburg to Birmingham

While Garry Wills concedes the "mystical" hold that the *Declaration of Independence* has in American political life he argues that it is nevertheless a "lost" text that has become "dark with unexamined lights" from persistent "misreadings."[1] He argues that Lincoln is the primary source for "many intervening filters that distort the text," which by now has become a "misshapen thing in our minds." I do not intend to deny Lincoln's contributions to our understanding of the *Declaration*—indeed I intend to acknowledge them. Rather I hope to show that Lincoln's readings, along with Martin Luther King's, illustrate the character of the *Declaration* as an exemplar of American Exceptionalism as a *merged* text.[2]

This character of a merged text is the source of its newness, for unlike the *Federalist Papers,* which reestablishes its authority through its mastery of the old and the new, the *Declaration's* authority rests upon its capacity for reapplication to new circumstances. Thus the Declaration of Independence mirrors American identity itself as a culture that defines itself as an eclectic mixture of the "old" and the "new."[3] These reapplications thus become part of the text itself, for to read the *Declaration without* the acts of merger at Gettysburg or Birmingham is to miss its contribution to American identity. The newness of the *Declaration* is axiomatic, for it is the original locus of American identity (We "declare these United colonies are and of right ought to be free and independent states. . ."). But since there is an oldness in the document itself, which Lincoln emphasized (its "birth" generations ago), only the most extraordinary circumstances can make it new or "re-born." Such a rebirth requires monumental circumstances and monumental readers for the rendition becomes the text itself.

Unlike Wills, I make no attempt here to critique the Declaration of Gettysburg or Birmingham nor to remove alleged alien encrustations upon Jefferson's text. For in terms of American identity, the *Declaration of Independence* is no longer Jefferson's or, at least, Jefferson's alone. Still, the Declarations of Gettysburg and Birmingham reveal a certain wear even in their monumental merger with the document of Philadelphia, for the two central propositions of the first Declaration must be accounted for: "all men are created equal" and "the right of the people to alter or to abolish" their government. Not even readers as monumental as Lincoln or King could completely satisfy both these demands, and thus we can conclude that it is in this commix of propositions (equality and rebellion) that the *Declaration* makes its claim to exceptionalism.

From Philadelphia to Gettysburg: The New Lincoln Text

The *Declaration* at Philadelphia, of course, contained its own tensions between old and new as well as between the equality and rebellion propositions. Jefferson was so insistent that he had only placed before mankind "the common sense of the subject" that Wills wondered why he had listed the *Declaration* as one of his three great legacies: "What is so memorable about saying what everybody else is saying?"[4] So too in terms of ambiguities was the axiomatic assertion of equality in the midst of a society that included the institution of slavery and visions of virtue from classical antiquity. What is so overwhelming, however, in the Philadelphia version of the *Declaration*, is its performative status as a statement of rebellion. The declaration of newness in the sense of the creation of a new polity as natural right is an authorization that still fascinates. The very circumstances of the drafting and signing of the *Declaration* at Philadelphia (the secrecy, the alteration of minutes, the obsession with spies and informers) and its subsequent plans for public readings highlight the distinction between the treason and independence and establishes what one nineteenth century observer called the "physical courage" of the signers.[5] Thus the incompleteness, indeed the hypocrisy of the equality proposition from the standpoint of later generations, does not diminish the boldness of the *Declaration* as an act of (successful) rebellion.[6] Rather it serves as a sanction for merger but one that must also acknowledge the singular triumph of independence.

In fact, Lincoln's success in galvanizing support for resisting secession rested on a set of arguments that respond to two core Southern propositions that traded upon the supreme authority of the rebellion proposition: the institution of slavery was not inconsistent with democratic society and the United States as a political unit contained the implicit right of secession on the part of one or more states. The first proposition appears ludicrous today while the second appears simply anachronistic since conventional wisdom asserts that it was the Civil War itself that resolved this question. Thus Gary Wills writes: "Up to the Civil War, the United States was invariably a plural noun: 'The United States are a free government.' After Gettysburg, it became singular: 'The United States is a free government.' "[7] Yet the South enjoyed a plethora of precedents supporting their later claim. Not the least of which were the Kentucky-Virginia resolutions written by two of the founders themselves and the Hartford Convention, which was supported by dissident New England Federalists in what became the heartland of abolitionism. Their trump card, however, was the *Declaration of Independence* at Philadelphia, which as the privileged revolutionary text asserted the right to revolution and did so on contractual terms. Thus, Jefferson Davis in his inaugural address explained the formation of the Confederacy thusly: "In this they [the CSA] merely asserted the right which the Declaration of Independence of 1776 defined to be inalienable."[8] It was the first proposition that Southern secessionists found much more difficult to defend. They were driven to seek "old" pre-liberal precedents in biblical interpretation and in Athenian democracy and by way of inversion, in their critique of the "new wage slavery" in the North as the less humane of the two economic systems.[9] In a sense, Southern secessionists strove to split rather than merge the *Declaration* by employing examples of the old and the new. Their arguments for secession became quite sophisticated and inventive—corresponding in essence to Lincoln's endeavor in the other direction—but unlike Lincoln's, the equality proposition could simply not be erased with the same degree of success.[10]

The young Lincoln argued as early as 1838 that the key document of nationhood was the *Declaration* and, implicitly, not the Constitution. In the Lyceum address Lincoln emphasized the fragility of the union whose fate now rested with the second generation of Americans. He warned that the edifice created by the fathers of the republic "must fade, is fading and has faded. . . ." But unlike Washington, who, in his Farewell Address urged Americans to pledge fidelity to the Constitution when tempted by the sirens of faction and designing politicians, Lincoln demanded filial piety centered upon pledging obedience to the "patriots of seventy-six."[11]

But as Lincoln developed his positions after the deepening crisis created by the Kansas-Nebraska Act of 1854, he found that neither of the Southern propositions was easily refutable through a simple appeal to retrieve the oldness of the Revolution. There was a gaping hole, of course, in the Southern recourse to liberal contractarian arguments on the one hand and the very un-Lockean defense of a semi-feudal society on the other. But Lincoln too faced his own contradictions. If he used the *Declaration* as the ballast for his central anti-secessionist support, focusing on its assertion of equality ("all men are created equal"), then he must also confront the *Declaration*'s seeming support for rebellion ("the right of the People to alter or abolish" governments). In more immediate political terms, Lincoln faced marginalization if he adopted an abolitionist position that centered the former part of the text at the expense of the latter and indistinguishability from his rivals in both parties if he accepted various kinds of accommodations that would keep the Southerners from exercising their alleged right to separate.

In his Springfield speech accepting his party's nomination for the U.S. Senate, Lincoln moved dramatically away from the latter alternative by employing the biblical metaphor of a house-divided to predict that the union "cannot endure, permanently half-slave and half-free."[12] The symbol of a house-divided was not lost on the biblically oriented nineteenth century audience. The phrase Lincoln employed is derived from Matthew's account of the questioning by the Pharisees of Jesus' healing power. Jesus' response, "every kingdom divided against itself is brought to desolation; and every city or house divided against itself shall not stand" is an extremely complex statement that explores the nature of belief, faith and motivation. Simply summarized, the house divided metaphor seeks to show the confusion and desperation that accompany actions undertaken in absence of divine guidance. Lincoln, by employing the phrase, was contending that people will pay a price for ignoring "ancient truths" in their common heritage and tolerating evil. "Satan cannot cast out Satan" was part of Jesus' defense of his divine powers and Lincoln was applying this New Testament lesson to those who would accommodate the spread of slavery. Thus not only had Lincoln linked the slavery crisis to an ancient biblical narrative in which division is not a natural right but a certain sign of descent into perdition but linked those, like Douglas, who apparently sought compromise, to a conspiracy which amounted to complicity with evil.

The house-divided position still provided him some wiggle room, however. In the debates with Douglas, Lincoln variously contended

his comment was simple prediction and that he never advocated political or social equality for African-Americans. Nevertheless, the critique of Douglas' doctrine of popular sovereignty from which Lincoln
drew from the house-divided position, along with the vividness of the
metaphor, placed him in a position where the *Declaration* suitably re-
read became the central metonymy from which he attacked the legiti-
macy of secession.

As Lincoln moved into the national arena, he boldly chose
Jefferson—the joint author of the Virginia-Kentucky resolutions, advo-
cate of states' rights, and slave owner—as his exemplar. In Ottawa,
Douglas leveled the charge of "newness." He raised the question of
why the union could not endure "in the same relative condition that
our fathers made it"? Lincoln responded that he based his position on
the "original principles" in Jefferson "fashion."[13]

But Lincoln's Jefferson was quite different from the Southern hero,
as this commemoration offered a year after the debates indicates: "All
honor to Jefferson—to the man who, in the concrete pressure of a
struggle for national independence by a single people, had the cool-
ness, forecast, and capacity to introduce into a merely revolutionary
document, an abstract truth, and so embalm it there, that today and in
all coming days, it shall be a rebuke and a stumbling block to the very
harbingers of reappearing tyranny and oppression."[14] The *Declaration* could have been "merely a revolutionary document" had not
Jefferson the foresight to introduce the idea of an "abstract truth."
Note how Lincoln says the work is simply a revolutionary pamphlet
written under "concrete pressure" except for a singular abstract idea.
But the idea is "embalm(ed)"; Lincoln must bring a dead thing to life.
Thus Lincoln as president-elect is able to say that he never had "a
feeling politically that did not spring from sentiments in the Declaration of Independence" and that the *Declaration* was the "immortal
emblem of our humanity" and "all honor to Jefferson" because he
read the *Declaration*, not as a revolutionary document, but as one
entailing a moral commitment to equality. The rest was "merely revolutionary" reflecting the "concrete pressure" of the moment. Thus
Lincoln's explanation of the *Declaration* in 1859 reveals a major turn-
ing point in the merger of the Philadelphia document with its eventual
reformulation at Gettysburg, for he had found the key combination for
the mixture of old and new (embalmed) as contained in the equality
proposition, and he erased its rebellious element as old and irrelevant.

Freed of his own stumbling block in terms of opposing secession,
Lincoln was able to move in two directions.[15] One involved his insis-

tence that once the eternal meaning of the *Declaration* had been brought to life, it would be a tragedy to restrict its application to white males of English descent. Douglas' arguments about what the signers historically meant carried little weight under Lincoln's mythic reading of an embalmed-rejuvenated document. The document was adopted by "iron men" when we were a "very small people." But what was the connection between the "old Declaration of Independence" and these "old men"? If ancestry by blood was the nature of the historical connection, these "new" Americans have none. If, however, the connection could be traced to moral principle ("all men are created equal"), a kind of moral paternity could be established since its sentiment could be recognized as "the father of all moral principle in them, and that they have the right to claim it as though they were the blood of the blood, and the flesh of the flesh, of the men who wrote the Declaration, and so they are." To so read the document in Douglas' terms now would be to cut "the electric cord" (the connection between the old and new) that "links the hearts" of patriots.[16]

Moreover, Lincoln was not averse to laying the more profane arguments alongside his mythic one. In a multi-ethnic society Lincoln knew the import of his assertion that any restriction of equality in the *Declaration* challenged the rights of Germans, Irish, French and Scandinavians: "If one man says it does not mean the Negro, why not another say it does not mean another man?"[17] Thus *new* Americans should see the import of dedicating themselves to this *old* document.

The other direction Lincoln took involved pursuit of the implications of a moral founding that occurred in 1776 that was committed to the proposition of equality. Having erased from the *Declaration* the reading that it contained the right to revolution on part of its constituent units, and having emphasized its "embalmed" message now brought to life, Lincoln turned to the Southern secessionist statements and their new constitution. He noted the recurrent citations of the *Declaration* but asked why "unlike the good old one, penned by Jefferson, they omit the words 'all men are created equal'?" When he examined the preamble to the constitution of the Confederate States of America, Lincoln pointed out that "unlike our good, old one, signed by Washington," it did not begin with "We the people" but instead substituted "We the deputies of the sovereign and independent states." "Why," Lincoln asked, "this deliberate pressing out of view, the rights of men, and the authority of the people?"[18]

Though Lincoln argued that the Union had not originated in a contract among the states nor was dependent on the performance of mutual obligations among them, he never denied the contractual trope per se. In his Lyceum address, he responded to the problem of civil unrest with a call for reaffirmation of the American social contract, which emphasized obedience to the law: "Let every American, every lover of liberty, every well-wisher to his posterity swear by the blood of the Revolution never to violate in the least particular the laws of the country, and never to tolerate their violation by others. As the patriots of seventy-six did to the support of the Declaration of Independence, so to the support of the constitution and laws let every man remember to violate the law is to trample on the blood of his father, and to tear the charter of his own and his children's liberty."[19] Consistent with his later positions, the young Lincoln's contractual thought took the citizen, not the state, as the contractual party and based the pledge on the "blood of the Revolution." So important is this pledge to the future of the republic that Lincoln insists that it must become the "political religion of the nation" taught by "every family, every school and college, every clergyman and legislator."[20]

As Lincoln faced the prospect of civil war, his criticism of Southern actions borrowed upon this expansive contract to deny the right of secession in terms of the threat to order in general. Southern ideas about secession were invidiously "new." "No government proper," he argued, "ever had a provision in its organic law for its own termination." Even if the U.S. were a compact among states, a unanimous vote would be necessary for "plainly, the central idea of secession is anarchy."[21] Standing alongside this argument, however, was one that grew more prominent as the Civil War progressed, finally subsuming the other. As Lincoln, however, reread the *Declaration* as a document of a union dedicated to equality, he began to transform the nature of the contract in several significant, even monumental, ways. First, the contract tied national identity to a commitment to the grand (embalmed) proposition in the *Declaration*. As long as slavery was a regional practice, Lincoln was willing to tolerate its existence (although the house-divided speech at the least pointed to eventual extinction, as Southerners were quick to remonstrate). But, as he showed in his debates with Douglas, any policy of popular sovereignty threatened to place the institution on "a new basis, which looks to the perpetuity and nationalization of slavery."

Lincoln used a wide variety of arguments to support this judgment that slavery was in danger of becoming a national institution and as such was eroding the principles of the republic. In Peoria, he presented an economic argument that slave and free labor could not coexist in the new territories: "Slave states are places for poor white people to remove from, not move to. New free states are the places for poor people to go to, and better their condition." The nation "needs these Territories," warned Lincoln, in order to maintain equality of opportunity.[22]

But Lincoln's primary supporting arguments rested on the assertion that nationalized slavery would require the repudiation of those central beliefs that made America a free nation. To Lincoln, this paring down of the shining abstract truth of the document represented a threat to everyone. He argued that the founding fathers who framed the principles that defined us as Americans had been uncomfortable with slavery and always meant slavery to be a local institution. The *Declaration* asserted the doctrine of self-government as an "absolutely and eternal right." "If the Negro is a man, is it not to that extent a total destruction of self-government to say that he too shall not govern himself?" He closed his Ottawa, Illinois, address in the debate with Douglas by quoting Henry Clay. Clay had once said that those who wished to repress liberty in America would have to "go back to the era of our independence, and muzzle the canon which thunders its annual joyous return; they must blow out the moral lights around us; they must penetrate the human soul, and eradicate there the love of liberty. . . ." Douglas, in his policy of caring not whether slavery is voted up or down, was of necessity attacking the "sacred right of self government" itself. He was "blowing out the moral lights around us."[23]

Throughout the next two years, Lincoln continued to present his own constitutional history of slavery. But intertwined with this effort was the broader theme that slavery constituted a moral crisis for American that required national expiation. In his Cooper Institute speech (1860), Lincoln reviewed the efforts of the founding fathers to restrict slavery, much as he had done in Peoria six years earlier, but the address ended with the ominous, "Let us have faith that might makes right."

In his message before a special session of Congress in April 1861, Lincoln spoke before a house that had divided. In the chamber, the seats of Southern representatives were vacant. He told the assembled body that the upcoming war was a "people's contest," urging Americans to "renew our trust in God," and go forward "without fear and with manly hearts."[24] As battlefield deaths mounted, Lincoln began to explicitly interpret the war as a providential test for America. At Gettysburg, Lincoln states his conception in terms so simple and elo-

quent that the address is regarded as a masterpiece of political discourse. Birth ("four score and seven years ago our fathers brought
forth on this continent a new nation, conceived in liberty . . ."), trial
("now we are engaged in a great civil war, testing whether that nation
so conceived and dedicated can long endure"), and re-birth ("we here
highly resolve that these dead shall not have died in vain; that this
nation, under God, shall have a new birth of freedom . . .") were the
meanings he attached to the war.[25]

In the debates with Douglas, Lincoln contended that there were
compromises and appeals to self-interest that a political system could
not accommodate without losing its self-identity. Lincoln's minimal
line was drawn differently than that of the abolitionists (he objected
only to the extension of slavery). In the late 1850s and throughout the
war, however, Lincoln, borrowing directly from the abolitionists, created a broader, even more demanding conception of nationhood that
contained a more complex conception of political religion than he had
recommended in 1838. In essence, Lincoln was creating an argument
that not only contended that slavery challenged American identity but
that the fate of the nation had a world significance, that America's
struggle with slavery constituted an even broader struggle, the outcome of which was of immense importance to humankind. The *Declaration* of Gettysburg framed this perspective. Lincoln began the
address with the assertion that the war was a test of whether people
could govern themselves. His second inaugural, delivered near the end
of the Civil War, is generally regarded as a conciliatory document. The
address does close with the biblical injunction to behave with malice
toward none and charity to all. But the body of the speech interprets
the war as the result of divine retributive justice. Both sides "read the
same Bible" and prayed to the same God; both invoked "his aid against
the other." But Lincoln is clear about the righteousness of the Northern cause: "It may seem strange that any men should dare ask a just
God's assistance in wringing their bread from the sweat of other men's
faces. . . ." He also warns "if God wills that it continue until all the
wealth piled up by the bondsman's two hundred and fifty years of
unrequited toil shall be sunk, and until every drop of blood drawn with
the sword, as was said three thousand years ago, so still it must be
said, 'the judgments of the Lord are true and righteous altogether.'"[26]

Even from this brief summary, one can see Lincoln's attempts at
creating a merged text were complex and evolving. Yet it is still possible to discern the use of the themes of old and new as the grand

strategy in this project. Despite Douglas' repeated assertions, Lincoln rarely conceded that he was speaking from a merged text. The *Declaration* was our "ancient faith," a repository of "ancient truths." It was Douglas and others who had really rejected the principle of oldness as veneration and spoke instead of oldness as irrelevance and obsolescence. "Why that object having been effected some eighty years ago, the Declaration is of no practical use now—mere rubbish—old wadding left to rot on the battlefield after the victory is won."[27] But while Lincoln was insistent upon interpreting that "all men are created equal" proposition in terms of oldness, at the same time he insisted that the "right to abolish or alter" governments was itself "old wadding," the "merely revolutionary" aspect of the document had been superseded by the stumbling block Jefferson had placed in it. When Lincoln did confront the application of this proposition in the act of secession, he did so in terms of its newness in terms of its departure from the equality proposition.

Lincoln came closest to an acknowledgment of newness in the equality proposition in the Chicago debate in which his "moral paternity" argument paired his reading of the *Declaration* with Douglas'. Here he granted that those who could not trace their descent to the revolutionaries (the "old" men of the Revolution) by blood, could not "feel part of us." Only if the document were read as moral proposition (as the "father of moral principle"), could half the population be "part of us." Even here, however, Lincoln insisted that this "newness" was unavoidable and itself immanent in the "Old Declaration" and the words of the "old men" who wrote it. For who, he asked the audience, would not wish the document to be read in this way given the likelihood of a slippery slope ("where would it stop?") once excisions were admitted.

Thus, every argument that Lincoln employed relied upon a commix of the old and new and in ever more complex ways. Sometimes the merger was secluded. This pattern is set in the Lyceum speech even before Lincoln centered the equality proposition as the "stumbling block" to rebellion. "Rededication" was the motif that provided the essential theme for the commix. This demand for reaffirmation of the old, however, hides the newness of Lincoln's own project by revising Washington's own demand in his Farewell Address, which required generational resubmission to the Constitution as well as the change of sentiment required once passion was no longer available as a source of solidarity. When Lincoln did focus on the equality proposition, he offered the compelling metaphor of a house-divided, with all its biblical resonances of conflict and discord as the fate of a people who refuse to follow "ancient truths." Lincoln's detractors pointed out the newness in this formulation. Such a reaffirmation seemed to require not only the abolition of slavery but a "consolidated empire . . . vesting Congress with the plenary power to make all the police regulations, domestic and local laws, uniform throughout the limits of the Republic."[28] Lincoln responded that he made a "prediction only" and that he had no intention of abolishing pluralism—except in the case of "a vast moral evil" and then only in terms of eventual extinction. On the eve of civil war Lincoln asserted that the doctrine of the right to secession was a new doctrine of "rebellion sugar-coated" with which the South had been "drugging the public mind" for a generation. Secession, however, could not hide the old truth that the *Declaration* provided all the conditions for union in perpetuity. It was the *Declaration* that created the existence of states: "The Union is *older* than any of the States, and created them as States." While the secessionists have "adopted some declarations of independence," they are new ones, unlike the "good old one, penned by Jefferson" since they leave out the proposition that all men are created equal. Lincoln's assertion that the *Declaration* was the founding document and not the Constitution certainly had precedents in American political thought and jurisprudence. But what is secluded here by Lincoln is his application of his reading of the equality proposition to this interpretation. That the *Declaration* created a political union was an assertion that Federalist and Whig nationalists heartily accepted; that the *Declaration* created a moral union (dedicated to the proposition that all men are created equal) was a new formulation that Lincoln insisted was old—by American standards (four score and seven years ago).

But the most inventive aspect of Lincoln's merger involved not the arguments based upon its authority in terms of its oldness nor on his sequestering of the new, but rather on a commix itself of old and new. The embalmed metaphor perfectly captured the consolidation of both for the equality proposition was both dead and not-dead, both old and new. It is at Gettysburg, however, that Lincoln truly merged the Philadelphia text, for here he used his reading of the *Declaration* to address the most profound yearnings of the human condition.

Insisting that he had only plucked a truth from a revolutionary pamphlet concerned primarily with the controversies of the day, he spoke at Gettysburg of "a new birth of freedom." Every aspect of the speech has fascinated subsequent generations but it is the audacity of the

Address (its newness) that is responsible for the awe that it still conveys. Commentators are enthralled by its brevity, its simplicity, its abstraction. Indeed, by studying the Address in terms of what it does not contain, one can see more clearly the creation of a merged text. There is mention of no soldier's name nor any general, no mention of the enemy, no mention of slavery. Indeed there is no mention of the *Declaration* itself. The reader of the Address is rather propelled in rising crescendos to comprehend its messages: the war has a profound meaning; there is a national identity that has monumental historical meaning; there is a profound connection among generations of Americans. Each of these messages peels away to release its own higher levels of abstraction: the dead can and must be honored; humans are capable of monumental projects; one generation can atone for the actions of another. What remains is a statement of the horror and hope of human existence itself, in which the recognition of birth and death is consoled by the prospect of rebirth.

Thus at Gettysburg, Lincoln's commix of old and new in the *Declaration* transformed the document to one that was old in ways the Philadelphian version had never imagined and hence was new. The controversy, which Wills initiated, about where the ideological origins of the Philadelphia document lie—with Locke or the Scottish Enlightenment—remain largely irrelevant after Lincoln's creation of the merged text. For no reading of the Philadelphia *Declaration* contains the Gettysburg's delineation of America as a biographical narrative that centers fratricide as the central confirmation of its identity. The commemoration of death—which must be remembered as well as forgotten (that is, forgiven)—is as old as Cain's sin and is an insight that the Philadelphians did not confront. By connecting this myth to the equality proposition, Lincoln merged his text with the "old" one. Lincoln confronted the consequences of victory through violence even in a just cause and raised the issue of atonement not only for the sin of fratricide but the sin of slavery. The Enlightenment voice is not rejected, but it is now commixed with the oldness of collective sin.

For all of Lincoln's genius, however, the Gettysburg *Declaration* could not avoid the interpretation that the equality proposition merged was fulfilled and sealed and hence "embalmed" in a new way. That is, that the Gettysburg *Declaration* was itself an act of atonement discharged. Moreover, there was a sense in which Lincoln had not erased the rebellion proposition from Philadelphia but, as he contended Jefferson had done, rather embalmed it, waiting for later generations to bring it to life.

From Gettysburg to Birmingham: The New King Text

The *Declaration* was not without reinterpretations for the generations after Gettysburg. Franklin Roosevelt's addendum during the New
Deal that the *Declaration* required an economic reading, a "new"
social contract which included financial security, was certainly a major
rereading. But it is important to note that Roosevelt's efforts were
directed at the *Declaration* of Philadelphia, with all its Jeffersonian
sensibilities. The "utopia which Jefferson imagined for us in 1776"
was still within reach. FDR had thus skirted the Gettysburg merged
text and when he turned to it in 1940, to confront a world "half slave
and half free," the *Declaration* was focused upon the "spirit" of America
abroad.[29] As momentous as the victory over fascism was, the American triumph did not feel the need to confront the question of fratricide
and war guilt.[30] FDR thus left the equality proposition sealed, and the
economic addendum fitfully survived in the postwar political culture of
high consumption and full employment.

It was with the struggles of the civil rights movement that conditions arose for a new merger of the *Declaration*. Martin Luther King
unsealed the equality proposition at Gettysburg. Not only did he recast the proposition and expand it far beyond Lincoln's reading but he
did so through the portion of the *Declaration* Lincoln had attempted
to erase. The right to "alter" a government that refused to recognize
the rights of life, liberty and happiness was the opening that King
employed to accomplish his task. As Lincoln sought to recast the equality proposition through a silencing of the rebellion proposition, so
King sought to recast the equality proposition through giving voice to
the rebellion proposition. But as Lincoln brought the *Declaration* to
life and re-embalmed it, so did King. For the rebellion proposition, so
centered in King's analysis of the *Declaration*, is to be set aside once
the promissory note of the equality proposition has been fulfilled.

How did King bring to life the rebellion proposition that Lincoln
had so monumentally closed at Gettysburg? In his analysis of the Montgomery bus boycott, King offered his central contribution to newness
that would bring to life the rebellion proposition. "We have discovered
a new and powerful weapon—non-violent resistance," King announced.
"Although the law is an important factor in bringing about social
change," the "new legal decisions" create tension and violence. Nonviolent resistance accepts this outcome, but refuses to respond in kind.
"If we respect those who oppose us, they may achieve a new understanding of the human relations involved."[31] The "old order," includ-

ing white Southern liberals, had always contended that any change other than gradualism would create conditions in which "things get out of hand and lead to violence." Thus even incremental change had "revolutionary implications" that could not be justified in light of the additional black suffering that would inevitably occur. But the new doctrine of nonviolent resistance permits the demand for the "right of equality now" without the need to retreat. Thus King drew a new line between the two hostile camps: those who "reject equality and are prepared to use violence" and those who refuse to accept "defeat, retreat, or fear" but refuse to use violence in return.

King supplemented his strategy with two other arguments from newness. A "new age" was emerging: "It is an age in which a new social order is being born. We stand today between two worlds—the dying old and the emerging new."[32] In 1957 King connected three major incidences of rebellion: the colonial uprisings in Asia and Africa, the Hungarian revolution, and the civil rights movement in America. The freedom fighters in Hungary frequently received dutiful mention in his analyses (they reappear in the "Letter from the Birmingham Jail," for instance), but it is the independence movement in the Third World that for King becomes both the indicator of the "emergence of the new" as well as the measure for the success of the American civil rights movement. Paralleling these struggles was the emergence of a "new Negro," who had gained a "new" sense of self-respect and dignity from the Montgomery boycott and the Brown decision of the Supreme Court.

King's "Letter from a Birmingham Jail" became the equivalent of the Springfield address in the creation of another merged text. But unlike Lincoln's effort, which emphasized the unity of the nation, King employed the rebellion proposition, newly formulated as civil disobedience, as his opening for recasting the equality proposition. Like Lincoln's biblical metaphor of a house-divided, King's dichotomy between just and unjust laws drew upon ancient lessons. As Lincoln spoke of the consequences of division by region, so did King in regard to race. As Lincoln spoke of the consequences of compromise with evil in regard to slavery, so did King in regard to segregation.

But while Lincoln's application of oldness emphasized rededication to the equality proposition as a strategy, King's rested on the rebellion proposition. Lincoln himself (as well as Jefferson) was portrayed as a righteous extremist. King cited the house-divided speech in particular as evidence as well as the *Declaration*. He presented a panoply of

but he would (?)

narratives of refusal (resistance during the Babylonian captivity, Socrates' "civil disobedience," the early Christian martyrs, the Protestant reformers, the American revolutionaries, and resisters to Nazism and Communism) in his effort to diminish the charge of illegality. In fact, for King "legal/illegal" was a false dichotomy. Rather, "just/unjust" was the appropriate focus not only because so many injustices were, strictly speaking, legal but because the latter division carried with it the possibility for dissolving injustice, which a legal dichotomy did not. If injustice was a degradation of the human personality, it mirrored the separation of the sinner from God, which must be overcome. This struggle against injustice was thus as old as human existence itself, and the American revolutionaries were part of this long chain of resisters. Thus the *Declaration's* assertion of the extralegal right to alter or abolish governments was but one confirmation of the morality of resistance to injustice.

The civil rights struggle so connected to this long train of abuses placed opponents to King's reading in the same position that Lincoln had placed Douglas in regard to the equality proposition. It is notable in this respect that it is the white moderate who receives King's attention, for it is he who might recognize the equality proposition but counsels "wait!" when faced with the prospect of resistance. Lincoln's parallels derived from Matthew, as he placed Douglas in the role of the Pharisee who could not (or willfully would not) accept that genuine healing required the will to confront evil. King derived his connections from Amos. "Let justice roll down like waters, and righteousness like an everflowing stream" was Amos' exhortation for repentance. Those who refused to accept this admonition denied the "urgency of the moment" by refusing to grasp "the meaning of the social revolution" and the actions to necessary to implement it.

The crisis of which King spoke too had its oldness for not only were there those who failed to heed Amos' call for contrition and repentance but there were those who refused to acknowledge the early Christians who too were called "disturbers of the peace" and "outside agitators." It was these men and women who insisted that they "obey God rather than man" and who also brought an end to "ancient evils" like infanticide and gladiatorial contest. Imprisonment, with all its attendant consequences of confinement, mistreatment, and suffering, was the price paid for resisting evil. "Things are different now" because the contemporary church is "weak" and "ineffectual" but nevertheless "the judgment of God is upon the church as never before."[33]

At Springfield, Lincoln spoke of the abandonment of the equality proposition in terms of a conspiracy among the highest officers of government. The "new" house they were building for such an enterprise could never stand because, as ancient truths verified, conflict would never cease until a "crisis shall have been reached and passed." Thus the new efforts of men like Douglas, Buchanan, and Taney, who represented the three great institutions of American government, replicated ancient and failed attempts at leadership. At Birmingham, King spoke of rebellion as the method to resurrect the equality proposition and criticized the "church's silent and often vocal sanction of things as they are." Both men employed oldness in support of their readings, but King emphasized the oldness of suffering and imprisonment as well as the oldness of resistance as a recourse. Commitment to legality was a theme that suffused all of Lincoln's analyses from his first formulation in the Lyceum address. Newness was reserved for the rebellion proposition. King, on the other hand, reintroduced and revalidated "rebellion," redefined as "civil disobedience," in terms of oldness. Not only was "extremism" rejected as a new response since both Jefferson and Lincoln were extremists, but so too were Amos and the early Christians. It is thus through oldness that King justifies the rebellion proposition.

But as Lincoln sequestered the newness of his reading of the *Declaration* exclusively in terms of the equality proposition so did King in terms of his reading of the *Declaration* in terms of the rebellion proposition. As Lincoln acknowledged the newness of his reading in Chicago during his debates with Douglas, so too had King acknowledged newness in Montgomery when he asserted that civil disobedience was a new strategy that avoided both submission and violence. Thus while the rebellion doctrine formed the core justification for a re-reading of the *Declaration* in the "Letter from a Birmingham Jail," it was portrayed as an old doctrine with ample biblical precedent. As was the case with Lincoln's reading, King's relied then upon a complex commix of the old and new. What was new was the Negro's newfound sense of self-respect (derived from the successful resistance movements of blacks globally, "new" interpretations of the Constitution in the Brown case and new perspectives gained by geographical mobility) and what was old was the injustice of oppression and resistance to this condition.

By rereading the *Declaration*, King had replicated Lincoln's strategy of commixing the old and the new in general but, as Lincoln had so revised Jefferson, so had King revised Lincoln. King, however, retained the overarching Lincolnian narrative of an American destiny, which could be discerned from his rereading of the *Declaration*. "Our destiny is tied up with the destiny of America" was a trope that King employed with increasing intensity as he chronicled the suffering born by civil rights activists as the movement progressed. The address in Washington, D.C. before the Lincoln Memorial and on the centennial of the Emancipation Proclamation was the occasion for rereading Lincoln himself, and thus becomes the monumental reinterpretation of the *Declaration* that Lincoln offered at Gettysburg. Lincoln began his address with a poetic rendering of the Philadelphia *Declaration*; so too did King in Washington of the Gettysburg reading as he spoke on the "hallowed spot" of his memorial: "Five score years ago, a great American, in whose symbolic shadow we stand today, signed the Emancipation Proclamation."[34]

King acknowledged the monumental character of Lincoln's reading. He acknowledged its oldness. He also remarked upon the status of the old: "But one hundred years later, the Negro is still not free . . ." Lincoln's reading is read as a "promissory note" that has still not been redeemed. Thus it is the very oldness of the "magnificent words" of the *Declaration* and the oldness of Lincoln's "momentous decree," which was based upon his reading of those words, that makes the condition of the Negro so scandalous and the Declarations at both Philadelphia and Gettysburg so incomplete. "This note was a promise that all men, yes, black men as well as white men would be guaranteed the unalienable rights of life, liberty, and the pursuit of happiness."[35] The inclusion of all Americans formed the basis for the *Declaration* at Gettysburg, and Lincoln's equality proposition was thus still a "bad check"("embalmed abstract truth").

Like Lincoln's Gettysburg Address, King's speech in Washington contains no specifics. There are no detailed narratives of the struggle, no names, no specific demands.[36] Shorn of particulars, the Address focuses exclusively on the failure of Lincoln's equality proposition. Paired with the promissory note unredeemed is King's delineation of the rebellion proposition. There is an urgency, accentuated by the oldness of the unfulfilled pledge of "real promises of democracy." There is a "summer of discontent," a "whirlwind of revolt," "creative protest," a "marvelous militancy," a refusal "to turn back." Thus the Philadelphia *Declaration* re-emerges in King's reading. Those whom he commemorates are the "veterans" of the civil rights movement. These unnamed men and women, some of whom are at the rally "fresh from narrow jail cells," have suffered "excessive trials and tribulations."[37]

Lincoln had pledged that the men who died at Gettysburg would be remembered for bringing about a "new birth of freedom" and so too King announces that those who have resisted segregation would produce a nation that "will rise up and live out" the "American dream" that "all men are created equal." Thus the emblematic theme of newness, rebirth, is also offered by King as he closes the address with Isaiah's vision applied to American identity. King's quotations of Old Testament prophecy, national anthem, and Negro spiritual—all "old" evocations of national identity—at the end of the address are conflated to offer a "new meaning" to America.

The *Declaration* at Gettysburg created a new conception of American identity through a commemoration of fratricidal war as atonement for the sin of slavery. Lincoln seared the equality proposition into this sacrifice in a way that he had argued in his youth the revolutionaries had once done in regard to the *Declaration* at Philadelphia. The Declaration at Washington certainly pursued the themes of redemption and equality as well, but King's new merged text placed racial harmony at the center of the *Declaration* and he did so by insisting upon the centrality of the right to alter or abolish governments that failed to meet fundamental rights. No clearer confirmation of this new merger can be offered than by pairing Lincoln's resolve that the soldiers at Gettysburg be remembered to King's determination that those civil rights activists who resisted oppression and bore "unearned suffering" be honored.

We noted how Lincoln's merger was challenged both in the North and in the South by those who gave privileged status to the rebellion proposition. In an important sense it was only Lincoln's monumental interpretation of the Civil War itself that successfully "embalmed" this competing axiom. King too faced challenges to his merger not only from those who questioned his evocation of the rebellion proposition but from those who questioned his commix. For there was a seclusion of enormous proportion in King's recentering of the rebellion proposition. The *Declaration* at Philadelphia spoke of revolution. King's reopening of this old proposition, closed at Gettysburg, spoke of a new form of rebellion—nonviolent resistance. Thus secluded in King's merger by his own evocation of its newness was the encasement of rebellion in this form. What if, however, the authority of the old *Declaration* at Philadelphia was invoked to inspire revolt?

African American commentators began to question King's reliance, ambivalent as it was, on the *Declaration* at Gettysburg. Was the focus upon Gettysburg a fixation upon "the Great Man Theory of Emancipation," which itself must be overcome?[38] The Black Panther Party Platform of 1966 cited the *Declaration* of Philadelphia in support of their demand for a U.N. supervised plebiscite "to be held throughout the black colony . . . for the purpose of determining the will of black people as to their national destiny."[39] Malcolm X replaced the parameters laid down by King for nonviolent resistance with the slogan "by any means necessary" and used the American revolution in support of his claim.[40] As the focus upon the rebellion proposition broadened, so did the equality proposition. The latter, formulated initially as "black power," borrowed from the "newness" of anticolonial revolt that King himself had spoken to include equality as collective self-determination. One of the most detailed efforts in this regard was proposed by the Republic of New Africa. Its leaders presented its plan for the secession of five states (South Carolina, Georgia, Alabama, Mississippi, Louisiana) to the State Department and requested immediate negotiations between the two "nations."[41]

With his merger of the *Declarations* at Birmingham and Washington threatened, King responded with attempts to enclose the rebellion proposition. He spoke of the success of his new strategy of resistance in terms of the risks of rebellion being expanded. A global revolution of color was "at least fifty years away from being relevant." The "cold hard facts of racial life" required a successful revolution by the American Negro to "reform the structures of racist imperialism from within and thereby turn the technology of wealth in the West to the task of liberating the world from want." Talk of violent rebellion could not even provoke urban riots that were "unplanned, uncontrollable temper tantrums. All the sound and fury seems but the posturing of cowards whose bold talk produces no action and signifies nothing." The strategy of nonviolent resistance was tested and capable of success (no one has been killed in a nonviolent demonstration and "dramatic changes" have occurred throughout the South) while the new reading of the rebellion proposition involved "romantic illusions about freedom and empty philosophical debate."[42] Concessions were offered. Rebellion as nonviolent resistance was still new but now so in two senses: it involved "creativity and imagination," it was "bold" and was "substantially improvised and spontaneous," but it also "carried the blemishes of our inexperience."[43] The times required new efforts to influence the "course of events" in terms of ideological, economic, and political power. But King warned that the "American social revolution has been a revolution to 'get in' rather than to overthrow."[44] However, no matter how much King sought to contain the rebellion proposition, he faced a reconsideration of his own axiom: nonviolent resistance was justified to the extent to which it could persuasively be tied to the likelihood that it could redeem the "promissory note" of the equality proposition.

Conclusion

Lincoln's effort to give rebirth to the equality proposition at Gettysburg and his re-embalming of the rebellion proposition ultimately met with limited success. Reconstruction, which was itself a concerted effort at implementing newness, resulted in its own embalming of the equality proposition and hence provided the circumstances for King's new merger. The "second reconstruction," premised upon the *Declaration* at Birmingham, unleashed new conceptions of equality and rebellion that King, like Lincoln, seemed unable to continue to direct. The assassinations of both men represented another historical act of enclosure and even possible future commixes since it could be argued that both monumental acts of merger were incomplete. Thus the *Declarations* of Gettysburg and Birmingham remain both permanently old and new; old in the sense that they constitute venerated readings and new in the sense that neither one has been truly implemented.

Garry Wills closes his analysis by concluding that the *Declaration* at Gettysburg "has entered the mainstream with the Declaration, bathed in a light that makes them easy to see but hard to read." If we add the *Declaration* at Birmingham to this empyrean, we can see that the question may not be so much that the *Declaration* as merged text is so difficult to read, but that it is difficult to live by. Surely there are worlds of difference between Jefferson Davis and Malcolm X, but both, as nemeses of Lincoln and King respectively, stood for rebellion in its most pure form. The problem with America, stated so succinctly by Samuel Mitchell thirteen years after the *Declaration* at Philadelphia, was that everybody wanted independence: first independence from Great Britain, then independence of the states from each other, then independence of the people from government, and "lastly, the members of society be equally independent from each other."[45] To flee by force to start anew or to remain and force renewal represent two great hungers of Americans. Both Lincoln and King attempted to satisfy these twin urges. Thus the broader question that arises from these two mergers of the *Declaration* at Philadelphia is how the *Declaration* viewed collectively as a merged document helps us to answer the question, "What does it mean to be an American?" What, in other words, does it mean to live in a polity that authorizes both equality and rebellion?

Notes

1   Garry Wills, *Inventing America: Jefferson's Declaration of Independence* (New York: Vintage, 1979), xxiv.

2   I use the terms Declaration at Gettysburg and Declaration at Philadelphia as metaphorical anchors since Lincoln's and King's readings of the Declaration span their entire careers. The *Gettysburg Address* does constitute a recognized acme for Lincoln as does Birmingham for King, although Lincoln's inaugurals and King's "I Have a Dream" speech are considered here as part of their respective merged texts.

3   The definition of American political culture in terms of its constant interaction with "newness" has been a persistent feature of theorizations, although with quite different assessments. See, as examples: Louis Hartz, *The Liberal Tradition in America* (New York: Harcourt, Brace, 1955); Daniel Boorstin, *The Genius of American Politics* (Chicago: University of Chicago Press, 1953); Samuel Huntington, *American Politics: The Promise of Disharmony* (Cambridge: Harvard University Press, 1981); Jean Baudrillard, *America* (London: Verso, 1988); Frederick M. Dolan, *Allegories of America* (Ithaca: Cornell University Press, 1994); Houston A. Baker, Jr., *Blues, Ideology and Afro-American Literature* (Chicago: University of Chicago Press, 1984). For a review, see: Philip Abbott, "Redeeming American Exceptionalism," *Social Science Journal* 32 (Summer, 1995), pp. 219–34

4   *Ibid.*, 190.

5   Robert G. Ingersoll, "The Meaning of the Declaration" in *Our National Centennial Jubilee: Orations, Addresses, and Poems Delivered on the Fourth of July, 1876* (New York: E. B. Treat, 1877), 694. Johan Huizinga, writing like Tocqueville from the outside, was also impressed by the "adventure, violence, and . . . personal choice of the signers." *America* (New York: Harper and Row, 1972), 182.

6   Two recent commentaries on the *Declaration* at Philadelphia illustrate the continuing power of the Philadelphia *Declaration* in this respect. Hannah Arendt, while critical of the document's appeal to "oldness" in the form of its appeal to "nature's god," finds in the *Declaration*'s performative "We hold" an "entirely new concept of power and authority" which drives the revolution to success that eluded later attempts in France and Russia. While Jacques Derrida finds a hidden chasm in the signing and the performative, which he calls a "fabulous retroactivity," his focus on the paradox of rebellion ("the signature invents the signer") still focuses on the inventiveness of the act. Hannah Arendt, *On Revolution* (New York: Penguin, 1963), p. 160; Jacques Derrida, "Declarations of Independence" *New Political Science* 15(1986), 7–15.

7   Gary Wills, *Lincoln at Gettysburg* (New York: Simon and Schuster, 1992), 145.

8   "Inaugural Address" in *Echoes of the South* (New York: E. B. Treat, 1866), p. 138. Robert Barnwell Rhett's defense of the South Carolina secession included the assertion that the South was the repository of the "revolutionary" tradition ("We but imitate the policy of our fathers . . ."). "Address to the Slaveholding States" in Frank Moore, ed., *The Rebellion Record* (New York, 1861–71), vol. I, 396.

9   I rely here upon Louis Hartz's classic analysis in *The Liberal Tradition in America* (New York: Harcourt, Brace and World, 1955), chs. 6, 7. For a more recent view of Southern culture as historically self-defined in terms of its "mythic 'oppositeness,'" see: Larry J. Griffin, "Why Was the South a Problem to America?" in Griffin and Don H. Doyle, eds., *The South as an American Problem* (Athens: University of Georgia Press, 1995), 10–33. Eugene D. Genovese attempts to place Southerners closer to the views of Northern conservatives on some issues in *The Southern Tradition* (Cambridge: Harvard University Press, 1994), ch. 3.

10   John C. Calhoun contended that there was "not a word of truth" in the equality proposition, which was "inserted . . . without any necessity" as a justification for rebellion. "Speech on the Oregon Bill" (June 27, 1848). Davis argued after the war that slavery was the "occasion" but not the "cause" of secession which rested with "sectional rivalry and political ambition." *The Rise and Fall of the Confederate Government* (1881) (New York: Da Capo, 1990), vol. I, 66–67.

11   "Lyceum Address" (1838), in Abraham *Lincoln: Selected Speeches*, T. Harry Williams, ed. (NewYork:Holt, Rinehart, Winston, 1957) 14. All following page citations are from this edition unless noted.

12   "Speech at Springfield" (1858) , 76.

13   *The Complete Lincoln-Douglas Debates of 1858*, Paul M. Angle, ed. (Chicago: University of Chicago Press, 1991), 110, 121.

14   "Letter to Henry Pierce" (1859), 114.

15   Thus, even Harry Jaffa, who argues forcefully for Lincoln's overall orthodoxy in regard to Jefferson, admits the insertion of some newness: Lincoln "exaggerated Jefferson's nonrevolutionary purpose." *Crisis of the House Divided* (Garden City, New York: Doubleday, 1959), 322.

16   "Speech at Chicago" (1858), 92.

17   *Ibid.*, 93.

18   *Ibid.*, 161. The Southern response was to interpret Lincoln's populism as a form of praetorianism. *Daily Delta*, February 26, 1861.

19   Lyceum Address (1838) in *Selected Speeches*, 14.

20 *Ibid.*

21 "First Inaugural" (1861), 144.

22 "Speech at Peoria" (1857), 49. As President, Lincoln introduced the concept of a "national homestead" and repeated that the republic must remain whole in order to renew itself without "embarrassing and onerous trade regulations" to take advantage of new technology (steam, telegraph) in the new territories. "Annual Message to Congress" (1862), 199–200.

23 "Speech at Ottawa" (1858), 102.

24 "Special Message to Congress" (1861), 162.

25 "Address at Gettysburg" (1863), 247.

26 "Second Inaugural Address" (1865), 283.

27 *The Complete Lincoln-Douglas Debates*, 424.

28 *Ibid.*, 19.

29 For FDR's employment of the Declaration at Gettysburg, see: Philip Abbott, *The Exemplary Presidency: Franklin D. Roosevelt and the American Political Tradition* (Amherst: University of Massachusetts Press, 1990), ch. 8.

30 The two unfathomable tragedies of World War II, the holocaust and the use of the atomic bomb, required no Lincolnesque response. Reflections upon the former did involve confrontation with universal questions of human responsibility, but war guilt was centered upon the Germans. Americans struggled briefly, and largely in isolated terms, with the moral import of Hiroshima and Nagasaki. See: Paul Boyer, *By the Bomb's Early Light* (New York: Pantheon Books, 1985).

31 "Our Struggle" (1956) in Martin Luther King, Jr., *I Have a Dream* (New York: Harper San Francisco, 1992), 7. All subsequent addresses and works by King are from this edition.

32 "Facing the Challenge of a New Age" (1957), 15.

33 "Letter from a Birmingham Jail" (1963), 97.

34 "I Have a Dream" (1963), 103.

35 *Ibid.*, 102.

36 The single exception is King's description of the governor of Alabama, who is unnamed. *Ibid.*, 105.

37 *Ibid.*, 103, 104.

38 For discussion of the challenges to the Declaration at Gettysburg after the Washington address, see: Merrill D. Peterson, *Lincoln and the American Memory* (New York: Oxford University Press, 1994), 356–58.

39   "Black Panther Party Platform" (1966). The Panthers later experimented with strategies designed to substitute the nation-state with alternative political structures. Huey P. Newton, *To Die for the People: The Writings of Huey P. Newton* (New York: Vintage, 1971), 31–37.

40   "Message to the Grass Roots" (1963) in *Malcolm X Speaks* (New York: Grove Press, 1965), 7. Malcolm X claimed that the march on Washington was a "picnic, a circus." (16).

41   "The Republic of New Africa" in Charles V. Hamilton, ed. *The Black Experience in American Politics* (New York: Putnam's, 1973), 60. For a review of the arguments of other "territorial nationalists," see: William L. Deburg, *New Day in Babylon* (Chicago: University of Chicago, 1992), 132–52.

42   "Nonviolence: The Only Road to Freedom" (1966), 127.

43   "Black Power Defined" (1967), 154.

44   "Nonviolence: The Only Road to Freedom" (1966), 130.

45   Samuel Latham Mitchell, "An Address to the Citizens of New York" (New York, 1800), 7.

Chapter 7

Entangled Texts
"Exceptionalism-within-Exceptionalism" in *The Souls of Black Folk* and *I'll Take My Stand*

It is part of the majesty of Lincoln's and King's achievements that their isolation as reinterpreters of the *Declaration* was rewarded by the recognition of their heroic role in their great respective mergers. Like many great American political theorists, Du Bois' and the Southern Agrarians' reputations have risen and fallen in dramatic proportions not unlike those of Lincoln and King. But there is a special air about these works, an atmosphere of irrelevance, even in a culture that regularly finds a place for the jeremiadic outsider.

Du Bois' irrelevance is captured perfectly by the close of his life. What can epitomize the irrelevance of a political persona in America more than the decision to join the Communist Party in 1961, a few months before his ninety-fourth birthday, and a year later to renounce America and become a citizen of Ghana? Du Bois thus missed the incipient Second Reconstruction. He was buried with state honors in Accra in August 1963. Nevertheless, he was memorialized before a hushed crowd before the Washington Monument in what became the acme of the civil rights movement's campaign for racial integration.

In 1963 W. E. B. Du Bois was honored for his "oldness" as a veteran of the struggle for civil rights. His recent acts of emigration were forgiven by a sympathetic movement. Roy Wilkins said: "Now, regardless of the fact that in his later years Dr. Du Bois chose another path, it is incontrovertible that at the dawn of the twentieth century his was the voice that was calling to you to gather here today in this cause."[1] "Choosing another path," what Wilkins was willing to forgive, became a guide to political action. For here were refrains that reverberated through the 1960s and beyond as Du Bois' voice "called." The key to

Du Bois' call is *The Souls of Black Folk*, a work both old and new and a work in which its newness and oldness have been reinterpreted by subsequent generations.

The irrelevance of the Southern Agrarians is no less demonstrated by the publication of *I'll Take My Stand* at the onset of the Great Depression. For if the laissez-faire conservative was discredited, what can be said of the Agrarians' plea for tradition and locality at the moment when New Deal experimentation and cosmopolitanism swept a terrified nation? The "stand" the Agrarians took was not even the one that was about to be displaced.[2] Then there is the enormous irrelevance of some of the Southerners' racism. For if Du Bois missed the Civil Rights movement he could at least be viewed as a precursor. The Agrarians seem to speak from another planet and when they don't— that is, when there are connections to the Second Reconstruction— they take ugly forms such as Donald Davidson's participation in the White Citizens Council movement. Even during the great conservative renaissance of the 1980s, the Agrarians and their small group of contemporary followers were at the margins of the Reagan revolution.

Yet, though the Southern Agrarians might as well have been buried in a far-off land, for the one they so prized has long gone, we still hear their "call" as well. Recently, Eugene Genovese has spoken of the "belated tribute" owed to the Agrarians and the need to recognize these "nonpersons" for their "outstanding contributions to American social, political, and cultural thought."[3]

Newness does manage to peek through. *The Souls of Black Folk* has been declared "old" for its reliance upon the good will of white Americans, for its Enlightenment belief in education, for its elitism, and for its paternalism. It has been declared "new" for its militancy, for the truth of its prophecies, and for its pioneering theorization of African-American culture. *I'll Take My Stand* has been judged "old" for its failure to acknowledge the contribution of the African American and for its fantasies of antebellum life. It has been judged "new" for its "premature environmentalism," for its skepticism of industrial progress.

Thus these two works, regarded by their writers as texts of dispossession, and regarded by the majority of Americans more harshly as texts of irrelevance, make their cases for two different kinds of exceptionalism—African American and Southern. Although both rarely use the term, *The Souls of Black Folk* and *I'll Take My Stand* are the texts of two defeated nations in America.[4] In what were often hoary conversational asides, white Southerners would repeat to anyone who would listen that only they—not the Northerners—"understood" Negroes, and African Americans would offer the conclusion that at least white Southerners were more honest than Northerners and thus were preferable as antagonists.[5] Du Bois refers to America as "the foster land" of African Americans and one Southern Agrarian separates the "Southern idea" from the American.[6]

These assessments, marked by huge elements of self-deception and disillusionment, show the strange (one wants to say, exceptional) common nature of these two great exceptionalisms in an exceptionalist nation. States more often than not contain many nations, defeated or not. But locked in mortal battles with one another and regarded as alien, what defeated nations must contend with a Lockeanism culture as triumphant as ours? And what two nations, with such a horrific heritage of mutual distrust and hatred, should find a common bond in their struggle against a more powerful exceptionalism? Without suggesting, even implicitly, a moral symmetry between the white American Southerner and the African American, each offers to America his own exceptional tale of tragedy in a nation that understands only progress, an exceptionalism thus doubled. No nation came to America under the condition of the middle passage except the African and no American ever faced military occupation as a defeated power except the Southerner. Both then speak in a political language that is exceptional; it is a language of grievances unacknowledged, of worlds lost or rather stolen, of histories exceptional, of resistance remembered and sworn. And both acknowledge the exceptional nature of America. *The Souls of Black Folk* and *I'll Take My Stand* are thus entangled texts. Nowhere is this entanglement better illustrated than in the preoccupation with foundings, real and imaginary, in both analyses. This chapter attempts to identify these foundings as both indicators of a political discourse in America that can be characterized as "exceptionalism—within—exceptionalism" and as a search for the nature of American identity. The focus upon foundings thus permits both Du Bois and the Southern Agrarians to confront the "newness" of America with the "oldness" of their claims and the "newness" associated with their own foundings.

Entangled Histories and Imagined Foundings–I

There is no question that for Americans at large the Civil War represents a monumental event in their nation's history. It is, in fact, Lincoln's theorization of that event in the Gettysburg *Declaration* that forms an essential part of American identity. It was in Lincoln's words a "test" that America reluctantly but heroically undertook, and it produced a "new birth of freedom." In these two great texts of exceptionalism-in-exceptionalism, however, there are two major alterations. First, the Civil War becomes not a monumental event but "the" monumental event of the republic. Each polity has its own way of measuring time and each nation within has its own independent gauges. For these exceptionalists, the Civil War is the founding moment; indeed rarely is any other event even acknowledged. The War and its aftermath anchors all the analyses of both texts. For Du Bois, it is the symbols of Frederick Douglass, the Freedmen's Bureaus, the 13–15 constitutional amendments, Port Royal, the *Emancipation Proclamation*, the "Revolution of 1876," the Klan, and Jim Crow. For the Agrarians, it is Chickamauga, Gettysburg, Cold Harbor, Sherman, Sheridan and Grant, Appomatox, Lee, and the Conventions of 1867. Mind not, just for the moment, the dramatically different perspectives on the Civil War and Reconstruction for we do speak of two counter-histories. Look rather on the intensity and centrality that these exceptionalists give to the War.[7]

If the Civil War is the defining moment for America for these exceptionalists magnified by huge proportions in terms of the general population, it is also given exceptional interpretation. There was no uniform national assessment of the War in 1903 nor in 1930. Yet the competing analyses all placed the War in larger perspectives that these exceptionalists denied. Du Bois, in fact, anticipated the interpretation of the Dunning School and returned in the 1930s to systematically refute Reconstruction as a hopeless experiment. The Agrarians poised themselves for direct assaults on the "New South" thesis and inverted the progressive's economic interpretation.

At the beginning of *The Souls of Black Folk*, Du Bois asked his readers to consider "how does it feel to be a problem?" For Du Bois the problem of the twentieth century was the "color line—the relation of the darker to the lighter races of men in Asia and Africa, in America and the islands of the sea."[8] The Civil War was a "phase of this problem" and no matter how many "technical points of union and local autonomy" were argued, they were "shibboleths," for what caused the great armies to march North and South in 1861 was the question of Negro slavery. And no sooner had Northern armies occupied Southern soil, than the "old question, newly guised, sprang from the earth—

What shall be done with the Negro?"[9] Frank Lawrence Owsley argued passionately against this thesis ("Without slavery the economic and social life of the South would not have been radically different"[10]) but accepted Du Bois' interpretation that the war was fought on terms other than preservation of union. Instead, he contended that the issues of the War involved a battle between industrial and agrarian civilizations. But for Owsley and the other Southern Agrarians, the Civil War was a defeat for the South that was not complete. While the South "fingers the weapons of industrialism," its citizens are "unregenerate" in their attempt to "live the agrarian life."[11] Thus for both exceptionalists, the Civil War continues to define the only real issues facing the republic: the color line and industrialization.

These revisions can be traced to the exceptionalism-within-exceptionalism thesis that the War constituted an act no less than the founding moment of the American republic. For Du Bois, the Civil War was a missed, or deformed founding; for the Agrarians it assumed the proportions of an anti-founding, a conquest.

Du Bois discusses the first ad hoc attempts at reconstruction on the part of Northern generals and traces the compromises and urgency that led to the formation of the Freedmen's Bureaus in 1866. Like all founding moments, the postwar period was one of crisis, opportunity, and Herculean obstacles. It was especially one in which the "new" became visible in extraordinary ways in "so vast a work . . . It was a tremendous undertaking. Here at the stroke of a pen was erected a government of millions of men—and not ordinary men either, but black men emasculated by a peculiarly complete system of slavery, centuries old; and now suddenly, violently, they come into a new birthright, at a time of war and passion, in the midst of the stricken and embittered population of their former masters."[12]

The bureaus noticeably failed, tragically failed, in their ability to systematically provide land for former slaves. For Du Bois, the financial collapse of the Freedmen's Bank was particularly fatal: "all the hard-earned dollars of the freedmen disappeared; but that was the least of the loss, all the faith in saving went too, and much of the faith in men . . ."[13] Still, the bureaus did manage some successes, particularly in education. Du Bois' overall assessment is quite positive. With only fifteen million dollars, they "set going a system of free labor, established the beginnings of peasant proprietorship, secured the recognition of black freedmen before courts of law, and founded the common school system in the South."[14] Nevertheless, Southern resisters found a weak point in the Northern psyche. By playing upon qualms about constitutionality, the North was left with one alternative. If it was unconstitutional for the nation to "stand guardian" over freedmen, then make them "guardians by arming them with the ballot."[15] "The Freedmen's Bureau died, and its child was the Fifteenth Amendment." Suffrage, however, "ended a civil war by beginning a race feud." Although not a single Southern legislator stood ready to admit a Negro, the North "felt gratitude toward the race thus sacrificed in its swaddling clothes on the altar of national integrity. . . ."[16]

Du Bois thus places conditional blame on Northern political sensibilities. But how, in a Lockean nation could a culture fail to be vulnerable to the charge of concentrated power? How long could it support, however justified, an agency that in Du Bois' words, "made laws, executed them, and interpreted them"? How, in a Lockean nation, could the argument that free men be their own guardians fail to persuade? Thus as Du Bois laments the "passing of this great human institution before its work is done," he must acknowledge the complicity of American exceptionalism in the legacy of the failure of the Freedmen's Bureaus.

Nevertheless, there is in Du Bois' analysis the lament of a Publius who failed. For if a Lockean nation could proceed with Reconstruction as it had done but proceed no further, then there was little possibility that the Civil War could have produced a "dawn of freedom" even without certain historical contingencies such as the crash of the Freedmen's Bank, the passing of Lincoln, etc. Yet this insight does not prevent Du Bois from considering what the Civil War as founding might have looked like if only the Freedmen's Bureau had remained a permanent institution. Instead of "economic slavery" in the rural South and a "segregated servile caste" in its cities, there could have been "a great school of prospective citizenship" that broke the color line. Imagine, if you will, a reader of Publius in the second generation of a failed republic whose citizens had not heeded his warnings. Imagine a republic under the Articles of Confederation plagued by all the horrors he had predicted—economic chaos, secession movements, roving armies—and imagine how he might react to the failure of the founding moment and one gains a perspective on Du Bois' analysis of the War. Our imaginary reader would still have the imagined founding in his mind; that is, he might be able to speculate on what America might have been had the warnings of Publius been heeded. He could dream of a prosperous nation, free of foreign interference and free of the same animosities that Europe suffers from. And so does Du Bois imagine. Had Reconstruction constituted a founding, the African American "double-consciousness" would have dissipated; the veil that separated the races would have dropped; the historical narrative of the African American would have been drastically altered.

These three concepts are, of course, those with which Du Bois is justly remembered. They, in essence, constitute the call of *The Souls of Black Folk* for later generations. These three concepts constitute as well the essence of African American exceptionalism. For it is the African American who "ever feels his twoness,—an American, a Negro; two souls, two thoughts, two unreconciled strivings; two warring ideals in one body, whose dogged strength alone keeps it from being torn asunder."[17] This twoness afflicts the craftsman, pastor, and intellectual alike and leads each to false paths to salvation and self-doubt. Double-consciousness is maintained by the veil that assures the African American a kind of absence of self-consciousness since America "only lets him see himself through the revelation of the other world." Nevertheless, there is also a kind of "second sight" that comes with the veil and certainly part of this exceptional consciousness is derived from an awareness of the sources of this double identity. "The shadow of a mighty Negro past flits through the tale of Ethiopia the Shadowy and of Egypt the Sphinx."[18] For Du Bois the African American harbors three thoughts about his experience as American that are exceptional: the "death ship" of the middle passage; the experience of slavery in the "old South"; the striving for emancipation. The latter, described by Du Bois as "The confused, half-conscious mutter of men who are black and whitened crying, 'Liberty, Freedom, Opportunity'— vouchsafe to us, O Boastful World, the chance of living men!" represents the possibility of a new exceptionalism that the Civil War and Reconstruction failed to produce but which Du Bois can still imagine.

Had another founding occurred, there would then have been added two momentous additions to American identity. The three thoughts would not, of course, have been erased but a fourth would have been appended. This striving for freedom would have been completed, and instead of a continued history of denial by a "headstrong, careless people," there would have been a "dawn of freedom." To Du Bois, the imaginary completion of this narrative—from death ship, old South, the long striving *and* to freedom—would have created a new exceptionalism for both white and black Americans. For whites it would have halted the process of racial contamination of the idea of Freedom and brought the nation to the kind of Hegelian fulfillment that is its destiny. For blacks, it would have provided a glorious conclusion to a historical quest, "a sweeter beauty than ever stretched before the eyes of wearied Israelites."[19] There would have been a national recognition then of a new exceptionalism, not only in the completion and conflation of these two histories of Freedom, but in an acknowledgment of the African American as *the* exceptional American. For Du Bois often repeats his belief that no American has "such unquestioning faith" in freedom than the African American.[20]

The call of the *Souls of Black Folk* has led many to accept Du Bois' theorization of black history as a single-minded striving for Freedom and to see in African American exceptionalism an unrecognized exemplification of American character.[21] There is in Du Bois' analysis, however, also an argument that had the two nations been joined in Reconstruction as a racial founding, America would have found a "new" strong bulwark in defense of freedom. For as Jefferson saw in the proposed ward system the structure for the defense of liberty and Tocqueville saw the same in Puritan culture and the township, so did Du Bois see in the free African American. No one knew better the "pure human spirit of the Declaration of Independence than the American Negroes," who seemed "the sole oasis of simple faith and reverence in a dusty desert of dollars and smartness."[22]

Du Bois also explored another feature of American Exceptionalism in his imagined founding. The historical striving of the African-American behind the Veil had hidden a significant question: "Would America have been America without her Negro people?"[23] As two nations, white America conceived itself as one country, but Du Bois asked: "Your country? How came it yours?" Du Bois closed *The Souls of Black Folk* with an analysis of the "sorrow songs" as an expression of African-American culture that would have provided the foundation for a new American identity in his imaginary founding. For in these folk songs—part African, part African American and part "Caucasian"— lay the "gifts" of a people to America. Du Bois argues that these songs constitute not just the gift of music but the "most beautiful expression of human experience born this side of the seas." "Neglected," "half-despised," "mistaken and misunderstood," the "sorrow songs" include the gift of story in an "ill-harmonious and unmelodious land"; the gift of Negro labor to America that helped "lay the foundations of this vast economic empire"; the "gift of the Spirit."

These observations, however, are based upon a founding in the imagination only. As such, they constitute what can be called a "new" exceptionalism. For the most part, Du Bois must deal with the consequences of a failed founding and thus must return to the "old" exceptionalism of an outcast nation. He views the landscape of the South, particularly of Georgia and the Black Belt, to describe the remains of the Confederacy. He surveys the "big houses" in half ruin with unkempt lawns and untrimed great magnolias still guarded by rusted gates and the slave cabins stretching on either side "like wings" and on the whole unaltered. Here was once the "Egypt of the Confederacy" before the kingdom would "sway and fall."[24]

In the context of the failed founding, the South as a slave society—itself a founding—is, of course, destroyed. But in the midst of its remains, the old exceptionalism has taken hold in the form of a new form, the crop lien system and Jim Crow. The Veil is as pervasive as it was in the antebellum South; the economic structure is a copy of England's before the Factory Acts and Du Bois notes the irony of that Georgia, "the world-heralded refuge for poor debtors, should bind her own to sloth and misfortune as ruthlessly as ever England did."[25] The plantation elite has disintegrated and "passed to those men who have come to take charge of the industrial exploitation of the New South . . ." The two races, in terms residential, economic, cultural, and social, are like "two great streams: they ripple on the same sunshine, they approach and mingle their waters in seeming carelessness, then they divide and flow wide apart."[26]

It is in fact the emerging connection between industrialization and segregation (the new form of the old exceptionalism) that especially troubles Du Bois. He compares Atlanta to the mythical Atalanta who stopped to fondle the golden apples placed in her path and thus was caught by the wily Hippomenes. There is even a wistfulness on Du Bois' part in the passing of the old South: "something was vanquished that deserved to live, something killed that in justice had not dared to die; to know that with the Right that triumphed, triumphed something of the Wrong, something sordid and mean, something less than the broadest and the best."[27]

As Du Bois proceeds with his mythical comparison, his ambivalence becomes so prominent that it deserves extended examination:

> She [Atlanta/Atalanta] forgot the old ideal of the Southern gentleman,—that new-world heir of grace and courtliness of patrician, knight, and noble; forgot his honor with his foibles, his kindliness with his carelessness, and stooped to apples of gold,—to men busier and sharper, thriftier and more unscrupulous. Golden apples are beautiful—I remember the lawless days of boyhood, when orchards in crimson and gold tempted me over the fence and field—and, too,

the merchant who has dethroned the planter is no despicable parvenu. Work and wealth are the mighty levers to lift this old new land; thrift and toil and saving are the highways to new hopes and new possibilities; and yet the warning is needed lest the wily Hippomenes tempt Atalanta to thinking that the gold apples are the goal of racing, and not mere incidents by the way.[28]

In his dissection of Reconstruction, Du Bois had words of praise—even reverence—for the New England school mistress, but when he pairs Yankee acquisitiveness, rather than moralism, to Southern culture in the context of the failed founding, Du Bois prefers the Southern gentleman. *The Souls of Black Folk* is constructed upon the careful interposition of myth, African-American and classical. But the apples that invite childhood memory of adventure and daring don't really correspond to the appended defense of thrift/toil/saving that follow.

Du Bois' fears about Atlanta could at this point have been written by one of the Southern Agrarians:

Atlanta must not lead the South to dream of material prosperity as the touchstone of all success; already the fatal might of this idea is beginning to spread; it is replacing the finer type of Southerner with vulgar money-getters; it is burying the sweeter beauties of Southern life beneath pretense and ostentation. For every social ill the panacea of Wealth has been urged,—wealth to overthrow the remains of slave feudalism; wealth to raise the "cracker" Third Estate; wealth to employ black serfs, and the prospect of wealth to keep them working; wealth as the end and aim of politics, and as the legal tender for law and order; and finally, instead of Truth, Beauty, and Goodness, wealth as the ideal of the Public School.[29]

Du Bois' argument seems extremely jumbled at this point. His imaginary founding offered no place for antebellum Southern virtues and, in fact, the Freedmen's Bureaus were to have transformed Southern culture. Even the autobiographical memory that pops up in the midst of his defense that partially excuses market morality seems to treat gold in a pre-capitalistic sense as an exotic object. Uncharacteristically, in regard to Du Bois' mythic glosses, the reader asks what do the apples signify? In the Greek myth, Atalanta's detours over the apples were evidence of the price of distraction, and Hippomenes' trick (with the aid of Aphrodite) an example of the power of intelligence over physical talent and beauty. But for Du Bois, do the apples signify materialism? Or do the apples signify "lust for gold"? Or do the apples signify loss of purpose (much as the fruit of St. Augustine's pear tree was not the real object of his desire)? Do the apples signify surrender to the temptation of "lawless" impulse? More troubling, if the soul of Atlanta is Atalanta, is the soul of the South the Southern gentleman? This, whatever might be said of Du Bois' elitism, cannot be, for his whole project has been to lift the veil and show the achievements of black folk.[30] But the soul of the South for Du Bois does lie outside the spirit of acquisition and the Southern gentleman sufficed to epitomize an alternative to the vulgarity of a market culture on one side of the veil. Thus it is here that these two texts of great exception-within-exception entangle. Had a refounding occurred, the new exceptionalism would have brought to America a sense of the spirit and a beauty that America lacked, save "the rude grandeur God himself stamped upon her bosom." Lacking such a transformation, however, Du Bois is not ready to accept the "newness" of a "new South" as a solution to the color problem and hence he forges a cultural alliance with the old plantation class. Admittedly, it is a strange coalition but Du Bois had begun his essays with the assertion that African-Americans had been born with a second sight. The "finer type of Southerner" had rejected the "lawless lust" of Hippomenes that the African American had been denied. Even now behind the Veil in Atlanta and in the South where it "makes little difference . . . what the Negro thinks or dreams," the Negro teacher and preacher are being replaced by a "new" man: "He is passing away just as surely as the old type of Southern gentleman is passing, and not from dissimilar causes,— the sudden transformation of a fair far-off ideal of Freedom into the hard reality of bread-winning and the consequent deification of Bread."[31]

Du Bois knows that the Southern gentleman as Atalanta built his "old ideal" upon racial oppression, but he also knows that the pursuit of the gold apples will mean the end of African-American exceptionalism, the collapse of the possibility of a new exceptionalism-within-exceptionalism, and its envelopment by the more powerful exceptionalism of a Lockean nation. An unsympathetic reader might conclude that the "new" Negro in an industrial South would simply become an American. For what could be more American than devotion to freedom as "deification of Bread" and what more irrelevant than the dispossessed "new-world heir" of the Southern gentleman?[32] There is even here some suggestion then of another imaginary founding set in the future, one that Du Bois fears:

> Here stands this black young Atalanta, girding herself for the race that must be run; and if her eyes be still toward the hills and sky as in the days of old, then may we look for noble running; but what if some ruthless or wily or even thoughtless Hippomenes lay golden apples before her? What if the Negro

people be wooed from a strife for righteousness, from a love of knowing, to regard dollars as the be-all and end-all of life? What if to the Mammonism of America be added the rising Mammonism of the re-born South, and the Mammonism of this South be reinforced by the budding Mammonism of its half-awakened black millions?[33]

Part of the call of *The Souls of Black Folk* rests upon Du Bois' critique of the agenda of Booker T. Washington. His famous essay, "Of Booker T. Washington and Others" compares Washington's strategy of accommodation to the great chain of resistance in American history that extended from "the fire of African freedom" burning in "the veins of the slaves" to Nat Turner, Daniel Walker, Frederick Douglass, and Alexander Crumwell. But from Du Bois' perspective, Washington's accommodation included not only the surrender of civil rights per se but also the "gift of the spirit" that constituted the African American's claim to exceptionalism. Washington's focus upon the "accumulation of wealth" made him a Hippomenes who was placing golden apples before African Americans. In fact, one can conclude that those mythical, mystical apples are, for Du Bois, America, or more accurately, an America without African-American exceptionalism. As such they signify all the meanings we have reviewed. America/apples is a sign of distraction from the striving for recognition of a people who were here "before the Pilgrims landed." Should African Americans/Atalantans stop for the apples, they will be caught in the embrace of Hippomenes, either in the form of black leaders like Washington or in the form of wily entrepreneurs from the North who have already destroyed the exceptionalism of the Southern gentlemen. For Du Bois, America/apples signifies the life of acquisition, which is the "lawless," undisciplined, lowly existence of America. The coming universities of the South can never completely "bear the maiden past the temptation of the golden fruit. They will not guide her flying away from the cotton and the gold, for—ah, thoughtful Hippomenes!—do not the apples lie in the very Way of Life!"[34] In this imaginary founding of the future, however, the Atalantan—now both the white and black Southerner—can remedy the great failing of the Old South. "Despising the education of the masses and, niggardly in the support of colleges . . . her ancient university foundations dwindled and withered under the foul breath of slavery . . ."[35] But a "new" Southern university system could fly above the "sordid aims and the petty passions," the "social unrest and commercial selfishness" of the rest of America. These Atalantans who would fly past the golden apples—"a few white men and a few black men"—would give America a "broad culture, catholic tolerance, and trained ability" that it never has enjoyed.

There are thus no less than four foundings of Du Bois, imaginary and real: the missed founding that came with "dawn of freedom" in 1865; the real founding of Jim Crow in its aftermath; the possible founding that would come with an industrialized New South seduced by Hippomenes; the possible founding if Atalanta should fly past the golden apples. In each Du Bois explores the old and the new as forms of African-American exceptionalism-within-exceptionalism. Certainly, the Agrarians do not imagine the same foundings nor do they give the same interpretations as Du Bois did of the actual ones. But the text of the Southern Agrarians is entangled with Du Bois', both with his preoccupation with foundings and with the consequences of exceptionalism-within-exceptionalism.

Entangled Histories and Imaginary Foundings–II

Du Bois explored both the newness and oldness of African-American exceptionalism. *The Souls of Black Folk* closes with the reminder that we were here before you, and Du Bois constantly explored the newness that could come with a recognition of the gift of African Americans. The Southern Agrarians are loathe to validate newness. They burn with anger at the designation "old-fashioned" as a term of disrepute, and the newness of the North, and especially its attempt to impose newness on the "old" South ("they can always propose new worlds to conquer"), is a source of endless frustration for them.

Still, the Agrarians must acknowledge a newness to the Southern project in America. In fact, there are on several occasions the assertion that it is the North that in a peculiar way continues to replicate European civilization, and that it is the South that struck out on new ground. Allen Tate, for example, notes the New Englander's "disguised and involved nostalgia" for the land—"the New England land being old England," his attempt to imitate the homes and universities of England that make it look like "a European museum, stuffed with dead symbols." It is the North that still suffers from a colonial mentality and can still not understand the "South's independence of Europe." The South, of course, "could be ignorant of Europe because it was Europe."[36] Herein lies that Southern Agrarians' pride in newness, partially disguised as it is in the constant, obsessive focus on oldness. For while the North prided itself on its grand founding of a new society, the South had engaged in an even more enviable project. It transplanted a European society on American soil: "The South is unique on this continent for having founded and defended a culture which was according to the European principles of culture . . ."[37]

As the Agrarians pursue their own version of exceptionalism-within-exceptionalism, the outlines of the newness of their founding intermittently come into focus. The Southerners were pioneers who created a "comfortable and rural sort of establishment." Its social orders were not as fixed as those of Europe. It lacked an aristocracy (Ransom prefers the term "squirearchy"[38]) despite the pretensions of its plantation class. Its culture was not as finished as that of Europe but it had just "got beyond the pioneering stage." Its people eclectically appropriated Greek culture and a "lively medievalism from the novels of Sir Walter Scott."[39] Southern architecture was exceptional, "adapted from classic models into something uniquely Southern." The South was "rich" in the folk arts, developed in "mountain fastnesses and remote rural communities."[40] It was a society that was Protestant without a reformation. Southern society had a strong democratic element owing to its frontier. It had a capacity to produce an abundance of leaders, perhaps in part because of the political competition with the North. And, of course, the Southern economy was based upon slavery.

All of these features suggest the "newness" of the Southern founding. If the South had completely, and without revision, founded European culture in America, that itself would have constituted a significant form of newness since that itself would have involved a transplantation as an act of political will. For what could be more "new" than the founding of a society based upon eighteenth-century sensibilities in the midst of capitalistic America? But the Agrarians acknowledge multiple sources of newness. In fact, their argument seems to devolve into a plea for the moral superiority of their founding in the context of a dual endeavor, both new though in different ways.

Yet, however new the Southern founding might have been, it now exhibits the ultimate designation of oldness—death. "Dead days are gone" is the beginning assessment of Stark Young's essay on the old South, and the project the Agrarians pronounce is one of restoration. There are allusions to imaginary foundings here of course. Had the South won the Civil War, had the South been able to preserve its exceptionalism-within-exceptionalism without recourse to violence, had Lincoln not been elected, America would have been different.[41] But "the Southern idea today is down" and the Agrarians focus upon their sights on the nature of the founding of 1867 and its consequences.

Frank Lawrence Owsley is the Agrarians' point man who sets his sights on Reconstruction as a founding. Reconstruction is assessed in terms directly inverse to Du Bois' analysis. Owsley briefly notes individual acts of respect for Southern generals and troops but the Freedmen's Bureaus, the fifteenth amendment, the attempts to "re-educate" the South are all noted, not as efforts at liberation but of subjection: ". . . so there commenced a second war of conquest . . ."[42] Owsley, however, insists that this founding was the result not of a conflict between slavery and freedom but "between the industrial and commercial civilization of the North and the agrarian civilization of the South."[43] This alteration of the origins of the Civil War in which Northern politicians used the slavery question as a feint to "get their party into power . . . with an industrial program for business" provides Owsley himself with an entree to examine the Civil War as an illegitimate founding in two ways. First, the South, in its massive attempts to assert its exceptionalism-within-exceptionalism, becomes the repository of republican wisdom in Western civilization, while the North represents the "new" doctrines of centralized state control in industrial form. Second, the South becomes the exemplary example of a people subjected to conquest and as such their moral position must be compared to those that Locke described in chapter 26 of the *Second Treatise*.

In Owsley's account of the founding of 1867, it is the "old" Southern tradition that was dislodged. Southern agrarian life is the New World repository of ancient republicanism. The colonial Southern founders were not "gentlemen" but were of the "yeomanry, and they were from rural England with centuries of country and farm lore and folk memory." They "dreamed of America, free from England, as a boundless Utopia of farms taking a thousand generations to fill."[44] This account is similar to Tate's, Davidson's, and Ransom's in its validation of the exceptionalism of the Southern project. Owsley, however, places special emphasis on the republican roots of the South. Southerners so loved the soil that they "sought out in literature and history peoples who had lived a similar life." From the Greeks they appropriated the value of leisure, oratory, and especially their architecture. The Greeks, however, tended to neglect their farms in favor of trade and so the Southerners turned to the Romans of the early republic. Here were people who, like the Southerners, "reeked of the soil, of the plow and the spade; they wrestled with virgin soil and forests; they built log houses . . ." They admired Cato's works on Roman agriculture but though Cato was "a fine gentleman with liberal ideas about tenants and slaves and a thorough knowledge and love of the soil," he did live in a villa. "It was Cincinnatus then, whose hands were rough with guiding the plow" and who received the Southerner's great affection along with the Gracchi who "died in the attempt to restore the yeomanry to the land."[45] In America, it was Washington who "kept vigil with his sick horses and dogs, not as a capitalist who guards his investments, but as one who watches over friends," and Jefferson, whose provincialism and liberal views on religion, that appealed to the Southern mind.[46] Southern political thought rested upon "the old Anglo-Saxon principles expressed in the Magna Carta, bill of rights, habeas corpus act, supported by the American Revolution, and grafted finally in every state constitution of the independent states, as 'bills of rights.'"

This lineage, which is traced to "the Anglo-Saxon and Scotch way of life," and "partly grafted" from the Greeks and Romans and confirmed by the American revolutionary experience, was smashed by Reconstruction and replaced by "the doctrine of intolerance, crusading, standardizing alike in industry and in life." Northern industrialists had to remove agrarian values and states' rights in order to build an economic infrastructure "at national expense. The South had to be crushed out; it was in the way; it impeded the progress of the machine."[47] To crush the South, "a war of intellectual and spiritual conquest" was waged. Southerners were told that they had no history. The "Northern schoolma'm" taught Southern children that "the Puritans and Pilgrim fathers were the ancestors of every self-respecting American," and that the South must accept the "stigma of war guilt, slave guilt, of treason."[48]

If the South was the sole agency of the republican tradition in America and was placed under military occupation for ten years and under an indefinite program to "remake every Southern opinion, to impose the Northern way of life and thought," what is the moral status of this founding? Though Owsley does not cite Locke, his response parallels his famous argument about the morality of conquest. Locke's account is quite frank about the actual powers of a conqueror: "the conqueror's swords often cut up governments by the roots, and mangle societies to pieces, separating the subdued or scattered multitude from the protection of and dependence on society which ought to have preserved them from violence."[49] But he is also quite clear that conquest never constitutes a founding in a moral sense: "But conquest is as far from setting up any government as demolishing a house is from building a new one in the place. Indeed, it often makes way for a new frame of a commonwealth, by destroying the former; but without the consent of the people, can never erect a new one."[50] The conqueror has a despotical right over all those who have resisted him and may even seize property as compensation for the cost of the conflict. On the other hand, this despotical power does not extend rightfully to the children of the resistors nor to their property. Thus, though the conqueror in practice may force the subdued to submit "to such government as he pleases," his right is solely one of force comparable to the victim who hands over his wallet to "the thief who demands it with a pistol to my breast."[51]

To Owsley, the South stands before the "Northern conquest" practically impotent before the "Juggernaut" and so deprived of consent. He describes the military surrender, the "selling empires of plantations," the "levying taxes," the "combing . . . for anything left by invading armies." He notes the enfranchisement of African Americans and the withdrawal of the "old Spartans" from politics. He describes the Northern project to "set the rising and unborn generations upon stools of everlasting repentance."[52] The South, "confused, ill informed," and unconsciously accepting "portions of the Northern legend and philosophy"; "sullenly and without knowing why" rejecting other portions, and "withal knows not where to turn" must come to know where to draw the moral line in regard to this conquest and learn that powerlessness is not consent.

For Owsley, the key lies in resisting the "conquest of the Southern mind." He cites the president of Harvard who wrote that the older generations, the hardened campaigners under Lee and Jackson, were too tough-minded to re-educate. The North must "treat them as Western farmers do the stumps in their clearings, work around them and let them rot out." This branding of the new generation of Southerners as "war criminals" and the attempt to industrialize the South thus constitute for him not only an act of conquest rather than founding but a conquest that exceeds the moral boundary of submission. When Locke asked how the children of the conquered might seek remedy against a robber who has broken into his father's house, he answered that he must "appeal to heaven" to have their "yoke cast off."[53]

Neither Owsley nor the other Southern Agrarians recommend violence, but there is a faint whiff of resistance, armed or otherwise, as a moral alternative that can be detected throughout *I'll Take My Stand*. Ransom speaks eloquently of Scotland's relative independence as an example of the prize for stubbornness, and Tate speaks wistfully of Irish resistance.[54]

For the Agrarians then, their history is one of founding/defeat in war/conquest/resistance. None of the Agrarians contends that the antebellum South can be restored. What then are the features of an imaginary founding of the future? There is among the Southern Agrarians a scenario of a South that capitulates to the North, permitting "herself to be so industrialized as to lose entirely her historical identity." Here America would lose her exceptionalism-within-exceptionalism, for without the "last substantial barrier that has stood in the way of American progressivism" the nation would be in a "condition of eternal flux" and the "new South" would become "only an undistinguished replica of the usual industrial community."[55] The old South would still live in the new South, of course, but as an embalmed idea fit for fiction and museums in which Americans bored by the "sterility" of their lives would themselves imagine "some state of living in which there is less exhaustion, colorless repetition, and joylessness . . ."[56]

The Southern Agrarians, however, cling to two other imaginary foundings paired with clarity by Ransom. One would involve an aggressive assertion of sectional loyalty and "resistance on the part of the natives to the salesmen of industrialism."[57] Andrew Lytle gives this imaginary founding a kind of Ghandian flavor in which the pursuit of a "natural economy" is uncompromising: "as for the bric-a-brac, let it rot on their hands. Do what we did after the war and Reconstruction; return to our looms, our handicrafts, our reproducing stock. Throw out the radio and take down the fiddle from the wall, forsake the movies for the play-parties and the square dances. And turn away from the liberal capons who fill the pulpits as preachers. Seek a priesthood that may manifest the will and intelligence to renounce science and search out the Word in the authorities."[58] If the Southerner continues to live in a "divided world, he will always be forced to suck the hind tit because the suck of the others is so unreservedly gluttonous." There is in Lytle's ode to agrarian life in the South a frank recognition of the newness of this strategy: "as for those countrymen who have not gone so deeply in the money economy, let them hold to their agrarian fragment and bind them together, for the unreconstructed fragments are better than a strange newness which does not belong."[59] Henry Blue Kline reiterates Lytle's strategy from the standpoint of the deracinated educated Southerner (William Remington) who returns from his wanderings with "something like Roman fighting fervor to keep his chosen spot" from becoming like a Northern city like Detroit. He avoids a life of consumption through "careful buying," engages in civic activity to "discourage promoters and exploiters from working their way" into his community and devotes himself to being something rather than becoming something.[60]

In the lone analysis by the Southern Agrarians that lifts the Veil at least partially, Robert Penn Warren suggests a monumental newness by including the African American in this imaginary founding that preserves exceptionalism-within-exceptionalism: "If the Southern white man feels that the agrarian life has a certain irreplaceable value in his society, and if he hopes to maintain its integrity in the face of industrialism or its dignity in the face of agricultural depression, he must find a place for the negro in his scheme."[61]

These imaginary foundings involve the "regeneration" of a Southern nation culturally and economically independent from the North. The other alternative is to find allies in "backward" regions of the union where there is a "lingering preference" for things "provincial, conservative, agrarian."[62] Western farmers and those who have "recently acquired, or miraculously through the generations preserved, a European point of view" would join the "old South" to form a "formidable bloc" that would be devoted to make the world safe for farmers.[63]

The Southern Agrarians thus offer three imaginary foundings of the future that can be built upon their real antebellum founding and the conquest that succeeded it. One leads to their extinction and the other two involve regeneration either through resisting America or recapturing it.

AMERICA

Houston A. Baker, who is himself an exceptionalism-within-exceptionalism theorist, has complained that African Americans have been too long under the thrall of what he calls AMERICA. For Baker, the designation in capitals inscribes America as "immanent idea of boundless, classless, raceless possibility." The great break with a Europe of aristocratic privilege and division has been filled by "virtuoso riffs on AMERICA as equalitarian promise, trembling imminence in the New World."[64] Without embracing Baker's strategy of forsaking AMERICA, we can at least see from these two texts the authority and power of AMERICA.

We began this essay with the contention that *The Souls of Black Folk* and *I'll Take My Stand* can profitably be reviewed as entangled texts, not just in terms of their entanglement in their dual history of oppression and resistance, but also in their dual entanglement with America as AMERICA. The entanglement is expressed in the mutual fascination with foundings. The narration of foundings, real and imagined, is, of course, a framework in which the writers of both texts can present their claims against America as AMERICA. Both resist AMERICA as Hippomenes and urge refusal to his strategy of seduction. Du Bois can instead chronicle Reconstruction as a failed founding and imagine its successful counterpart. The Agrarians can redefine Reconstruction as illegitimate founding (conquest) and dream of a South as culturally (re)founded or as a nation (re)captured. The necessity of founding is a way, in other words, to relocate one's relationship to America as AMERICA in the strongest terms possible.

But the founding narratives also attempt to express exceptionalism-within-exceptionalism through their evocation of the new. If AMERICA is a sign of exceptionalism as newness as possibility, the alternative foundings of these exceptionalists provide them with their own version of the new. As spokespeople for defeated nations, Du Bois and the Agrarians based a significant part of their claims for recognition on the basis of their oldness. The African American is a descendant of Ethiopia and Egypt; he was here "before the Pilgrims landed." The Southerner brought the oldness of Europe to the New World. Yet America as AMERICA values only the new. For Du Bois its fixation on "material prosperity as the touchstone of all success" not only refuses to acknowledge "how heavy a journey" is African American history but threatens to abolish the "gift" of the African American. For the Agrarians, Southern culture is "stupid" to an America "fascinated by materialistic projects, men in a state of arrested adolescence." "Where can," in the words of Allen Tate, "an American take hold of Tradition?"[65] New foundings remedy this dilemma. They confirm that these exceptionalists are indeed American for they are capable of creating new foundings in fact or in imagination. Yet the search for foundings also validates their irrelevance in another fashion by highlighting their own exceptionalism.

Herein, however, lies the call of *The Souls of Black Folk* and *I'll Take My Stand*, for in their very irrelevance—their resistance to nationally acknowledged foundings, their fear of absorption into the new as AMERICA, their insistence upon recognition of alternate forms of newness that would carry us in directions unknown to AMERICA— they call America to reexamine the nature of its exceptionalism. At the close of *The Souls of Black Folk*, Du Bois asks "Would have America been America without her Negro people?" From the perspective of entangled texts, we can ask more generally would America be AMERICA without her exceptionalism-within-exceptionalism?

Notes

1   See David Levering Lewis, *W.E.B. Du Bois: Biography of a Race* (New York: Henry Holt and Co., 1993), 1–3 for an account of the announcement and reactions.

2   In the Southern Agrarian framework, Hoover and Coolidge are routinely conjoined with Beard and Dewey as "progressives." See especially: John Crowe Ransom, "Reconstructed But Unregenerate" and Lyle H. Lanier, "A Critique of the Philosophy of Progress" in Twelve Southerners, *I'll Take My Stand* (New York: Harper and Row, 1962), 6–11, 122–54.

3   Eugene Genovese, *The Southern Tradition* (Cambridge: Harvard University Press, 1994), pp. 13, xi. Also see: Thomas Daniel Young, *Waking Their Neighbors Up* (Athens: University of Georgia Press, 1982) and William C. Havard and Walter Sullivan, eds., *A Band of Prophets* (Baton Rouge: Louisiana State University Press, 1982) for positive assessments.

4   For a fascinating comparison of common nationalist strategies in *The Souls of Black Folk* and Slavic texts, see: Dale E. Peterson, "Justifying the Margin: The Construction of 'Soul' in Russian and African-American Texts," *Slavic Review* 51(Winter, 1992), 750–757. For the centrality of nationalism in the African-American historical experience generally, see Sterling Stuckey's contemporary classic *Slave Culture: Nationalist Theory and the Foundation of Black America* (New York, 1987). The most systematic exploration of a comparative nationalist perspective in terms of the Southern Agrarians is John Shelton Reed, "For Dixieland: The Sectionalism of *I'll Take My Stand*" in Havard and Sullivan, eds. *A Band of Prophets*, 41–64.

5   As these emblematic assessments suggest, entanglement does not suggest racial fraternity. See Houston Baker's forceful rebuttal of any union on these terms. "Completely Well: One View of Black American Culture" in Nathan J. Huggins, eds., *Key Issues in the Afro-American Experience* (New York, 1971), 1–22. For a different view, however, see: Jimmie Lewis Franklin, "Black Southerners, Shared Experience, and Place: A Reflection" in Larry J. Griffin and Don H. Doyle, eds., *The South as an American Problem* (Athens: University of Georgia Press, 1995), 210–33.

6   W.E.B. Du Bois, *The Souls of Black Folk* (New York: New American Library, 1969), 270; John Crowe Ransom, "Reconstructed But Unregenerate" in Twelve Southerners, *I'll Take My Stand*, 3.

7   It is important to note of course that Du Bois wrote *The Souls of Black Folk* less than forty years after the conflict. But Du Bois was offering the same analysis, now overlaid with Marxist perspective, in 1935. The Agrarians' relationship to the Civil War, psychologically and theoretically, is as close to Du Bois' 1903 outlook and reexamined so in subsequent "reunions."

8   W.E.B. Du Bois, *The Souls of Black Folk*, 54.

9   *Ibid.*, 55.

10   Frank Lawrence Owsley, "The Irrepressible Conflict" in Twelve Southerners, *I'll Take My Stand*, 76.

11   John Crowe Ransom, "Reconstructed But Unregenerate" in Twelve Southerners, *I'll Take My Stand*, 16, 20.

12   *The Souls of Black Folk*, 62.

13   *Ibid.*, 75.

14   *Ibid.*, 74.

15   *Ibid.*, 76.

16   *Ibid.*

17   *Ibid.*, 45.

18   *Ibid.*, 46.

19   *Ibid.*, 47.

20   *Ibid.*, 47, 52.

21   See, especially: Albert Murray, *The Omni-Americans* (New York: Ourtbridge and Dienstfrey, 1970), 13–66; Dexter Fisher and Robert B. Stepto, eds., *Afro-American Literature: The Reconstruction of Instruction* (New York: Modern Language Association, 1979), 18ff.

22   *The Souls of Black Folk*, 52.

23   *Ibid.*, 276.

24   *Ibid.*, 65, 158. Robert B. Stepto places great weight in his analysis of *The Souls of Black Folk* on this journey as an attempt on Du Bois' part to evoke the spirit of communitas and thus, on our terms, to conceive potential foundings, even while traveling in a Jim Crow rail car. This "valiant search . . . involves nothing less than his envisioning fresh spaces in which black and white Americans discover bonds beyond those generated by social-structured race rituals." *From Beyond the Veil: A Study of Afro-American Narrative* (Urbana: University of Illinois Press, 1991), 66–82.

25   *Ibid.*, 155.

26   *Ibid.*, 204.

27   *Ibid.*, 110.

28   *Ibid.*, 112.

29   *Ibid.*

30 See Lewis, who notes how this language is "embarrassing in later years." *W.E.B. Du Bois: Biography of a Race*, 284. Compare Du Bois' threat to the "Southern Gentleman" in the next chapter (136–37). Note, however, that Du Bois contends that this threat is not "wholly justified."

31 *The Souls of Black Folk*, 113, 114.

32 V. P. Franklin raises this point in regard to Du Bois' "talented tenth" in *Black Self-Determination: A Cultural History of African-American Resistance* (New York: Lawrence Hill, 1992), 21.

33 *Ibid.*, 114.

34 *Ibid.*, 117–118.

35 *Ibid.*, 118.

36 Allen Tate, "Remarks on Southern Religion" in Twelve Southerners, *I'll Take My Stand*, 170–71.

37 "Introduction: A Statement of Principles," in Twelve Southerners, *I'll Take My Stand*, 3.

38 The Southern Agrarians did not present a uniform position on the class structure of the Old South and its implications for exceptionalism-within-exceptionalism. At the extremes, Stark Young presented the most direct defense of the planter class while Davidson emphasized the centrality of folk culture.

39 Tate, "Remarks on Southern Religion" in Twelve Southerners, *I'll Take My Stand,* 172.

40 Donald Davidson, "A Mirror for Artists" in Twelve Southerners, *I'll Take My Stand,* 55.

41 Lewis P. Simpson argues that there was an implicit assumption among the Southern Agrarians that the Confederacy failed in large part because its leaders failed to include men of letters in its founding and thus was unable to replicate the founding of 1787. "The Southern Republic of Letters and *I'll Take My Stand*" in Havard and Sullivan, eds., *A Band of Prophets*, 67–70.

42 Frank Lawrence Owsley, "The Irrepressible Conflict" in Twelve Southerners, *I'll Take My Stand*, 63.

43 *Ibid.*, 74.

44 *Ibid.*, 69, 70.

45 Ibid., 70–71.

46 Owsley argues that Southerners abandoned Jeffersonian views on religion and "became devoutly orthodox and literal in its theology"(81) as a negative response to his abolitionist arguments.

47 *Ibid.*, 91.

48 *Ibid.*, 66.

49 John Locke, *Second Treatise on Government*, sec. 221, p. 177. Radical reconstructionists did offer stratagems remarkably similar to Locke's description, arguing, of course, that the South required massive changes to make it a "true republic." See Thaddeus Stevens, for example:

> . . . the foundation of their institutions . . . political, municipal and social must be broken up and relaid. . . This can only be done by treating and holding them as a conquered people. Thus all things which we can desire to do, follow with logical and legitimate authority. As conquered territory Congress would have full power to legislate for them. . . They would be held in a territorial condition until they are fit to form State constitutions, republican in fact not in form only, and ask admission into the Union as new states. . . If their Constitutions are not approved of, they would be sent back, until they have become wise enough to purge their old laws as to eradicate every despotic and revolutionary principle—until they have learned to venerate the Declaration of Independence. . . The whole fabric of southern society must be changed. . . Without this, this Government can never be, as it has been, a true republic. (Paul Escott and David Goldfield, eds., *Major Problems in the History of the American South*, vol. I (Lexington, Mass., 1990), p. 563

50 *Ibid.*, sec. 175, 148.

51 *Ibid.*, sec. 186, 159.

52 Owsley, "Irrepressible Conflict," in Twelve Southerners, *I'll Take My Stand*, 63.

53 Ruth W. Grant, relying upon the discussion in sec. 192, contends that Locke is speaking of a national right of self-determination, "a right belonging to a distinct people with political and territorial claims that continue across generations." *John Locke's Liberalism* (Chicago: University of Chicago Press, 1984), 147–48.

54 Ransom, "Reconstructed But Unregenerate," in Twelve Southerners, *I'll Take My Stand*, p. 24; Allen Tate, "Remarks on the Southern Religion," in *Ibid.*, 168–69. Tate especially is quite direct in answering his own question on means of resistance: "The answer is, by violence." (174)

55 Ransom "Reconstructed But Unregenerate" in *Ibid.*, 22, 5; "Introduction: A Statement of Principles," in *Ibid.*, xxi.

56 Stark Young, "Not in Memoriam, But in Defense" in *Ibid.*, 333–34. Davidson also pursues the scenario of Southern culture embalmed for Northern amusement in detail in his contribution, "A Mirror for Artists."

57 Ransom, "Reconstructed But Unregenerate" in *Ibid.*, 23.

58 Andrew Lytle, "The Hind Tit" in *Ibid.*, 244.

59 *Ibid.*, 245.

60 Henry Blue Kline, "William Remington: A Study in Individualism" in *Ibid.*, 324–25.

61 Robert Penn Warren, "The Briar Patch" in *Ibid.*, 263. It is important to note that Warren supports the Booker T. Washington agenda in his formulation (250). Some of the Agrarians had strong objections to the inclusion of the essay. See Young, *Waking Their Neighbors Up*, 17.

62 Davidson, "A Mirror for Artists," in *Ibid.*, 52.

63 Ransom, "Reconstructed But Unregenerate," in *Ibid.*, 25.

64 Houston A. Baker, Jr., Blues, *Ideology and Afro-American Literature: A Vernacular Theory* (Chicago: University of Chicago Press, 1984), 65–66.

65 Allen Tate, "Remarks on the Southern Religion," in Twelve Southerners, *"I'll Take My Stand,"* 169.

Chapter 8

(Re)newed Texts
Thoreau's and Luhan's "Agri-Cultural" Settlements

Despite the pervasiveness of their search for community, a sense of place remains a largely unexplored feature among Western political theorists. Whether this absence is the result of the nature of theorizing itself, in which portability is a central requirement, or a particular feature of the origins of Western political development, in which its political theorists "quit the hearth and its area" in order to pursue community on a "basically psychological phase of like-mindedness," the epic political philosophers have confronted their own communities with an attitude of resentment or open hostility or more often with silence and obliviousness.[1] The philosophers of modernity, when they theorize community, emphasize the same universalizing features. There are, of course, some exceptions to this rejection of a sense of place but they are sporadic and circumscribed.[2] Invocations of place do appear in the works of Cicero, Machiavelli, and Rousseau, as well as in numerous narratives of national origins and history. But if we define a theoretical sensibility that focuses upon a sense of place as one which centers upon a particular geographical locale and engages in a project of moral instruction about its history and preservation as a site for the formation of homes and households across generations, we can locate a form of communitarianism that is still different from even these formulations. For here the hearth and the area have not been quit or transcended as the major focus of community.

Once the exceptionalism-witihin-exceptionalism of the Southern Agrarians is acknowledged, searching for such a sensibility among American political theorists would seem to be a futile effort. One of the core definitions of American Exceptionalism places this nation as the exemplar of modernity in which a sense of place would seem to be least predominant or first obliterated. In John H. Schaar's assessment, for example, "such primary experiences are nearly inaccessible to us" as a people given over to "restlessness and rootlessness. We do not and cannot love this land the way the Greeks and Navaho loved theirs."[3] Yet if one examines two projects nearly one hundred years apart by Mabel Dodge Luhan and Henry David Thoreau, there are strong elements of a sense of place in their theories even though the result of this struggle to theoretically capture this sensibility is often flawed. Thus, exceptionalism there is in these texts, but it is an exceptionalism *of* place rather than *from* place.

As political personae, Mabel Dodge Luhan and Henry David Thoreau appear to occupy vastly different positions. Luhan was a socialist, a modernist, an epitome of cosmopolitan gregariousness. She was, in the words of one of her critics, "another rich and restless woman, a footnote in the cultural history of Bohemia." Thoreau, on the other hand, was highly critical of any form of political action, a provincialist and the epitome of a solitary individualism. He was convinced of the "indifferency of all places" and believed that "the best place for each is where he stands."[4] Thoreau's account of his venture has been acclaimed as an American masterpiece, while Luhan's is very much a "lost" text rejected or neglected by its natural audience of feminists and socialists. The only possible link between the two personae appears to be derived from critiques of their solipsisms.[5] Yet both Thoreau and Luhan can be studied in terms of their common project to form an identity through the re-creation of a sense of place. Thoreau formed Walden outside the town of Concord and Luhan, Los Gallos outside Taos. Both re-creations involved extractions from the existing place to form a new one that existed as a projection of their respective struggling identities. Thus Thoreau's Walden and Luhan's Los Gallos, as theorized in their works, which we shall call texts of (re)newal, reconstituted the place as self. In both efforts Thoreau's and Luhan's places involved the founding of new villages, the delineation of new "economies" and cultures, and included the creation of an "alternate household," which dramatically altered the gender distinctions prominent in the communities of their birth. Thoreau described a household in Walden stripped of material possession and kinship in which the roles of male/female were distilled through Thoreau's own persona. Luhan collected a household in which she was the "founding mother" who determined its cultural agenda.

The Walden Settlement

Reactions to the projects of Thoreau and Dodge as being driven exclusively by their hyper-individualism have obscured their efforts to found new communities. Part of this assessment is derived from Thoreau's and Dodge's own explicit attacks on their own villages by birth or adoption. Thus Thoreau's *Walden* is often theorized in terms of a dichotomy between communitarianism and individualism. Suffocated by the materialism and cultural conformity of the New England village, he expresses his outrage and wins his personal liberation through flight to Walden pond. Writing in this framework, Emerson described Thoreau as "a protestant a outrance, and few lives contain so many renunciations."[6] Yet this mythical reading of Thoreau as an American St. Simon Stylite has always been subject to qualifications. Sometimes his physical and psychological proximity to the village is taken as a sign of hypocrisy. Thus an early reviewer complained that Thoreau "ingeniously confesses" to his frequent visits to Concord and the frequent guests he entertained from the village. His selection of his pillar so close to Concord makes one "suspect" that he was "happy enough to get back among the good people of Concord."[7] Even Emerson, whose relationship with his young friend was extremely complex, noted in his eulogy that this "hermit" had "dedicated his genius with such love to the fields, hills and waters of his town, that he made them known and interesting to all reading Americans, and to people over the sea."[8]

Certainly Thoreau's critique of Concord is extensive and damning. Walden begins with this negative assessment: "The greater part of what my neighbors call good I believe in my soul to be bad . . ." Concordites toil without reward, "enslaved" by the mortgages on their farms and houses; they are given over to gossip and business competition, each "buried by this other's brass." There is "no play" in them; they lead "mean and sneaking lives."[9] Yet one can proceed quite far in reading *Walden* as an attempt not to present an individualist alternative to community but to present another "renewed" community. In this framework, Concord assumes the status of anti-village, a community that has lost its way and Walden, a new and purified village. It is true that Thoreau is unable to hold to this project throughout *Walden*. In fact, his new village idea recedes significantly as he remembers struggling through the New England winter and his conclusion derives more from his personal psychological rebirth in "Spring" than from a collective renewal. In this reading, however, Thoreau's failure is the inverse of the mythic individualist narrative, for he fails here at precisely the juncture that he allegedly succeeds. For the farther Thoreau removes himself from the anti-village, the more he is unable to collect himself to pursue the features of his own village, and the latter portion of *Walden* seems thus devoted to saving himself. This achievement is nonetheless so heroic that a reading of the essay as the triumph of individualism rather than the failure of community does seem fitting.

In the individualist narrative, Thoreau's awkward status in Concord, which he himself seems to substantiate in his description of himself as "the self-appointed inspector of snow storms and rain storms," provides the background for assessing his experiment as offering the lesson "that individuals must depend only upon themselves if they are to achieve personal autonomy" and that "authenticity is a matter of private and, in fact, literary experience."[10] It is true that Thoreau had difficulty finding a satisfactory role in Concord but his struggles had more in common with other men of his generation than that of the traditional town pariah or eccentric.

Founded in 1635 by a military captain and pastor and settlers from East Anglia, Concord had a more notable place in New England than other small towns, a point that Emerson emphasized in his prideful account of its contribution to the success of the American Revolution at its bicentennial. Like all American towns, Concord was a coveted community whose origins rested uneasily upon economic advantage and religious principle.

At the time of Thoreau's experiment, the town was being made over in two different directions.[11] Commerce and banking establishments began to fill the old village green, replacing light industry and crafts. Factories were being created in its environs. Concord village residents now included bankers and insurance agents as well as Irish immigrants. When Thoreau walked through the village at the end of the day in Walden the "signs" that "were hung out on all sides to allure" unnerved him. He reminded himself of Orpheus' solution, and he would also bolt into someone's house for relief. Thoreau in his journals wrote sympathetically of the plight of the farmers who lived outside the village. As Concord became more and more a capitalist town, the farms that surrounded it appeared more remote and provincial. He wrote of the "despair" of the life of the young Hosmer who lived in what was now a "stagnant-heart-eating-life-everlasting gone-to-seed country." This new distance between village and farm might be acceptable for an old man who may decide to "rust it out" but was heartbreaking to one like Hosmer who "pines to get nearer the post-office and the Lyceum" and is "restless and resolves to go to California because the depot is a mile off."[12] One alternative that some farmers undertook to accommodate these changes involved conversion to dairy farming since the Fitchburg railroad now provided a market just an hour from Boston. To Thoreau this transformation was hardly more acceptable since market farming entailed a rationalization of place. The new farmer "would carry the landscape" and "his God" to market, "if he could get anything for him." These "model" farms were "a great grease-spot, redolent of manures and buttermilk!"[13]

As Concord moved rapidly, though uncertainly, into a capitalist world in which space was reorganized, many of its prominent residents were also engaged in making over the community. Massachusetts' separation of church from state in 1833 unloosened already declining church influence. Emerson and Channing, of course, were major figures in reconstituting religious authority and belief; the Alcotts offered their own communal experiment at Fruitlands; others were involved in the Brook Farm project in West Roxbury. Party activities attracted others and new organizations rapidly formed, such as the Temperance Society, the Anti-Slavery Society, and the Female Charity Society. This Concord, the Concord that was to produce the first autonomous expression of American literature, offered a new conception of community based upon the recruitment of like-minded citizens.

Although it had little in common except in embryo with the avante garde experiments in Luhan's age, this new Concord culture exhibited certain features of the modernist cultural project. For example, an *milieu artiste* structure emerged in which participants "create their own caste, a society within a society" and form "alternate modes of behavior befitting those living on an island surrounded by alien waters." The proliferation of journals and manifestos is one indication of this "world within a world"; for each journal and manifesto suggests "not the larger world but its own terms, the miniature as whole."[14] In regard to this modern cultural transformation, Thoreau could be as hostile as he was to the capitalist conversion of Concord. The author of *Walden* seethes with anger over the projects of "dyspeptic" reformers and philanthropists. But however much Thoreau might have resented the implication of a culture of reform, he could not escape the fact that his own identity as an aspiring literary figure was tethered to this cultural makeover. Even during the Walden experiment, while speaking of the satisfaction derived from the "solitude of an early settler," Thoreau remarked that there still was the "lyceum in the evening, and there is the book shop and library in the village, and five times a day I can be whirled to Boston within an hour."[15]

Thoreau's project at Walden then can be seen as a reaction and inventive resolution to the economic and cultural transformation of Concord. Confronted with the following alternatives: flight to the West, a "heart-eating" existence on isolated subsistence farms; capitalist agriculture, factory life, commercial ventures, cultural projects, Thoreau assumed the role of founder (or re-founder) of a new kind of village. He selected a site outside Concord as a new village offering in mock recitation the municipal covenant of New England village foundings and the current boosterism: "I have thought that Walden Pond would be a good place for business, not solely on account of the railroad and the ice-trade; it offers advantages which may not be a good policy to divulge; it is a good port and a good foundation."[16] A focus of disappointment to individualist readers, the founding itself involved communal participation. The initial act of clearing trees was made possible through the loan of an ax by a neighbor (his cultural compatriot Alcott), and the raising of the frame of the cabin in May was a collective effort "rather to improve so good an occasion for neighborliness than from any necessity."[17] Thoreau insisted that his moving-in day on July 4 was by "accident," but he was quite explicit that his cabin was modeled after what was for him a more momentous event, the "first dwelling houses" of the "first settlers of this town" in the "beginning of the colonies."[18]

The genius of Thoreau rests upon the praxis he created for his project, which is recognized in the individualist narrative. The first and by far the longest chapter in *Walden* is devoted to the economic foundations of his enterprise.[19] Dedicating his effort to the desperate youth of Concord, Thoreau insisted that choices were still possible and that "one generation abandons the enterprises of another like stranded vessels." "Economy" thus appears to capture the spirit of the success guides for youth that have been a staple of American popular culture since Franklin and that enjoyed enormous popularity as a genre in Jacksonian America. Thoreau emphasizes the virtues of thrift and his accounting of expenditures is so minutely detailed and packed with such "a nightmare maze" of economic terminology that some readers have concluded that the chapter represents a parody of the genre.[20]

Whether the intention is to burlesque or not, Thoreau does deconstruct this genre while employing its structure. He denies the utility of geographical mobility, asserting that even if the rail graded the entire planet, the project would not help the youth who spends "the best part of one's life earning money in order to enjoy a questionable liberty." He concludes that "trade curses everything it handles" and complains that the "poor" student who reads Smith, Ricardo, and Say "runs his father in debt . . ."[21]

Thoreau's own heterodox religious convictions prevented him from making over the village along the lines of Puritan conceptions of community. The religious thematic nevertheless glides through the chapter on economy as Thoreau seeks to recover a "simple and irrepressible satisfaction with the gift of life" and "memorable praise of God," which he believes is absent from the cultural reformers.[22] The economy that Thoreau relies most heavily upon, however, involves an attempt rather at retrieving a classical conception of *oikonomia*. Cato's *De Re Rustica* is Thoreau's professed "cultivator" and his delineation of the Walden economy includes the following significations: (1) the focus on a house, household, family, or estate as the self-contained unit, the *point d'appui*, devoted to husbandry (the cultivation of the flora of a property, especially of fruits and vegetables); (2) frugality (in the sense of getting much out of little); (3) directives, rules or precepts designed to preserve a sense of the whole; and (4) stewardship (putting to the best possible use that which one has received or that which one is expected to administer).[23] The Franklinesque conception of virtue is thus still retained in form (though not in substance) in regard to thrift and pedagogy (2); the Benedictine rule is apparent (3,4) and the arcadian element (1) which so fascinated the Concord participants at Fruitlands and Brook Farm is given an ancient Roman rather than Fourierist gloss.

Thoreau undertakes this eclectic act of retrieval by reducing economy to those elements "necessary of life": food, shelter, clothing, and fuel. Only in respect to clothing does Thoreau fail to provide an account of acquisition, noting only that durability and use are appropriate standards. Otherwise, he builds a house, cultivates a garden, and adds a chimney for the winter within his oikonomic model.

Despite the elegance of Thoreau's delineation of a "new" economy for his Walden "settlement," the actual undertaking of the project, which was essential for conveying its authenticity, was more problematic. *Walden* was, of course, a text much revised and rewritten. Its status as a guide to "success," as Thoreau recast the term, depended upon its portrayal of the success of the enterprise as he himself noted in his demand that a writer be required to offer a "simple and sincere account of his life." Nevertheless, even after so many revisions, the contingency of the experiment is still prominent. Thoreau's pride in his accomplishment is apparent in the first pages of *Walden* as he relates the curiosity of his townsmen ("some have asked what I got to eat; if I did not feel lonesome; if I was not afraid; and the like"). Thoreau understood that he was ill-prepared as a farmer for his venture. As a participant in the cultural remaking of Walden, his persona had been one of traveler rather than settler.[24] *A Week on the Concord and Merrimack*, which Thoreau composed during his Walden experiment, systematically pursued this persona of the naturalist-anthropologist who promised "you shall see men you never heard before, whose names you don't know . . ."[25] Even in *Walden* Thoreau prefaces his experiment with the statement that he is now a "sojourner in civilized life again."[26] He confesses that he never owned a house before, and his comic battles with the weeds that invade his bean field convey the wonder and frustrations of the novice gardener: "What was the meaning of this so steady and self-respecting, this small Herculean labor, I knew not." This unpreparedness gives Walden a perpetual sense of excitement that is portrayed in the individualist narrative as a journey of the self; the awkwardness of his efforts, his satisfaction with projects successfully completed (like building the chimney and baking bread), and those less so (the purchase of a stove), and the delight in unanticipated events (the effect of the cabin on his senses, the mice that cohabit the cabin and the uneven freezing of Walden pond) also convey the firstness of the founding settler in which providing for the necessities of life is an ongoing adventure. The fact that Thoreau sees everything anew, even the smallest occurrences, suggests the vitality entailed in rebuilding a new community of which he excitedly speaks at the close of the chapter "Where I lived, and What I lived For": "Let us settle ourselves, and work and wedge our feet downward through the mud and slush of opinion, and prejudice, and tradition, and delusion, and appearance . . . til we come to a hard bottom and rock in place, which we call reality, and say, This is, and no mistake; and thus begin, having a point d'appui, below freshet and frost and fire, a place where you might found a wall or a state . . . that future ages might know how deep a freshet of shams and appearances had gathered from time to time."[27]

Perhaps the most serendipitous aspect of Thoreau's settlement involves the impact of his hut upon his view of the world. His confession that he was never a homeowner and his examples of previous ownership (a boat and a tent) convey his persona of traveler. When he moved in at Walden, he regarded the hut more as "a defense against the rain" than the "sort of crystallization about me" whose implications he began to explore. While he continues to follow his own advice concerning simplicity and refuses to close-off the cabin from the outside (even permitting a nest of wasps to cohabitate), Thoreau exhibits all the qualities of a house-proud new owner. He marvels each morning over the view from his cabin, first from a window, then from the door, enjoys the ventilation ("I did not need to go out doors to take the air, for the atmosphere within had lost none of its freshness"[28]), makes some of his own furniture, and lists for his readers the cooking utensils he has bought. Thoreau's major "home improvement," the building of a chimney, is described in great detail: how difficult it was to remove the old mortar from the used bricks, how he didn't even get a stiff neck from his labor, how satisfying it was to see "my work rising so square and solid by degrees," and how he learned "more than the usual of bricks and trowels."[29] When he finished, he "lingered most about the fireplace, as the most vital part of the house." Thoreau now had a hearth.

The remaking of the family and the home was also part of the new Concord cultural project as its participants lurched from celebrations of domesticity to explorations of new family forms in communal experiments and the promotion of new female friendships. In "Home," Emerson had praised the "sense of stability and repose" within the home but noted the disruption of the home under modern conditions. Sons "have scattered" and parents were forced to spend their time alone together. On the other hand, this loosening of family ties gave the member of this new generation an opportunity to transfer "his affection to his cause; to his trade and profession; to his connection in society; to his political, religious, literary parties." As to the communal reorganization of the family into "consociate" units, Emerson concluded that he would reform "without pulling down my house" as he turned down an invitation to join Brook Farm.[30]

Thoreau's renewed home represented some of this ambivalence. The Walden cabin was fundamentally a bachelor's home. He ate alone and visitors were largely male. *Walden* is, as Stanley Cavell says, "Emile grown up. The absence of Sophie only purifies the part."[31] Thoreau's

discussion of the azad at the close of his initial chapter is often interpreted as a parable of his personal freedom, but in the context of
homemaking this tree, which bears no fruit and has "nothing to give
away," is a theorization of his single status. "If thy hand is plenty, be
as liberal as the date tree," so goes the sage's advice, but Thoreau
must be content to accept that each plant "has its appropriate produce." But Thoreau also attempts to transcend his fruitlessness in the
garden-home-woods place in which he has situated himself. As a solitary homemaker, he employs female and male deities indiscriminately
(Hebe, Diana, Isis, Actaeon, Osiris) as he presents an "eroticized nature" of which he is a part. Sometimes he employs male sexual metaphor in searching for Walden's "bottom" and observing how in spring
the creator is "strewing his fresh designs about," and sometimes he
acts as midwife to a world in which there is "nothing inorganic" and
the Earth "stretches forth baby fingers on every side."[32]

Thoreau had shown that a sense of domesticity could still be achieved
in the context of singlehood as he cheerfully performed both conventional male and female household tasks (". . . whatever satisfaction
parent or child, master or servant derive from living in a house, I
enjoyed it all").[33] On the other hand, his "apartment" also served as a
model for a "purified" model home that could include a spouse and
children but without the architectural and domestic "adornments" that
so infuriated him. Thoreau detested the Concord parlor as an attempt
to enclose visitors in the alleged act of hospitality as he did the kitchen
in which cooking was performed with "so much secrecy" as if the host
"had a design to poison you." Visitors were thus shut off from seven-
eighths of the house; "nowadays the host does not admit you to his
hearth . . ."[34] No doubt there is a sense that Thoreau's complaints
about the openness of a home to visitors reflected his own status as
frequent guest, but his advice was part of his project in which the
homes of the new village would be designed to minimize housekeeping and material acquisition and maximize the mutual sharing of hearth
and dining. In this respect, Thoreau's home (to the extent to which it
is theorized beyond his particular form as a bachelor's apartment,
which constituted his practical achievement) represents a compromise
between the isolation of the bourgeois nuclear family home from the
world of which Emerson spoke and the conflation of individual families in communal experiments.

The economic settlement of Walden as new village and its first
home, however, represented only part of Thoreau's founding. He ex-

pressed his strong distaste for the Concord cultural project's devotion to philanthropy in "Economy," and in "Reading" asks derisively "What does our Concord culture amount to?" The merger between the oikos he set out to retrieve and culture proved to be frustratingly contradictory for other Concord intellects in their own cultural projects. Hawthorne, for example, complained bitterly to his fiancee about his experience at Brook Farm: "After a hard day's work in the gold mine [the manure pile] my soul obstinately refuses to be poured out on paper . . . A man's soul may be buried and perish under a dung heap or a furrow in the field, just as well as under a pile of money."[35] Thoreau too has moments in which he wonders whether the cultivation of his small plot might not prove to be Augean labor and make "study impossible." He is convinced, however, that the oikos he has constructed leaves time for cultural enhancement and argues that "his residence was more favorable, not only to thought but to serious reading, than a university." Thoreau keeps the *Iliad* on his table and makes the case that only in the context of his oikos can the nobility of the classics be properly contemplated as an enhancement to the nobility of this particular existence. "Books, the oldest and the best, stand naturally and rightfully on the shelves of every cottage."[36] This project of creation of a material culture at Walden is told with considerably more self-assurance than the economic endeavor. Thoreau is clearly more "settled" in the construction of a cultural space of dwelling-reading-woods than in the construction of his economic habitat of dwelling-gardening-woods in which, as we suggested, his role as settler is more contingent and awkward (though consequently, more exciting). In fact, though the replication of his oikos requires the replication of his settlement in ways Thoreau does not outline apart from his autobiographical example, he confidently proposes that the old village itself be made over from this experiment: "It is time that villages were universities, and their elder inhabitants the fellows of universities, with leisure—if they are indeed well off—to pursue liberal studies the rest of their lives."[37] In a sense, this proposal represents the Concord cultural circle's project magnified and utopianized with the village as a collective taking "the place of the nobleman of Europe," pushing aside economic activities ("foddering the cattle" and "tending the store") altogether. Thoreau, however, admits that his proposal of village as "uncommon school" is utopian in a negative sense, and he reserves an entire chapter to outlining Walden as a rural, democratic salon in which he welcomed "children, railroad men, fishermen, hunters, poets and philosophers—all honest pilgrims."[38] The cabin, with its curtainless windows open to the woods, is the setting for reading and study, but it is also designed for visitors (except that its smallness is tight when "big words" are uttered). His house is "always ready for company," and Thoreau proudly states that it has held twenty-five to thirty people.

These interconnected economic and cultural constellations (excepting the proposal of the old village as university) complete his vision of a new village. But despite Thoreau's assuredness about Walden as cultural settlement, he does face two examples (one as visitor and one as host) that challenge his own vision of oikos and culture. In "Baker Farm" Thoreau reports coming across an Irishman's hut. His enjoyment of the pastoral setting is marred, however, when caught in the woods by a summer shower, he espies the hut of John Fields and discovers rural poverty. Fields' "cone-headed" infant sits on his father's lap as his wife, "with round face and bare breast" and "never absent mop" cooks "many successive dinners" over a primitive stove. Chickens overrun their living space as Thoreau listens to the family's lament. Fields works very hard at bogging for a neighboring farmer and is "still thinking to improve her condition some day."[39] He compares his "tight, light, and clean house" to Fields' as he tries to tell the immigrant of his experiment "as if he were a philosopher." But the struggling Fields responds only with a sigh, and Thoreau concludes in exasperation that "alas! the culture of an Irishman is an enterprise to be undertaken with a sort of bog hoe."[40]

If Fields' oikos challenges the practicality of Thoreau's new village by suggesting that others cannot see how to "make their port" under conditions of sharecropping, Therien, the "free" woodland trapper, creates questions about his cultural project. Thoreau is clearly fascinated by Therien who, unlike Fields (and Thoreau himself) is unburdened by family obligations and shows a complete absence of Yankee ambition ("He didn't care if he only earned his board"). But Thoreau, who initially thinks Therien is a natural poet and philosopher as he asks him question after question about money, reform, religion, and work and receives enigmatic responses, is horrified to learn that while the woodchopper reads Homer he understands none of it, responding happily only to the rhythms of the text. Fields cannot grasp Thoreau's oikos and Therien's culture. Thoreau simply exits from the dilemma posed by Fields, declaring that "he is a poor man, born to be poorer" through "want of enterprise and faith . . ." He is more reluctant to give up on Therien for he fights against his own observations: "There was

a certain positive originality, however light, to be detected in him . . .
yet his thinking was so primitive and immersed in his animal life . . . it
rarely ripened to any thing which can be reported."[41]

The examples of Fields and Therien, as dual challenges to the agri-
cultural foundations of Walden—along with Thoreau's own near psychological collapse in the winter—give this renewed community an
exceptional flavor that characterizes his sense of place. For there is a
bravado in Thoreau's efforts (which we have attributed to his pioneering) that is so prominent that some readers find the tone insufferable.
Yet alongside this boosterism, there is an acknowledgment of the threat
of place as an extension of self. No way will I become a Fields or a
Therien, so says Thoreau, both of whom seem more anchored in place
than he.

The Taos Settlement

Thoreau left the village of his birth to found a new village on its outskirts. Mabel Dodge Luhan's project of village re-founding was more
circuitous and involved the creation and re-creation of two new villages. Nineteenth-century Buffalo was a "cozy town" and "although
everybody knew everybody else," the "occupations were so unvaried
and the imaginations so little fed," the village provided no sustenance
for any kind of meaningful inner life. No one talked about how they
"felt" and the young Mabel saw the insane asylum on the outskirts of
town as the most likely source of escape.[42] Instead she fled to Paris
and then Florence and participated in a salon that included Gertrude
Stein, Picasso, and Matisse. In 1912 Mabel Dodge, now twice married, returned to New York and was a founder of one of the great
cultural projects in American history—the creation of Greenwich
Village.[43]

The idea of an enclave of freedom and rebellion in the midst of
bourgeois society did not, of course, originate with the American "lyrical
left." The Village itself had a bohemian existence before the arrival of
the lyrical left, and many of its new residents had attempted to create
American bohemias in other cities before they arrived in New York.
But the creation of what Floyd Dell called a "quiet island" at the turn
of the century had more immediate and general American origins.
Village radicals were, though they might not wish to think of themselves in this light, very much an efflorescence of Progressive reform.
Dell, for example, was shocked to find an "unexpected general toler-

ance" for his ideas among people "whom I regarded as my class enemies—the lawyers and other professional men whom I met as a reporter."[44] The first settlement house in New York was set on Delancey Street in 1893. Many new arrivals to the Village came to volunteer for settlement work. The Village was a place to study and "write about life in the tenements." The Socialist Party, ever hopeful to collect reformers, opened up the Rand School on East 19th Street in 1905 to both study poverty and educate the poor.

The new sense of public purpose awakened by Progressive reform also brought to the attention of the sons and daughters of the middle and upper-middle classes the existence of a world beyond the friendly but intellectually stultifying one of the small town. Jane Addams, although she was to travel a different route from the village radicals, spoke not only for women but an entire generation when she recounted her autobiographical experience of feeling lost, "sickened," and "smothered." Middle-class youth were "as pitiful as the other great mass of destitute lives."[45] Hutchins Hapgood, who came to Greenwich Village relatively late in his life, described his life in Alton, Illinois, as the same as the town itself—"ugly, arid, and sterile."[46] Susan Glaspell arrived in the Village from Des Moines, Iowa; Mary Heaton Vorse from Amherst, Massachusetts; and Neith Boyer from a small town in California. Max Eastman grew up in a series of small upstate New York towns. In each he felt estranged from the "family rings" of his parents' ministerial circles. At the end of 1906 he left a sanatorium for the Village.[47] Onboard ship to New York, Mabel was struck with the same sense of suffocation at the thought of returning to America as village writ large full of "dull, grubby men and women, street cars, cigar stores, electric signs, and baseball games" that she suffered a brief nervous breakdown.[48]

This nervousness, which not only afflicted Village radicals but their parents as well, did give the attempt to create in the Village an atmosphere of a sanatorium.[49] Eastman explained for the readers of the *New York Tribune* in 1914 why he resided in Greenwich Village: "I want to be very close to that exciting current of life and business that flows north and south on the main avenues. I want to be able to rush into it for pleasure and profits on a moment's notice. But I don't want to live right in it, because I can't stand the strain. And so I seek out the little low roofed cove . . . where only an occasional backwater eddy of the mainstream reaches me, and I live in complete quietness."[50] Dell described the village as "a quiet island . . . where the pace of life slowed down a bit and left time for dreams and friendship and art and love." He compared the Villagers to persecuted Christians hiding from the barbarians of the north.[51]

If the Village was a place of escape and psychic retreat, the Villagers, at least the early ones, also created their own sanatorial institutions. The Village radicals never completely made over the neighborhood. Their relationships with the poor were very limited; they seemed to literally fail to see the communities of ethnics that surrounded them.[52] Floyd Dell meticulously described the class structure among villagers (old and new inhabitants, those talented and those less so) as if those who arrived for reasons other than bohemia did not exist. The communities that Village radicals created were thus laced among the churches, stores, and families that either supplied the radicals with their daily wants or begrudgingly tolerated their neighbors. The common link between the institutions formed by the radicals—the salons, the political clubs, the theater groups, the magazines—was intellectual. Here were places to talk and to write and to talk about what one wrote. "It seems as though everywhere," remembered Dodge, "barriers went down and people reached each other who had never been in touch before; there were all sorts of new ways to communicate."[53]

These creations gave the Village radicals a sense of place denied to them in their small towns. In fact the very idea of bohemia is the small town recreated. Gone, at least psychically, are the bank, the church, and the family. Gone too are the rotary clubs, the lodges, the women's reading groups—the official structures of bourgeois sociability. These are replaced by bohemian institutions. Thus the small town is transformed and transcended. Its features of sociability are magnified, indeed made nearly the whole of community. Talk among neighbors, a major feature of small town life, is the "Village idea" as much as Christian affection or a place to bring up a family were the ideas of the American village in general. Mabel Dodge's characterization of Hapgood could fit all the Villagers: "Talking was his principal outlet— so he talked and talked, always advocating resistance to authority."[54]

Talk among neighbors was the salve that eased the minds of the expatriates from other villages. Opinion, disconnected from the restraints of family, church, and business, developed in new and unanticipated directions. As youth were introduced to talk of syndicalism and revolution at the Liberal Club, perhaps after a dinner downstairs in which post-impressionist art was discussed, and went to the experimental plays of the Provincetown Players and browsed at Boni's bookstore, in which *The Masses* or *Seven Arts* carried on the discussion with play and gallery reviews and reportage of a strike, who could not fail to feel the exhilaration of participation in a newer, more fulfilling, more "modern" community? Eastman described the atmosphere created by the Village idea as one of "universal revolt and regeneration, of the just-before-dawn of a new day in American art and literature and living-of-life as well as in politics." And regeneration was axiomatically conceived as "talk," which he insisted "was radical; it was free-thought talk and not just socialism."[55]

The "spiritual center" of this new village was Mabel Dodge's salon at 23 Fifth Avenue. Every Wednesday and Thursday evenings "you might find . . . a learned and eminent professor from Columbia University, holding forth on Freud's theory of psychoanalysis . . . or it might be that Mr. Haywood and the IWW would be expounding to the uninitiated what the IWW stood for. Or Lincoln Steffens, or Walter Lippman, would be talking about 'Good Government'; a correspondent just back from Mexico telling about the war, or a scientist from England would make eugenics a topic; or it might be feminism, or primitive life . . ."[56]

During her first years in this new village, Dodge acted more as a broker of ideas but at the suggestion of A. A. Brill she began to write and lecture in her own person. As an advice columnist her eclectic topics included feminism, communism, the popularization of Freud, quilt-making, and child-rearing. These efforts are briefly stated and her philosophy is inchoate but two themes emerge. One involved a fascination with human will and its relationship to community. In "The Crime of Stealing Energy" she concluded that the worst human crime was taking the "life out of another. Release your energy! Release your money! Release your love!" she demanded of both the American bourgeoisie and radicals alike, both of which sought "power without vision" in machine technologies. Another involved feminist topics. She complained about the female obsession with father figures. "For the mature woman, there is no father. There is no master. There is only herself, free and alone, in the brotherhood of man . . ."[57]

By 1917 Dodge had come to the conclusion that the Greenwich Village experiment had failed. Her life had become effete, "striving and striving and ending in nothing." She arrived in Santa Fe in December to rendezvous with her latest estranged spouse. While she thought this was the "strangest American town" she had ever visited, her "restlessness" continued until she visited Taos. Here she witnessed a religious ceremony at the Taos pueblo and concluded that here "a different instinct ruled" and "felt a new life was presenting there unfolding me."[58] On January 1, Mabel Dodge rented a house outside of town from an Englishman who once planned to create a country estate. Here she attempted to found her second new village.

Mabel Dodge wrote extensively about her village experiment, chronicling her second attempt to found a salon at her new home, Los Gallos (*Taos and Its Artists*; *Lorenzo in Taos*) and exploring her relationship with her Native-American spouse in the last volume of her autobiography (*Edge of the Taos Desert*). But *Winter in Taos* is her masterpiece, "her finest literary work, the one that comes the closest to sustaining the richly integrated sense of self and environment, form and content" and the account that permits "one to glimpse the regenerate vision that is sometimes hers."[59]

Like Thoreau's *Walden*, *Winter in Taos* is a narrative structure organized around the seasons, focusing upon what the Taos natives called the "Time of Staying Still." Unlike Walden, however, winter is the season of "the sweet melancholy of renewal" for it provides Luhan with the means for expressing her own sense of settlement. Partially bedridden with a cold, Luhan at first feels a sense of panic at the prospect of a new winter day: "Something like a shiver went over me at the thought of winter thickening still more, covering us, clamping us down . . ." Then she remembers what "I learned long ago, but always forget and have to learn anew each year: that if one gives up and lets it come right down over one, if one sinks into the season and is a part of it, there is peace in this submission. Only in resistance there is melancholy and a sort of panic."[60] Her narrative encompasses a single winter day as she recalls the other seasons that bound her current existence. The salvation of her self (for Luhan's account too contains strong individualist elements) occurs at the end of the day. Near midnight she becomes increasingly unnerved by the ferocity of the storm outside and the closeness of the howls of coyotes. At the "zero hour of truth," her spouse arrives, takes her to the window and says, "Don't you know the moon is shining?" The storm has passed and "the desert was spread out so clear and visible that I could see the shadow of the house, a dark reflection of itself upon the snow."[61]

Luhan's oikos is more complicated than Thoreau's, but she describes, with the help of Hesiod, her "moderate sized farm" of wheat and alfalfa as one in which there is a "great satisfaction that goes beyond economic ones." In Luhan's economy "unpaying guests" or "family" such as horses and pigeons get a "cut" of an alfalfa field. The yield of the oat field is used to buy corn and beans for household consumption. In mock recitation of the problems of "economy" she tells of her travails in keeping both pigeons and cats in her yard. It is "delicious to participate with the cat in the deep within the domestic quietude of the somnolent interior, yet it is also so precious and uplifting as the tender, wakeful participation with the birds." She cuts back tree branches that enable the cats to reach their prey but no matter what safety measures she undertakes the placita is strewn with feathers the next morning. Luhan is determined to renounce the cats but when a stray walks into her yard, she evades the responsibility of economy and takes her in.[62]

Like Thoreau, Luhan was a traveler and like Thoreau she is enthralled with her home. Surveying her house, she thinks about others still wandering ("people who float around the world in hotels and boarding houses, the aging women, and men of all ages, who are looking for climates or distractions or something, they don't know what . . . .") and concludes that it is the "small household gods that give a person more heart-warming than theaters, art galleries, or any public festivity in the world. . . ." If only they could "find a little house of their very own, where every corner means something intimate and special, something planned for comfort and convenience, where the kettle sings on the hearth and the flower blooms in the window."[63] Most of Luhan's attention is focused upon the gardens she has created around Los Gallos rather than the fields of alfalfa. The placita is filled with hollyhocks, irises, lilies, and burning bushes, which in winter each snow storm "moistens and soaks until a rich liquor runs down to the roots." Spring gardening is like "mid-wifery," and "we, are, every one of us, always aching to deliver the unborn, if not in ourselves, then outside in some vicarious fashion."[64]

This chaos of garden color is continued inside Los Gallos itself, for while Thoreau's cabin was designed spartanly, Luhan's is comfortably ramshackle. The simplicity of the cabin at Walden is designed to reduce the divide between home and nature so that the sun and moon "should look in." Luhan's Los Gallos achieves the result by imitating the profusion of the garden. The house, like the garden, was created in stages; it had "grown slowly, room by room" and it "stretches and sprawls out beneath" her. Sometimes Luhan even wonders whether her house is not the picturesque "patchwork of a home" suitable as a "background for the Holy Family" but instead a "run down, inefficient

. . . eyesore." For the most part, however, Luhan is delighted with the casual anarchy of her dwelling and prefers it to the "spick and span" farms of her youth.[65]

In her salon in Greenwich Village, Luhan described herself as a "Head Hunter" procuring "Heads, of things, Heads of Movements, Heads of Newspapers, Heads of all kinds of groups of people."[66] Despite this status as "new woman" she never escaped the role of modernist hetaera whose persona was determined by her abilities, primarily sexual, to surround herself with talented men. At Los Gallos, however, Luhan's settlement in the private space of her new home and new village gave her a sense of independence that her public life lacked. It is true that she continued to engage in head hunting, asserting that she "willed" D. H. Lawrence to come to Taos. Her injunction, stated in *Lorenzo in Taos* ("Come, Lawrence! Come to Taos! became in me, Lawrence in Taos") carried all this ambivalence. Her "Lawrence project" was "not a prayer but command. Only those who exercised it know its danger"[67] and thus Luhan continued her persona of a feminist Nietzsche, which contemporary critics have concluded involved an unconscious desire to submit rather than to dominate.[68] Yet in *Winter in Taos* she chooses only to speak of local visitors and her extension of her self is carried through her home and garden. Her winter knitting forms a rhythm of "thinking, feeling breathing . . . like a dance or like the slow, sure emotion of a constant star." In spring, the irises in her garden are "moving purple and quiet, like women gossiping with their heads together. . . . "[69] This creation of a "new woman" inside the home rather than outside is a major reversal of the historical feminist agenda, a transformation of domicile not unlike Thoreau's act of bachelor homemaking.[70]

Like Thoreau's cabin, which is situated across nature as old village-garden-cabin-forest, Luhan's is signified by old village-garden-house-mountains/desert and like Thoreau's cabin, Luhan's constitutes a "liminal" space "betwixt and between" cultural and natural sites.[71] But in one respect Los Gallos stands in something like an inverse relation to the village of Taos, as did Walden to Concord. Thoreau's settlement was designed to serve as a beacon to a disintegrating village. Taos, on the other hand, for Luhan emits a sense of settlement and strength that energizes her founding of her new village as "the spiritual center of America" and extends to her feminist garden household. The adobe ovens are shaped "like breasts" and the pueblo children in their running games, "teeth bared, heads back . . . putting forth every bit of energy they can summon up . . . are giving back to earth and sun what they have received." The Tiwa women, husking corn, look like "queens, sitting with these riches surrounding them."[72] Though, like Thoreau's, Luhan's project threatens to collapse into a plan to save her self, she was determined that the salvation of the "whole culture and agriculture of the pueblos" could be the basis for "a social experiment" that would also save America. Her home would be "a kind of headquarters for the future. It would be a wonderful and a new work on earth if it could be done," she wrote in 1922.[73]

In *Winter in Taos* Luhan secludes what became the most famous part of the culture-agriculture experiment: the creation of a salon in the "new" center of America. Between 1917 and 1939 Luhan lured Edna Ferber, Leopold Stokowski, D. H. Lawrence, Robinson Jeffers, Georgia O'Keeffe, Ansel Adams, Carl Jung, and others to Taos. While few of her guests stayed, preferring to regard her new village in the mode of the Greenwich Village sanatorium, Luhan planned the construction of a "theater of a new culture" at the base of the San Christobel mountains. The Tiwa sense of the mountains' sacredness would revitalize American culture and re-merge life and art. Instead, *Winter in Taos* records only her sense of cultural transformation as founder and first settler.

These grandiose hopes for the new Taos village, as well as Luhan's own salon, do reveal a tension in her project as founder that Thoreau confronted in his own relationship to the Concord circle. For if swarms of artists did arrive in Taos and stay, the new village would be transformed in ways Luhan did not envision. The cultural project would assume an autonomous existence crowding out its symbiosis with agriculture. Taos and its environs did in fact become a professional artist colony, an artiste milieu with the old pueblo culture a minor aspect of this new village. There are asides of this future in *Winter in Taos* despite Luhan's narrative of agri-cultural pioneering. Artists, whatever their striving for cultural renewal and isolation, attract a cosmopolitan audience. Tourists follow art and the Tiwa respond to the economy of tourism. By the late twenties, natives had begun to open curio shops and "let the earth lie fallow" as they sold "cheap little drums, bows and arrows, small, uninspired pots, and even oil paintings of the Pueblo, Indian horses, and men." Luhan is also distressed that the Tiwa prefer canned goods and white bread "that has no taste and no virtue." She hoped that the Pueblo Relief Act would alter these kinds of economic incentives but they did not. In a moment of self-doubt she wonders if she is not some kind of pioneering tourist herself in this "Garden of Eden."[74] It does not occur to Luhan that the economy she planned did not offer the same dilemma as the one she confronted in her effort to find a balance between the birds and cats in her yard. She insisted on both culture and agriculture (as did Thoreau) in her new village without fully resolving how the cats she brought to Taos could exist alongside the first residents.

Luhan's marriage to a Tiwa (as disruptive as such an affair must have been to the Pueblo since Anthony Luhan was already married) represented a union of the agri-cultural project at a personal level. Mabel Luhan's reliance upon Anthony was total (he is described as more than a "rock"; he is like a "mountain, that will support all the weight I can put on him.")[75] He is her savior at the close of the narrative and is her cultural eye to Tiwa culture, guiding her through the mountains and canyons on foot or horseback. But there is a subtext in her account that suggests that Tony has similarities to Thoreau's Therien. Her spouse's knowledge of English is limited. While "naturally patriarchal," he sometimes seems more like Luhan's field hand, responding obediently to her requests to do chores ("'I stop by Mares' and see if he got any more them fatted sheep.' 'See if he can butcher it and bring it by tomorrow, will you?'" is one such conversation) and sometimes like a primitive beyond Mabel's comprehension (he insists that deer and eagles communicate with one another despite her skepticism).[76]

Conclusion: New Village—New Home—New Place

Though intertwined with their efforts at individual salvation, the settlements described in *Walden* and *Winter in Taos* do manage to delineate a sense of place. Walden pond and the Sangre de Cristo mountains are the locale for Thoreau's and Luhan's struggles to discover and recover their own fragile identities, but they are also settlements in which both writers offer a moral map of village-home-place. In *Walden*, Thoreau spoke of the dangers of the new signs that proliferated in commercial Concord, some designed to "allure" the passerby, some designed to "catch him by the appetite," some designed to capture his "fancy."[77] His work, as well as Luhan's, is an attempt to offer other signs, signs to aid readers to retrieve lost economies and lost homes. The peculiarities of their political agendas (Thoreau's antagonism to reformers and Luhan's efforts to preserve Taos culture in opposition to the modernist assumptions of New Dealers) at least in part are connected to their vision of their sense of place, which valued the recovery of hearth and its area more than the promotion of new political communities rather than simply a consequence of their alleged hyper-individualism.

But these efforts at renewal are also undertaken in the contexts of foundings, for Walden and Los Gallos are foremost "created" places (although they lean heavily both psychologically and theoretically on the "old villages" of Concord, Buffalo, and Greenwich Village respectively) in which Thoreau and Luhan assume the role of first settlers and pioneers. The sense of place theorized as founding constitutes an essential act of (re)placement for Thoreau and Luhan for they examine the moral qualities of settlement from the standpoint of their persona as the displaced, as the traveler. As such, they provide an authenticity in a culture that is often given over to restlessness and rootlessness. Their efforts are thus fundamentally different from the Heideggerian project in which the significance of thinking about "dwelling" carries none of this emphasis on the inventively cultural contingent nor does it include the constant examination of the role of the sojourner in terms of the costs and benefits of settlement.[78]

Nevertheless, though Walden and Taos capture the dominant American vernacular of traveling and settlement in their projects, place becomes an extension of their selves in ways different from those who theorize place from the vantage point of inherited residence. When Michael Gold complained about "Mabel Luhan's slums" when he visited New Mexico in 1936 he was expressing the conventional Marxist aversion to the idiocy of rural life.[79] On the other hand, Gold inadvertently captured a tension in both Thoreau's and Luhan's projects. From Luhan's perspective, she could avoid Gold's critique of Taos as a place "stretched tight, league after league""with human misery just as Thoreau could avoid the charge that he was defending small town moral smugness because both writers had rejected their villages as they stood in all their historical moral ambiguity. Luhan need not balance the serenity of pueblo life with medicine men who killed their patients and Thoreau the moral enclosure of the small town and its treatment of others like the Irish except in their respective novice encounters with "primitives." Their "agri-cultural" projects avoided this kind of moral reckoning in a way that say, the Southern Agrarians could not. Derived from an imaginative distillation of the communities of intellect of which they had been participants, Thoreau's and Luhan's efforts constituted a theoretical reconstruction of a sense of place and re-anchored it in their own autobiographical founding.

The central question raised by Thoreau's and Luhan's project thus becomes one of assessing whether their settlements constitute a creative moral response to the moral weight that any theorist of place must bear or whether their foundings represent an act of moral irresponsibility. In the former, both Thoreau and Luhan revitalize farming through the form of the garden-home and tame the modernist drive of the *milieu artiste* through the marriage of "agri-culture." To find antecedents in Thoreau's and Luhan's agri-cultural experiments in the formation of America's first villages (which also were radically eclectic foundings) simply extends the debate since detractors can frame their critique on more general cultural terms.[80] It may be, however, that the projects that both Thoreau and Luhan outline, the abandonment of place and the creation of another, constitute dual lessons. First, they illustrate the exceptionalism of the *American* sense of place though this may, in fact, be finally no place at all (as critics suggest). But they also illustrate the price paid for a heightened awareness of the sense of place through the experiencing of the consequences of its loss and the benefits of attempted recovery.

Notes

1   George E. Gordon Catlin, "The Meaning of Community" in Carl J. Friedrich, ed., *Community* New York: Liberal Arts Press, 1959), 119. Also see the speculations of Iris Murdock in *Metaphysics as a Guide to Morals* (New York: Penguin, 1993), ch. 12.

2   Robert Nisbet pieces together a tradition of "ecological" community extending from St. Benedict to Kropotkin. *The Social Philosophers* (New York: Crowell, 1973), ch. 5.

3   John H. Schaar, "The Case for Patriotism," *New American Review* (May, 1973), 64–65. See also: D. H. Lawrence, "The Spirit of Place" in *Studies in Classic American Literature* (1923) (Baltimore: Penguin, 1977), 7–14 and Wallace Stegner, "The Sense of Place" in *Where the Bluebird Sings to the Lemonade Springs* (Baltimore: Penguin, 1992), 199–206. Lawrence's argument about the absence of a sense of place in America leans heavily on the absence of class (Americans do not know their "place" because "men cannot live without masters"). Stegner contends that the American would like to be a "placed" person but cultural traditions work more strongly in the opposite direction.

4   Christopher Lasch, *The New Radicalism in America* (New York: Knopf, 1965), 107; Ralph Waldo Emerson, "Thoreau" in Donald McQuade, ed., *Selected Writings of Emerson* (New York: Modern Library, 1981), 790–91.

5   See the following for examples of other harsh critiques: Perry Miller, *Consciousness in Concord* (Boston: Houghton Mifflin, 1958) and Vincent Buranelli, "The Case Against Thoreau," *Ethics* 67 (1957), 257–88; Leon Edel, *Henry David Thoreau* (Minneapolis: University of Minnesota Press, 1970) and Emily Hahn, *Mabel: A Biography of Mabel Dodge Luhan* (Boston: Houghton Mifflin, 1977); Malcolm Cowley, "Fable for Russian Children," *New Republic* (November 25, 1936) 122; Granville Hicks, "Portrait of a Patroness," *New Masses* (November 24, 1936); Arrell Morgan Gibson, *The Santa Fe and Taos Colonies* (Norman, Okla.: University of Oklahoma Press, 1983), 218–29 and Max Eastman's and Carl Van Vechten's fictional satires, *Venture* (New York: Boni Liveright, 1927) and *Peter Wiffle* (New York: Knopf, 1922). Perhaps the most severe analysis of at least a portion of Luhan's life is her self-criticism in *Movers and Shakers* (New York: Harcourt, Brace, 1936).

6   *Selected Writings of Emerson*, 782.

7   Charles Frederick Briggs, "A Yankee Diogenes," *Putnam's* (October, 1854), 443–48. Also see Llewelyn Powys, "Thoreau: A Disparagement," *Bookman* 69 (April, 1929), 163–65.

8   *Selected Writings of Emerson*, 789.

9   *Walden and Civil Disobedience*, Owen Thomas, ed. (New York: Norton, 1966), 5,6. All subsequent references to *Walden* are from this edition.

10   *Walden*, 11; Richard Lebeaux, *Young Man Thoreau* (New York: Harper and Row, 1975); Leo Marx, *The Machine in the Garden* (New York: Oxford University Press, 1964), 264.

11   For discussions of economic and cultural changes in Concord, see: Townsend Scudder, *Concord: American Town* (Boston, Little, Brown, 1947); Paul Brooks, *The People of Concord: One Year in the Flowering of New England* (Chester, Conn.: Globe Pequot Press, 1990); Lebeaux, *Young Man Thoreau*, 18–27.

12   *Journal* in *The Writings of Henry David Thoreau* (Boston: Houghton Mifflin, 1906), vol. III, 237. Hosmer left Concord for Chicago in 1857.

13   *Walden*, 131–32.

14   Frederick R. Paul, *Modern and Modernism: The Sovereignty of the Artist, 1885–1925* (New York: Atheneum, 1985), 17. Paul's assessment is based upon analyses of modernist culture in European metropoles. Emerson, who himself was a major figure in this project, offered a self-criticism of the new Concord culture as a "congress of kings, each of whom had a realm to rule" in "New England Reformers." *Ralph Waldo Emerson: Selected Prose and Poetry* (New York: Holt, Rinehart and Winston, 1962), 144. For studies that emphasize this aspect of Concord culture, see: Taylor Stoehr, *Nay-Saying in Concord* (Hamden, Conn.: Archon Books, 1979) and Anne C. Rose, *Transcendentalism as a Social Movement*, 1830–1850 (New Haven: Yale University Press, 1981) although Rose exempts Thoreau from her analysis as one opposed to its collectivism.

15   *Journal* in *The Writings of Henry David Thoreau* (Boston: Houghton Mifflin, 1906), vol. IV, 478.

16   *Walden*, 13–14.

17   Ibid., 30.

18   Walden, 26.

19   Thoreau delivered a version of this chapter at the Concord Lyceum in 1847, which gained enough attention to place him on the lecture circuit.

20   See: Neufeldt, *The Economist: Henry Thoreau and Enterprise* (New York: Oxford University Press, 1989), 156–186; Stanley Cavell, *The Senses of Walden,* revised ed. (Chicago: University of Chicago Press, 1992), 88–98. Jane Bennett offers the intriquing proposition that this, and other minutiae, in Walden are part of an effort to recover the self. *Thoreau's Nature: Ethics. Politics, and the Wild* (Thousand Oaks, CA: Sage, 1994), 16–43.

21   Walden, 35, 47.

22   Stanley Cavell (*The Senses of Walden*, 15–22) contends that the prophetic scriptural mode is a prominent trope in Walden, with Thoreau assuming the

role of Ezekiel. While it is undeniable that *Walden*'s dramatic swings of mood and strident criticism of Concordians who have lost their way are in the prophetic tradition, Thoreau's project, to the extent to which it leans upon a religious sensibility, is more Benedictine in its message of serenity and simplicity.

23   I modify here Neufeldt's schema. *The Economist*, 174.

24   The relationship between traveling and settling in Thoreau is extremely complex. The author of several "travel" books and many "travel" essays, his travels took him no farther North than Canada, South than Staten Island, and West than Minnesota, and these were relatively brief excursions despite the advice of friends such as Hawthorne and Emerson to leave Concord permanently, or at least travel more extensively. Yet Thoreau was clearly fascinated with the persona of traveler and at the same time defensive about the geographical limitations of his experience. See: John Aldrich Christie, *Thoreau as World Traveler* (New York: Columbia University Pres, 1965) for an examination of this paradox.

25   *A Week on the Concord and Merrimack Rivers*, ed. Carl F. Howde (Princeton: Princeton University Press, 1980), 13.

26   *Walden*, 1.

27   Ibid. 66.

28   Ibid., 57

29   Ibid., 160.

30   Emerson, "Home" in *The Early Lectures of Ralph Waldo Emerson*, Robert E. Spiller, et al., eds. (Cambridge: Harvard University Press, 1972), vol. 3, 26; *The Letters of Ralph Waldo Emerson*, ed. Ralph L. Rusk (New York: Columbia University Press, 1939), vol. 2, 371.

31   Cavell, *The Senses of Walden*, 86.

32   Douglas Anderson explores the connections the azad metaphor of Thoreau's self and his portrayal of a corporeal Nature in terms of Thoreau's domestic experiment in *A House Divided: Domesticity and Community in American Literature* (Cambridge: Cambridge University Press, 1990), 72–80. Sherman Paul examines much the same material and folds it into the individualist narrative of rebirth. *The Shores of Walden: Thoreau's Inner Exploration* (Urbana: University of Illinois Press, 1958), 348–50 and Perry Miller emphasizes Thoreau's disgust with aspects of procreation and birth. *Consciousness in Concord* (Boston: Houghton Mifflin, 1958), 126 ff.

33   *Walden,* 161. Thoreau's account of "housekeeping at Walden" (as Emerson once described the experiment) parallels Catherine Beecher's popular how-to *A Treatise on Domestic Economy* (1841) employing her topics and themes such as "On Economy of Time and Experience" and "On the Preparation of Healthful Food." In the individualist narrative of Walden, however, since Thoreau is regarded as an opponent of domesticity, the similarities are treated

as parodic. See, for example, Linck C. Johnson, "Revolution and Renewal: The Genres of Walden" in *Critical Essays on Henry David Thoreau's Walden*, ed. Joel Myerson (Boston: G. K. Hall, 1988), 221–23. But aspects of Beecher's project were quite hospitable to Thoreau's since Beecher argued that housekeeping need not be drudgery and the democratic household did not require outside salaried labor.

34 Ibid., 161, 162.

35 Brooks, *The People of Concord*, 89.

36 *Walden*, 69. See Joan Burbick's analysis of *Walden* as cultural "settlement" in which Thoreau attempted to delineate a "cultural space in nature." *Thoreau's Alternative History* (Philadelphia: University of Pennsylvania Press, 1987), 60.

37 Walden, 73.

38 Ibid., 103.

39 Walden, 136.

40 Ibid., 137.

41 Ibid., 101. Thoreau's more negative assessment represented something of a self-critique since earlier versions of *Walden* presented the trapper in a more positive light.

42 Mabel Dodge Luhan, *Intimate Memories: Background* (New York: Harcourt, Brace, 1933), 5–6. Despite her critique, Luhan dedicated the volume to the town of her birth, even suggesting that its movement to a more tolerant atmosphere ("there are fewer taboos, fewer fears, and less unhappiness") was costly since now there was a corresponding "lack of savor and of charm."

43 The following discussion of Greenwich Village is adapted from my *Leftward Ho! V. F. Calverton and American Radicalism* (Westport, Conn.: Greenwood Press, 1993).

44 Floyd Dell, *Homecoming: An Autobiography* (New York: Farrar and Rinehart, 1933), 142.

45 Addams, *Twenty Years at Hull House* (1910) (New York, 1961), 64–65.

46 Hutchins Hapgood, *A Victorian in the Modern World* (New York, 1939), 49.

47 Max Eastman, *The Enjoyment of Living* (New York: Harper and Brothers, 1948).

48 Mabel Dodge Luhan, *Intimate Memories: European Experiences* (New York: Harcourt, Brace, World, 1933), 447.

49 Robert E. Humphrey traces the entire village experiment to an attempt to recover and re-live adolescent experience. *The Children of Fantasy* (New York: John Wiley and Sons, 1978).

50   *New York Tribune* (December 20, 1914).

51   Floyd Dell, *Looking at Life*, 125.

52   See Carolyn Ware's *Greenwich Village* (Boston: Houghton Mifflin, 1935).

53   Rudnick, *Mabel Dodge Luhan*, 62.

54   Mabel Dodge Luhan, *Intimate Memories: Movers and Shakers* (New York, 1936), 187.

55   Max Eastman, *The Enjoyment of Living*, 399.

56   Rudnick, *Mabel Dodge Luhan*, 75.

57   Ibid., 137–42.

58   Gibson, *The Santa Fe and Taos Colonies*, 219–20.

59   Rudnick, *Mabel Dodge Luhan*, 271.

60   Mabel Dodge Luhan, *Winter in Taos* (New York: Harcourt, Brace, 1935), 102.

61   Ibid., 237.

62   Ibid., 9, 29.

63   Ibid., 78–79.

64   Ibid., 112.

65   Ibid., 60, 62.

66   Luhan, *Movers and Shakers*, p. 83.

67   Luhan, *Lorenzo in Taos* (New York: Knopf, 1932), 35.

68   Simone de Beauvoir, *The Second Sex* (New York: Bantam, 1949), 599.

69   Luhan, *Winter in Taos*, 97, 118.

70   See, for example, Dolores Hayden's discussion of six decades of proposals of "material feminists" who sought to overcome the "physical separation of household space from public space" in her *The Grand Domestic Revolution: A History of Feminist Designs for American Homes, Neighborhoods and Cities* (Cambridge, Mass.: MIT Press, 1981).

71   I borrow her from Sue Birdwell Beckham's analysis of the American front porch as a liminal space "neither sanctified as the hearth nor public as the road." "The American Front Porch: Women's Liminal Space" in Marilyn Ferris and Pat Browne, eds., *Making the American Home: Middle Class Women and Domestic Material Culture, 1840–1940* (Bowling Green, OH: Bowling Green State University Popular Press, 1988), 69–89. Both Thoreau's and Luhan's home within their settlements seem to be presented in this fashion. Their homes themselves are like these porches, more "private" than the for-

est or desert yet more public than the conventional home from which they were remodeled. Thus Thoreau as a bachelor "outside" the family hearth and Luhan as a middle-class woman "inside" are modified in terms of openness from two different directions.

72   Luhan, *Winter in Taos*, 31, 125, 232.

73   Luhan to Neith Hapgood in Rudnick, *Mabel Dodge Luhan*, 179.

74   Luhan, *Winter in Taos*, 35, 48, 155.

75   Ibid., 42.

76   Ibid., 42, 119.

77   *Walden*, 113.

78   See: "Building Dwelling Thinking" in Martin Heidegger, *Poetry, Language, Thought* (New York: Harper and Row, 1971), 145–161. Compare, for example, either Walden or Los Gallos to Heidegger's exemplar of the Black Forest farm house (160).

79   Michael Gold, "Mabel Luhan's Slums," *New Masses* (September 1, 1936).

80   Sumner Chilton Powell examines the "inventive" character of the economic, cultural, and political institutions of Sudbury, Massachusetts, in his *Puritan Village* (Middletown, Conn.: Wesleyan University Press, 1963). Also see Philip Abbott, *Seeking New Inventions: The Idea of Community in America* (Knoxville: University of Tennessee Press, 1987), 141–49.

Chapter 9

Texts of Regret
Radical Self-Critique in the Novels of Tess Slesinger, Mary McCarthy and Marge Piercy

Three novels by Tess Slesinger, Mary McCarthy, and Marge Piercy respectively can tell us much about American radical movements as well as the way in which the search for a post-exceptional America itself replicates exceptionalism in its own distinctive search for the new. The three works are in part an assessment of radical movements in the three successive generations who lived through the Depression, Cold War, and the Sixties. Each describes a different form of radical organization. Slesinger presents an account of a radical literary circle and McCarthy a utopian colony. Piercy's novel describes several sets of radical organizations: a national student group, SAW; a cadre of terrorists called the Network; two communes (one urban and one rural), and a feminist collective. All three writers were themselves veterans of major radical causes of their generation. Slesinger was a member of the *Menorah Journal* group, a secretary to V. F. Calverton, who edited an independent radical quarterly, and was a fellow traveler of the Communist Party. McCarthy was an editor of the *Partisan Review*, a fellow traveler in the mid-Thirties and then close to the Left Opposition. Piercy was a member of SDS and later a feminist activist.[1] In each work is contained what might be called the radical self critique that each writer offers for the failures of their generation's radical politics. I intend to argue that there are two sets of arguments common to these self-critiques and that despite the introspection and severity of the assessments of Slesinger, McCarthy, and Piercy there is an additional submerged critique that is not made but can be drawn from their own narratives. Together these critiques offer combinations of the old and the new, though it is, in fact, from this submerged critique that we can learn the most about the successive failures of American radicalism. For what these radicals discover is that their experiments were not as new as they had once thought. Despite their newness, each radical experiment was infected with the oldness of fetishism (not the kind precisely of which Marx spoke but nevertheless an attachment that hid the true nature of relations and objects) and the oldness of patriarchy. That their utopias may have failed because they replicated organizational forms bred by exceptionalism is a critique implied in their accounts but not fully grasped.

These chronicles of radical experimentation do contain accounts of newness as exhilarating moments, individual and collective hopes and dreams. Most, however, have occurred "off camera," before the events in the narrative. Bruno Leonard, the leader of Slesinger's radical circle, feels "a quick nostalgia" for the old meetings with a collection of students called the "Black Sheep," who with their "turbulent imagination" had "burned the campus with their angry pacifism."[2] The leader of one of two factions in McCarthy's utopian colony hopes that his efforts will create an example for "a network of autonomous, cooperative colonies" but remembers tenderly his "leap of faith" ten years ago when he embraced "the intangible values that eluded his empirical grasp," quit his job and "moved down town into Bohemia, painted his walls indigo, dropped the use of capital letters and the practice of wearing a vest."[3] During an intense theoretical debate among Network leaders, Piercy's Vida Asch daydreams about the early days of SAW when it was a "fiercely, totally democratic organization" and as "uncontrollable and lush as a vacant-lot jungle."[4]

It is the atmosphere of failure, however, that provides the structure for each of these narratives. Radical projects dissipate. The magazine of the literary circle never appears despite an obscenely chic fund-raising party. The utopian colony never succeeds in bringing its philosophical teacher to its community. Another plan, Operation Peace, which was to create a peace fleet to transport European refugees to America, never materializes. The Network finally abandons its terrorist strategy for environmental political education only to adopt a plan to blow up a caterpillar at a nuclear power plant. Radical organizations disintegrate. Bruno Leonard disbands the literary circle. The colony dissolves. The communes break up. The Network still remains, although smaller in numbers and ambition each day because of arrests and defections. Vida Asch flees from possible arrest at the novel's close with only "her history, her political intent, her ability to make trouble."[5]

The most significant failures, and those that receive the most attention, are the personal relationships among members of radical organizations. The marriage of Margaret and Miles Flinders disintegrates at the close of Slesinger's novel. Bruno Leonard is unable to respond to Elizabeth Leonard, the expatriate and ex-flapper, despite expressions of love from both parties. Jeffrey Blake's compulsive Don Juanism exacerbates the personal and ideological tensions of the circle. McCarthy's "oasis" is so divided from its inception by faction that the most minor personal incidents (a kitchen accident, a practical joke) are causes for crises. SAW, and its cadre successor Network, are complex tangles of personal animosities and sexual jealousies. Vida, who confesses that she was "always sexually curious about any new man who came into the SAW circle" suffers both personally and politically from a succession of lovers. Leigh betrays her as he moves gradually toward a successful career in counter-cultural journalism. Her relationship with Kevin is largely one of psycho-sexual domination. Her affair with Joel, a deserter, is marred by their age differential.

According to these writers collectively, the radical imagination in America collapsed in three successive generations. What was so new as different and new as vibrant ("uncontrollable and lush as a vacant lot garden") became—serially—old as stale and impotent and even debilitated and decayed. What explanations are offered for these massive failures in radical organization, agenda-setting, and personal relationships? These two closely related critiques offered by each of these writers suggest that in all three aspects of radical endeavor, the creation of new institutions and policies and the creation of new kinds of individuals, failure was inevitable because the participants were too debilitated by their experiences in America. In the words of Mary McCarthy this "secession from society," this "insurrection of slaves against the inner masters," failed because "habits die hard."[6]

The First Critique: Ideational Fetishism

The title of Slesinger's novel, *The Unpossessed*, suggests a critique, reversing Dostoyevsky's, based upon the inability to engage in commitment. Each of her characters in their own way is psychologically, and hence politically, immobilized. Bruno Leonard both revels and despairs in his inability to act. "A Jew," he concludes, "if he has any brains at all, had twice as much as anyone else; he saw all sides at once and so his hands were tied, his brain stood still, he couldn't leap here and he couldn't leap there." His protege, Jeffrey Blake, "who had no Idea," had written seven novels while he "who could conceive behind his desk of The Novel must content himself or not content himself with the knowledge that if he ever wrote a book at all it would be a better book than any written by his colleague Jeffrey Blake." Leonard even brags that in college he knew the "idea" of football better than the half back but admits "all the same it was the dumb bastard of an athlete that got his letter." The magazine represented the apogee of Leonard's individualized Hegelianism. "A Jew said Magazine and he was content, dancing on the point of a needle for his life thereafter to investigate the concept of Magazine, to explore the function of Magazine, to dream the fulfillment of Magazine conveying the Idea. . . ."[7]

In a brilliant satirical illustration of Leonard's intellectualism, Slesinger recounts the would-be editor's reaction to a file cabinet sales person's pitch. The file cabinet (hence referred to as the File Cabinet) typically elates and disturbs Leonard. The File Cabinet does represent a manifestation of the Magazine but also is "profoundly disturbing by its presence." A File Cabinet ordered, caused the Idea to be "tampered with," and the Idea of the File Cabinet "became less clear less dear to him." Leonard imagines how Jeffrey Blake (who placed the order) conceptualizes File Cabinet: "Jeffrey said Magazine and immediately he saw himself assistant editor of a Filing Cabinet; he saw the whole thing complete, in its concrete form; complete with office desks and typewriters, lavatories, water-coolers, telephones on hinges, office girls named Miss Diamond, waste baskets, desk calendars. . . . Where then was the Idea?"[8]

Leonard's reluctance to bring the Magazine to fruition rests in part from fear of failure. He realizes that he must "finally admit that no matter how lofty the hopes, how valid the Idea, reality must consist in dealing mediocre articles to mediocre readers."[9] Thus editorship reveals Leonard's own flawed Hegelianism. For him the real can never be rational since the File Cabinet materialized is "yesterday's blushing sweetheart turned coarsely to a bride." Moreover, the Idea realized ceases to be his Idea. The daydream of Blake's concretization of the File Cabinet concludes with the image of office paraphernalia, "all ticketed, docketed, billeted, and in all four corners threatening the editorial desk."[10] Thus when Leonard does make a courageous decision, such as his refusal to permit Communist direction of the magazine's content, it is not clear whether the reaction is the result of moral principle, fear of Blake as an editorial competitor, or a generalized dread of the loss of the Magazine as his Idea.

Slesinger does, however, assign to Leonard the primary task of the radical self-critique. It is noteworthy that the moment of revelation occurs when Leonard completely loses his psychological equilibrium. The occasion for the critique comes not from political sources (the fund raising party is the epitome of radical chic, with a sumptuous buffet set underneath a Hunger March poster) but from his personal failure to commit himself to his life long love, Elizabeth. His speech before an alternately hostile and bewildered audience is a rambling, disjointed tirade from a man in the midst of a nervous breakdown. But Leonard does manage to convey his critique. Intellectuals are lost individuals both collectively and individually. Leonard, parodying Marx, offers "TO THE INTELLECTUAL SEX IS THE SUBSTITUTE FOR ACTIVITY, THE HIGHEST SUBLIMATION, THE FINAL OPIATE" and "TO THE REVOLUTION, FELLOW-LICE; THE MOST INGENIOUS OPIATE OF THE INTELLECTUAL" as slogans. When the crowd mistakes his shouting for wit (one young listener replies, "hurray for opiates!"), Leonard attempts to give a sociological explanation for his assessment: "for too long we have wandered unorganized, unwitting members of the lost tribe, the missing generation, the forgotten regiment; outcasts, miscasts, professional expatriates . . . accidents of birth—for many of our fathers were farmers or tailors or jewelers—we have no parents and we can have no offspring; we have no sex: we are mules—in short we are bastards, foundlings, phonys, the unpossessed and unpossessing of the world, the real minority." Pursuing this normatively inverted Mannheimian analysis, he tells his audience: "We have no class; our tastes incline us to the left, our habits to the right; the left distrust, the right disposes us." Leonard calls on the former Black Sheep and the aspiring editors to admit that they are sick or dead individuals. For youth, he pleads with them to "go west . . . go south, go north—go anywhere out of our God damned city."[11]

Before his moment of self-critique, Leonard had blamed his malaise on his Jewishness. Slesinger's other characters never achieve this expansion of self-revelation. Miles Flinders is obsessed with the harshness of his New England boyhood. If Leonard represents the scholarly tradition of American urban immigrant radicalism, Flinders epitomizes the fierce moralism that once emerged in political form as abolitionism. He attempts to explain to his wife, Margaret, that his ancestors ("pioneers and zealots") "never should have landed where they did . . . they aren't farmers; they aren't peasants. They're people with brains who hate the soil; they stayed, they put up with it, only because

it challenged them."[12] His most vivid childhood memory is the shoot-
ing of the family dog for killing chickens. Flinders admired the dog for
returning to the farm to accept his fate but most of all he is in awe of
his uncle's resolve. He "knew well that day that there was something
bigger in men than themselves, that could drive them to do what alone
they would have never dared. . . ."[13]

Miles Flinders struggles to apply this lesson in determination to his
politics. Margaret sees his adoption of Communism as his "new God."
He becomes a resolute Leninist. But he cannot fit his new commitment to economic determinism with the individualism of his ancestors. Moreover, his uncle was an economic failure as a farmer attempting to grow tobacco in New England, and he is a failure as a low level
white collar worker. As much as Flinders insists that it is the "personal
struggle" itself that defines success, he is aware that there is some
existential difference between struggling against rocky soil and maintaining a sense of dignity in relation to a boss who periodically cuts
his salary in 10 percent decrements. The only successful connection
between the personal and the political for Miles is his insistence that
his wife have an abortion as some kind of act of rejection of bourgeois
society or, more likely, as some sort of replication of his uncle's act of
self-denial. But this act results in the dissolution of his marriage.

Jeffrey Blake represents the combination of hedonism and revolutionary politics of which Leonard had spoke. Blake is a personable
and moderately talented novelist who attempts to fulfill personal ambition through any medium available at the moment. He loves mixing
cocktails, engaging in sexual conquest, and planning his next novel.
Margaret, who is alternately attracted to him as an antithesis of Miles
and repulsed by his hedonism, wonders "if his Revolution existed just
as cocktails did, something for Jeffrey to enjoy."[14] There is a vague
moment of personal politics in another sense, however, when Blake
makes love to Comrade Fisher (who is later exposed as less than a
"genuine" communist and a member of the Left Opposition) above a
portrait of Lenin and is overwhelmed with gratitude when she tells
him that he has "the hands of a revolutionary leader."[15]

All of Slesinger's characters are unable to reproduce themselves,
literally and politically. They had hoped, as Leonard concluded, to be
founders but instead were "foundlings." McCarthy's utopians bear many
resemblances to Slesinger's literati. The colony is divided into two
factions, the realists and the purists. Will Taub, the leader of the realists, suffers, like Leonard, from ethnic self hatred ("a kind of helpless-
ness came over him when he became conscious of his Jewishness")

and, like Leonard, is theoretically addicted. But unlike Leonard, who is morally conscious of his leadership abilities, Taub savors the most minor exercise of power. He is "a politician even with thought" who is bored with other people's ideas "once he had placed them in his atlas."[16] MacDougal Macdermott, Taub's counterpart in the purist faction, is less expressively drawn, but he does represent aspects of the New England tradition that inspired Slesinger's characterization of Miles Flinders. "Mac" too is a prisoner of his own theoretical gifts. His detractors claim that his pacifism will lead him eventually to vegetarianism. Mac defends himself by believing that he did not "hold eccentric views gladly" but that they were "imposed upon him by the inexorable clarity of his intelligence."[17]

The warring factions and their respective leaders could have been used as an occasion to explore the ideological disputes between Marxists and individualist anarchists. Instead, McCarthy chooses to treat the political ideas of both groups as efflorescences. The realists are former Marxists, who having "recognized the failure of socialism in their time," have suffered "an excruciating personal humiliation." While in their newly assumed roles as anticommunists, they had "accomplished with credit" their "historic mission," "the awakening of the Left to the dangers of Red totalitarianism," the realists were men and women without new ideas. However much they searched through the pages of Marx and Engels, the realists could not decide whether to support capitalist governments and if so, on what terms. The only common belief that remained among this group was a fanatical adherence to the doctrine of historical materialism. In McCarthy's assessment, the realists, themselves victims of history, insisted that everyone was subservient to the doctrine of inevitability. But while "their materialism had hardened into a railing cynicism," they still "retained from their Leninist days . . . a notion of themselves as a new revolutionary elite whose correctness in political theory allowed them the widest latitude in personal practice." The only actual manifestation of this sense of *lese majeste*, however, appears to occur in their talented and ferocious skills in political intrigue. Taub's collapsing personality only reasserts itself at the possibility of a political contest. Indeed, the sole reason he joins the experiment is to prove "what fools they'll make of themselves."[18]

If the realists hope for failure as a political victory, the purists are uncertain about the experiment. Macdermott's commitment to pacifism appears to be genuine, but he is never sure where his political opinions will take him next: "He was never quite certain what he thought about anything until he had tested his opinion for seaworthiness in the course of some polemical storm."[19] The purists' devotion to their anarchist teacher's injunction that the only hope for the future lies in "small insurgent communities" is variable among the members of the faction. Moreover, the group is not quite sure itself how it should organize apart from its dedication to operate on the principle "from each according to his capacities."

For McCarthy, both factions and the utopian experience itself represent the disorientation of the American Left in the 1940s.[20] The interaction between the two groups ten or fifteen years earlier might have produced reams of brilliant polemical attacks. But given the opportunity at the end of the war to engage in continual combat at an old secluded summer hotel, the participants have difficulty finding a political discourse in which to converse. The realist faction is in the midst of an ideological transition that we now know will culminate in the creation of neoconservatism. Taub, in fact, had offered his services to the State Department as an expert on communist strategy (only to be rejected because his contact with the Party had long passed). The purists, with their devotion to the principle of personal happiness, are already moving away from an anarchist Jeffersonianism to a materialism American style, as McCarthy's description of the opening day of the experiment suggests: "And out of those loaded automobiles began to come a variety of definitions of happiness: happiness as ornament, happiness as utility, happiness as oblivion, happiness as squalor, happiness . . . in a French casserole or sterilizer, a kiddie-coop or gold evening dress, Spanish shawls, books, pictures, batik hangings, porch furniture, blue jeans, garden tools, carpentry sets. . . ."[21]

Amazingly, however, after a series of crises, the experiment seems to succeed. The two factions cease to maneuver and conspire; friendships blossom; there is "a lyrical phase of the community"; the realists experience the "dawn of a new ethical attitude, a certain subordination of self to the requirements of the general welfare."[22] Yet most of Taub's supporters insisted that this utopia born was an accidental and exceptional case, not appropriate for the formulation of a social theory and the purists express concern that the colony is "not doing anything."

And the utopia does soon collapse. The incident that precipitates the failure involves the discovery of a group of poor people who are picking strawberries on the colony's grounds. Katy Norell, a member of the purist faction, is so distraught by the intrusion that she encourages some colonists to drive off the pickers by gunpoint. Taub sees the incident as confirmation of the need for force in society. Macdermott is so shaken by the incident that he is without an effective response. It is Norell then who offers the explanation for the incident and the failure of the experiment at the colony itself.

The use of force in so minor a context did not prove that the colonists were "just like everybody else" in the sense that Taub asserted. According to Norell, the strawberries themselves were not the occasion for force, but it was the idea of the strawberries that was crucial. She and the colonists had converted the whim for strawberries into an ethical demand. In their minds they felt they needed the strawberries and hence were morally justified in taking any action to secure them. The colony had confused its "material triumphs with the triumphs of its idea." For Norell, the pursuit of the idea of perfection or goodness now appeared to her as a "shallow and vulgar craving, the refracted error of a naive and acquisitive culture which imagined that there was nothing—beauty, honor, titles of nobility, charm, youth, happiness— which persistency could not secure." This error led to a conception of utopia "as a kind of factory or business for the manufacture of morality" and explained the periodic crises of the experiment. "The spirits of the colonists rose and fell with the market quotation of the enterprise; at the moment, its stock was very low."[23] She is not, however, prepared to abandon utopia. At the novel's close, she is counting the number of members who can be relied upon to stay. Instead, the colony must turn its attention to the production of some commodity "more tangible than morality." Cheese, wine, furniture, books, and glass might be prospects, but Katy Norell knew that it would be presumptuous to fix upon a panacea.[24]

McCarthy then, in her radical self-critique concludes that the radical styles of the 1940s, rather than chastened modifications from the experiences of the 1930s, possess a common flaw, which might be called a kind of commodity fetishism of ideas that must be erased before the radical project has a chance of success.

Marge Piercy's first critique is more muted, in part because she is anxious to avoid a captious assessment of her generation and in part because most of her efforts are reserved for a second critique. There is, for example, no explanation for the transition from the "wildly democratic" SAW to the cadre structured Network apart from the implication that the successor emerged from the need to protect persecuted radicals. But Piercy's Vida and her compatriots are increasingly painfully aware of the growing political irrelevance of the Network. "We have to change or we're relics. Remember that fossils are also located underground," remarks one member of the Network board near the end of the novel.[25] In addition, Vida is troubled by the demise of SAW as well as the two collectives of which she was also a member. Indeed, Vida's first critique is partially submerged by her second one somewhat in the same manner as we will contend that a third is submerged in the case of the three writers.

Vida complains about the new radical recruits who never experienced the utopia that was SAW and appears to believe that the values internalized and skills attained in what one radical called "ancient history" enable the Network to preserve some measure of democratic spirit. Former SAW board members "had been trained to argue for a position, to lose gracefully, plotting to rise again in a parliamentary motion, to compromise for support by accepting a friendly or even moderately hostile amendment, to shift support for one candidate to another and withdraw behind the scenes."[26] "Used to counting votes in [her] head," Vida gains a sense of empowerment from her ability to frame her arguments in a manner that promotes coalition-building. But while these skills were helpful in the 1960s, they assume the cast of parody in the hermetic atmosphere of the Network. Piercy's characters are terrorist versions of McCarthy's Will Taub. Lark, a leading theorist of the Network, "read long articles on the latest ideas of Kim Il Sung and Enver Hoxa." Roger "adopted a working class style, dressing in baggy work clothes her father would never have been caught dead in when he wasn't lying under a truck."[27] Vida herself works sporadically on a theoretical piece on American imperialism, still trying to follow the Sixties injunction to name the system. And while Vida's adoration of SAW's participatory democracy is genuine, she describes meetings in which majorities are formed more on the basis of sexual ties and jealousies and ability to theatrically deconstruct an opponent than on parliamentary skills and rational discourse.

The Second Critique: Male Domination

The set of arguments we have reviewed in each novelist's account of her generation's radical politics trace failure of the radical project to an obsession with the idea of radicalism, which results in psychologically flawed leaders and dramaturgical gesturing. To the extent that these writers were participants in these efforts, their works represent a self-critique, at least broadly autobiographical, of their experiences, although Slesinger would not likely agree that she is Margaret Flinders or McCarthy, Katy Norell or Piercy, Vida. It is in the second critique, however, that these writers offer another set of explanations for failure that is even more closely a personal reassessment of the political than the first.

The second critique is feminist: The failure of American radicalism is the result of the failure of men to acknowledge the humanity of women despite their professions of radical imagination and, to a lesser extent, the failure of women to resist male domination. Of course, the second critique is variable in these works both in terms of the relative weight assigned in relation to the general self-critique and the actual substance of the accusation. Piercy's, for example, forms the dominant perspective of her account and could more properly be called her first critique. Feminist concerns are far more prominent in Slesinger's narrative than McCarthy's, but her vision of the role of women is unlikely to be accepted by either Piercy or McCarthy. Still the theme of the second critique in terms of self-criticism is sufficiently commonly explored to permit a general characterization.

In the male domination critique, radical projects and organizations are the projections of male power fantasies, and internal political conflict is the result of male contests for domination and prestige.[28] Men see women only tangentially or instrumentally related to these activities. Slesinger's Blake, McCarthy's Taub, and nearly every male character in Piercy's novel are collectors of women. Blake "tastes" women in the same spirit of gaiety with which he experiments with new cocktails. Taub mentally ingests "women like a snake." Leigh surveys a group of women as if they were "ripe plums," and Kevin approaches women like a "police dog" chasing prey.

In "The Grand Coolie Damn," Piercy's nonfictional critique of the New Left, this style of promiscuity is described as "fucking a staff into existence."[29] Dominant males bring women into voting blocks and cast them out and replace them. Vida becomes especially adept at identifying power shifts in both the SAW and the Network on this basis. At one point in the narrative she suspects that her sister is censored by the steering committee of SAW not for her political deviancy but because "the rest of [the women] were all, theoretically available as sex objects." But in 1968 Vida could not say so aloud "without everybody telling her she was crazy." Men ignore or belittle attempts to raise political issues of importance to women. Slesinger's Norah is chided for her attempt to introduce women's concerns as part of the magazine's agenda. "I think we'll add a happy womb in every home," responds Leonard "cheerfully."[30] Male SAW members react spitefully when it is Vida who appears on the cover of *Life* magazine. The press neglects to tell readers that the occasion for the clenched fist and the demonstration is an effort to promote day care. Preston Norell takes advantage of the "Utopian brotherhood" as an occasion to ignore his wife; Katy Norell realizes that "men were born to love each other." Even the ferocious debating styles of each generation's movements are seen as phallic identity rituals. Piercy's Vida calls this "waving one's prick"; Slesinger, writing in a more restrained era, has her female observer murmur, "Shuttledore and battlecock. Struttlecock. Struts the cock," during a heated exchange among male members of the literary circle.

Part of this second critique is also devoted to a success story amidst the failures of male radicalism. In each of the novels the rising awareness of patriarchy parallels the decline of the generational radical project. Female radical participants succeed as their male counterparts fail. Slesinger's Margaret devotes her life to nurturing her husband. She attempts to convince him that there are life enhancing memories in his childhood experiences, that his economic failures can be overcome by participation in the magazine and that, most of all, he can gain a sense of peace and self worth by rededication to their marriage. But except for a brief moment in the novel, which turns out to be more of a truce than a reconciliation, Miles regards his wife's efforts as part of an attempt to "swallow him whole" with her "amoeba-motherly" love. He resents her salary, the legacy of her "urban birth," and her refusal to accept "historical necessity."

The chapter "Missus Flinders," originally published as a short story, is a powerful narrative of the climax of Margaret's disillusionment with Miles and the men of her generation, a personal-political critique that parallels the political-personal critique by Leonard in the chapter, entitled "The Party." She had already recognized the "sterility" of the literary circle's radicalism. Now Margaret Flinders sees the sterility of male/female relations in her own sterility: "He was a man, and he could have made her a women. She was a woman, and could have made him a man. He was not a man; she was not a woman. In each of them the life-stream flowed to a dead-end."[31] Miles had given her a basket of fruit after the abortion, which to Margaret seems to represent an Edenic loss ("they were ashamed as though they were naked or dead").

The abandonment of a woman by a man, and the subsequent clarity of political and personal perception that emerges on the part of the woman, is replicated by Slesinger's Elizabeth. The distant cousin of Leonard, Elizabeth is the sexually liberated former flapper of the twenties who spends time as an expatriate. She too seeks solace in male monogamy, but this transformation is also aborted by the psychological immobility of Leonard. Slesinger refuses to give both characters the new improved self that is the romance of the conversion narrative. Both Margaret and Elizabeth in many ways are as lost personally and politically as the male members of the circle. But both also emerge at the end of the narrative as the only characters who attain political lucidity and still have their personalities intact.

McCarthy's Katy Norell is delineated in two crises that confront the commune. In the first, she is the victim of a minor kitchen accident when the stove is left lit. The person culpable is the only conventional bourgeois in the experiment. When colonists realize that the incident is likely to lead to a political crisis among factions over the question of his dismissal from the commune, Katy is so reluctant to explain the incident that her shyness brings recriminations upon the victim by both her husband and some of the members. Some feel she should have identified the culprit; others believe she should have accepted guilt for not checking the oil level of the stove or for the sake of avoiding a factional battle. Katy ends up pleading for forgiveness to the group. Her husband humiliates her ("Go in and get breakfast. . . . Pull yourself together. You disgust me"). The mortification continues for several days as her husband publicly ignores her.

But it is Katy Norell who is able to offer the self-critique precipitated by the strawberry episode. From two domestic incidents (cooking breakfast and berry gathering), Norell, who joined the experiment with the "same petty conviction" that she had shown in demonstrating the "absolute necessity of a new dress or an apartment," discovers the secret of utopia's failure. Taub's insistence that Katy recognize historical necessity and "know yourself" becomes in this critique a demand (rejected) that she accede to male authority. Her response, "then we must get out of history," is a personal and feminist victory that seems to place her at the center of a new utopian experiment. The moral commodity fetishism that forms the explanation for failure in the first critique becomes a mechanism for female liberation in the second.

The conceptual proximity of the two critiques is most pronounced in Piercy's *Vida*. She has described the origin of the novel in these terms: "Suppose you wrote about two sisters, one of whom is a woman whose politics is based on her own sense of oppression, her own situation, and who becomes a feminist, and the other sister is a woman whose politics is based primarily on the oppression of other people."[32] Vida is certainly the more focused character as the center of the narrative. But it is Vida, the political radical, whose activities are a chronicle of failure, and it is Natalie, the feminist radical, whose activities are accounts of at least small successes. In fact, as fugitive, Vida's contract employment (vigilante action against a rapist, transporting battered women to shelters) are feminist activities. At the close of the novel, feminists take over the governing cadre of the Network. Thus Vida's failures, and the failures of the New Left in general, are largely the results of patriarchal structure and behavior in the radical movement. Vida is slow to appreciate this insight and thus it is Natalie who assumes the role of political and personal mentor. Vida is repeatedly but patiently chastised by her sister for accepting and even excusing rape, for her aggressive heterosexuality (despite several lesbian experiments), and for her failure to form voting blocs with women. Although Vida is neither completely or personally free even after the death of Kevin, she gradually gains a sense of self-worth and adopts portions of feminist analysis. Vida, like the feminist movement, is still in the process of birth at the novel's close.

The Submerged Organizational Critique

These radical self-critiques have also been subjected to criticism. While Slesinger's novel was positively reviewed to the extent that it was perceived as a critique of the independent Left, many reviewers complained that the narrative neglected the political at the expense of the personal. Joseph Freeman, for example, praised the book for its critique of Left intellectuals but concluded that ultimately the novel was "bourgeois" and "reactionary" because it studied "social impotence without any real explanation of that impotence."[33] Sidney Hook, writing many years later, contended that the novel lacked presentation of a single political idea. Slesinger could "talk about Virginia Woolf, Jane Austen . . . but the political isms were something her 'obsessed husband and his odd friends' were concerned about—a concern which affected her life."[34] Richard Pell in his history of political ideas in the 1930s gives Slesinger credit for her effort to understand urban radicals but concludes that "the issues ultimately become more sexual than political."[35] One of McCarthy's reviewers admired the style of the novel but regretted the narrow landscape she had selected for this "mechanically arranged roman à clef."[36] Hook again has complained about McCarthy's reduction of the political to the personal, alleging that her radical "imagination seems to be limited only to individuals she knows" and to whom "she is sexually attracted."[37] A sympathetic critic of *Vida* argued that for all of Piercy's effort to describe the goals and passion of the New Left, the political explanations and perspectives of the characters are "superficial." This, she cautioned, was precisely the complaint that outsiders had about the movement in life "and now here it is exacerbated in art. . . ."[38] Another criticized Piercy for describing a "politics oddly severed from history" without the "amplitude and texture of European novels of the left."[39]

Perhaps the most powerful generalized critique of novels such as those of Slesinger, McCarthy, and Piercy is offered by Irving Howe in his *Politics and the Novel*. Howe concludes that the link between the American political novelists of the nineteenth and twentieth centuries is that both "cannot focus upon politics long and steadily enough to allow it to develop according to its inner rhythms. . . Personalizing everything they could not quite do justice to the life of politics in its own right. . . . "[40]

Are both the radical self-critiques we have described solipsistic evaluations of radical movements that were in turn solipsist? Or had the political imagination of the novelists failed as they attempted to diagnose their generation's radicalism? I would argue that both critiques, however insightful, fail to account for the generational failure of American radicalism but that a third critique is available from each of these narratives that accounts for the personal-political analysis but in a very different way than any of these novelists (or critics) formulate. Slesinger, McCarthy, and Piercy have indeed described accurately the process by which radical organizations emerge in a liberal society though they have confused this process with their self-critique. Thus, Howe, and many of the critics of these novels, are incorrect in their assessment that some political reality has escaped the focus of the self-criticism.

Radical (and many reformist) groups in a liberal society can best be understood as invented communities.[41] Emerson identified the emergence of the first set of these movements in the second generation of the republic. In America, and especially New England, there had been a "keener scrutiny of institutions and domestic life than we had known. . . ." He described a "spirit of protest" that had produced a "restless, prying, conscientious criticism." Emerson admired the climate of friendship and association that these efforts had created as well as their utopianism, although he thought the experiments themselves were misplaced. What Emerson had perceived was the intense mixture of personal and political motives in the formations of these groups. It is the idea of "union of friends who live in different streets and towns" that animated the experiments, as well as a "sincere protesting against existing evils."[2]

Generations have passed since Emerson's speech, but the questions and complaints that he heard in the 1840s continue to be voiced in America: "Am I not too protected a person? Is there not a wide disparity between the lot of me and the lot of thee, my poor brother, my poor sister?. . . I do not like the close air of saloons. I begin to suspect myself to be a prisoner. . . . I pay a destructive tax in my conformity."[43] What Emerson had described then is a generationally replicated form of personal-political protest that emerges from the structure of a liberal society and that is particularly prominent in America in the form of what we have called critical utopian exceptionalism.[44] The communities that emerge from it originate from two interrelated and complex goals: commitment to the resolution of a public problem (often politically and economically, but not psychologically, removed from the interests of the participants) and the commitment to create a new community of persons.

The organizational structure of these invented communities reflects their origin. Large and complex movements may emerge from the spirit of protest but the fundamental reproductive unit is the union of friends described by Emerson. The novels we have discussed faithfully imitate this structure. Slesinger's circle numbers less than two dozen; McCarthy's utopia has fifty members. While Piercy's Vida feels she can rely upon tens of thousands of movement members, her participation in collectives, communes, and cadres amounts to interaction with less than a score of individuals. But the natural aggregate limitations of this form of organization also require other structural features similar to conventional patterns of friendship: relative equality; rejection of specialization; homogeneity; personal restraint.[45] To borrow a term from Erving Goffman, participants in the formative stages of these invented communities must travel as "unacquainted pilots."[46] In Slesinger's account Miles Flinders complains about the tasks placed upon him in this regard. He asks: "I wonder if anyone can be successfully transplanted?"[47]

There are, of course, some organizationally natural ways for this union of friends to maintain their structure. Political and class homogeneity is guaranteed by the process of group formation itself. Slesinger's characters are defined by their common class positions, although haunted by their bourgeios backgrounds. The outsider, and source of conflict, in McCarthy's utopia is a "bourgeois," distinguishable only by his failure to examine his class origins. The other members are ministers, journalists (print and radio), teachers, and the sons and daughters of the middle class. Piercy's characters are awed by the appearance of non-middle class participants, whether red diaper babies or children of the working class.

The greatest challenge, however, to these forms of organization, and the one that makes them so structurally unstable, is that the two goals of the protests (reformist or radical) are inconsistent. Stated in simple terms, the task of one involves doing and the task of the other involves being. The magazine, the political object in Slesinger's account, is the organizational imperative that creates the circle of friends, but it is also a goal that destroys the same group. Leonard's friendship with Blake cannot withstand the professional jealousies that a journal would exacerbate. The magazine so awakens Blake's personal ambition that he searches for a different invented community with the Communist Party. In McCarthy's utopia, as factions dissipate, a "lyrical phase of the community" begins. When the colonists briefly reject the political basis of their experiment, life becomes like a "tone poem." It is when Katy Norell complains that "we are not doing enough" that political issues reemerge and the colony is propelled again into another crisis. Her concluding assessment that the colony must abandon a social purpose to survive is abandonment of doing for being. The members of Piercy's SAW are, of course, morally obsessed with ending the war, but Vida's emotive responses suggest that the political goal is instrumental. After a street brawl, she speculates not on the strategic value of her action but "how wonderful to be connected widely and richly . . . to a web of caring. . . . " The Red Wagon collective seems to veer functionally toward an intentional family until one member, a police agent, goads the group into undertaking a bombing as a political act. When the Network board debates whether its role is primarily the nurturance of fugitives and or "political education," it also is experiencing the antagonism between the antagonistic goals reflected in its organization between doing and being.

The first critique blames this disharmony upon the participants themselves. For Slesinger the "sterility" of the circle cannot bring forth marriage and children or a magazine. McCarthy's realists cannot accept the "multiple virtuousness" of the colony because "boredom and cynicism had become so natural to them that an experience from which

these qualities were absent seemed to be, in some way, defective."
Piercy blames failure to connect the personal and political upon the
absence of experience in SAW or, as when she confesses to her sister,
upon her own "mess" in the "sex and love" part of her life.

This is not to say that the first critique is not correct in another
sense for there are severe structural strains in the invented community
itself without the demands for doing. All three critics describe radical
organizations by family metaphors. The Black Sheep were a "family"
as well as the circle. The colony is located in an old family resort hotel
that takes even the realists back "to the dawn of memory, and the
archaic figures of Father and Mother." Each one of Vida's new institutions is a family. But while the metaphor captures the being aspect of
these institutions, it also reveals the ways each structure cannot quite
duplicate the family. Each unit described (literary group, commune,
etc.) may be devoted to equality, but father figures are prominent in
these undertakings. Leonard is weary from dealing with the problems
of his Black Sheep, and his speech is in a sense a father's demand that
his children leave the nest. The utopia has two fathers (Taub and
Macdermott) with all the problems this structure entails. Interestingly,
Piercy's various radical organizations are bereft of fathers (only con-
taining, it seems, brothers) which could have led to Freudian insights
had not she adopted the second critique in which all men are fathers.

But the structural incoherence of these invented communities rests
not primarily either upon the incomplete replication or existence of
authority figures (at least in the first critique). What these novelists
express by the family metaphor is the anticipation of a community as
durable as kinship. But while the obvious falsity of this claim is part of
the first critique (none of these structures endure for even a generation), the metaphor illuminates other aspects of these invented communities. The incest taboo prevents the family as a unit from disintegrating into dyadic units and assures the replication of family forms
generationally. In the invented community, to the extent that the family is a model of communal feeling, members who pair-off engage in
the functional equivalent of incest. One solution to this problem, which
Vida enacts, is to engage in sexual relationships with as many members as possible as a form of solidarity. To the extent to which sexual
behavior is relatively routinely rotated, it is robbed of its disruptive
aspects. But unless this promiscuity is bureaucratically managed, the
neutralizing function is incomplete and the structures suffer from sexual
tensions and antagonisms, as is the case with every organization described by the novelists.

Even if the "incest" problem is resolved, however, the invented community suffers from a defect recognized by radical critics of the family. In an anomic society the family tends to insulate and isolate itself from disruptive influences. These invented families engage in the same behavior. The Black Sheep are extremely suspicious of any group outside their circle. The colony described by McCarthy is the ultimate act of withdrawal. Each successive radical organization that Piercy describes is more remote from society than the other. Invented these groups may be, but their appreciation of their community leads them to regard themselves as members of "natural" institutions with a moral and political superiority over other structures in society.

While the second critique is meant as a diagnosis of the instability of radical organizations, it is in many ways another extension. Without rejecting the general validity of the feminist analysis, in the context of this form of invented community the examination of gender places new demands on the homogeneity of the organization. Although the challenge is part of a natural organizational progression in this sense, it is also a retreat from the community that has just been invented. Feminist consciousness may serve temporarily to prevent the consolidation of heterosexual dyads that threaten the community but at the same time new forms of personal/political sexual experimentation create the possibility of raising the demands on the unacquainted pilots to organizationally unacceptable levels.

More significant, however, is the power of the second male domination critique to replicate internally the very process that created the initial radical invented community. The community was initially formed by like-minded individuals in order to confront the dual needs of rejecting privilege and seeking solace among themselves. The second critique demands that the same process be repeated within the new community itself. Margaret and Elizabeth, Katy and Vida are twice new persons, first as the result of their participation in a radical project, and second as a result of their participation in the feminist project. Not only do these repeated transformations run the risk of producing a solipsistic consciousness, but they draw attention away from radical self-critique. Circles, colonies, and communes may fail but the belief that a new movement is born can become "radical organizations fail but I am reborn."[48] A conclusion close to this is, after all, the last thought of Vida's. Katy will re-make the colony, and Margaret will seek a new life without her husband and the circle. Algerism, admittedly of a different variety than the standard formulation, seems to be as much a consequence of the second critique as the first although it is largely unrecognized in these novels.

It would be unfair to blame this process of privatistic individualism-public/personal commitment-privatistic individualism on feminism and the second critique. The imperatives that push individuals to radical participation and back to privatism can come from many other directions, and the attraction of newness is almost impossible to resist in America. The point here is that the radical organization in America is unable to restrain this process and that the second critique may be sanctioning this transformation more than assessing it.

Conclusion

Both the ideational and male domination critiques argue that their generation's failure to resolve public problems is largely the result of personal failures. The submerged critique available from the narratives of Slesinger, McCarthy, and Piercy suggests that the diagnosis should, initially at least, begin the other way around. The failure to resolve personal problems is the result of the political failure to construct organizations capable of overcoming the solipsistic tendencies in liberal society. Given the nature and the origins of the movement of middle-class individuals to create these "free spaces" in the context of an individualistic culture, these organizations manage rather to produce new forms of free personal space rather than new forms of community. However much effort individuals in these structures expend in an attempt to reproduce their newly invented beloved community, they seem to fail. In this sense, these radical organizations can be seen as unanticipated replicative structures of American exceptionalism.

As we noted, the distinctive nature of group formation and maintenance in America was first given theoretical prominence by Tocqueville for it was Tocqueville who insisted upon the historical uniqueness of American society and raised the question of how civil society could be maintained in the absence of an aristocracy. The celebratory interpretation of his tentative reliance upon new forms of association for a liberal society on the part of contemporary American political scientists has been challenged by those who have raised important questions about the scope and character of American pluralism. But these self-critique narratives confirm Emerson's observations on the personal origins of political protest and also explain the theoretical and empirical difficulties faced by those who have focused upon social

movements as the primary agency for the revitalization or even radical restructuring of liberal society.[49]

Three alternatives in particular deserve attention. One involves teth-
ering these invented communities to a hierarchically organized political structure, much as the American Communist Party attempted to
do in the Popular Front period in the 1930s. Slesinger herself implicitly recommends this alternative in her first critique. [50] As Warren
Sussman concludes, "The genius of the Communist movement of the
1930s was its ability to use the obvious social and psychological needs
of the period. It recruited effectively individuals who had no other
place to go and who sought to belong. . . . The Party offered more
than political participation: there were its camps, its discussion groups,
its magazines, even its dances and social affairs."[51] But the strategic
cunning of the Communist Party was itself at war with the invented
communities it sought to control. As a result, even before the Nazi-
Soviet pact, Earl Browder complained that the Party had to recruit
seven people in the hope of retaining two.[52]

Another alternative entails splitting the radical organization's unstable combination of being and doing. This option is outlined by
McCarthy through the plan proposed by Katy Norell at the end of *The
Oasis* and has recently received some attention by those radicals who
bracket their theories as "post-Marxist." For example, Mark Gottdiener,
who has argued that "Marx was wrong" and the utopian socialists
were correct, has suggested that given the extent to which capital has
appropriated all forms of space, the formation of communities which
are simply committed to use rather than exchange value are themselves inherently radical.[53] It is far from clear, however, that "use communities of being," however radically structured and non-evangelist
politically, would not constitute what Henri Lefebre has critically called
in a slightly different context "privileged spaces" of relative independence and affluence, or would form no more than what Robert Bellah
and his associates have called "life-style enclaves."[54] Whatever the likely
form, the exploration of new ways of being, even though conceived
collectively, necessarily involves a dramatic withdrawal from public life
as presently organized. The assumption of a net gain in the creation
of public space is thus dependent upon the belief that by some exemplary process "use communities" will multiply, which, after all, is just
another way to reintroduce the demand for doing into the organizational theory. Thus the most likely positive scenario in this regard is
the existence of a few isolated neo-monasterial structures, which func-

tion as isolated beacons for liberal citizens, but the temptation to con-
vert this form of withdrawal to a critical utopianism through political
evangelism is enormous. And, as we have seen repeatedly in the texts
we have studied, the route between the critical and the celebratory in
America is circuitous. McCarthy perceived this in her description of
the multiple forms of happiness exhibited by her utopia's participants
on the first day of the experiment.

Perhaps the lesson of these narratives of three generations of radicals, however, leads us to a position that would argue for the abandonment of any form of radical organization as a structure for political
change and a consequent neglect of the post-exceptional imperative.
There are institutions in American society, admittedly atrophied or
dependent upon bureaucratic structure, such as political parties, unions,
schools, churches, and neighborhoods that could be transformed in
ways that meet both the redemptive and political needs of restless
individuals. These institutions have a history that extends well beyond
a generation as a recoverable resource for radical imaginations. They
have some, or the possibilities for some, multi-class character. They
have the remnants of the *Gemeinschaft* so earnestly sought. Though
unlikely to be followed, the central, though submerged and unintended,
political lesson derived from the self-critiques of Slesinger, McCarthy,
and Piercy would thus involve a moratorium on new magazines, circles,
collectives, communes, and cadres during the next wave of "restless,
prying criticism" that flows through American society before these are
really the only alternatives left.

Notes

1   For autobiographical and biographical analyses, see: for Slesinger, Shirley
    Biagi, "Forgive Me for Dying," *Antioch Review* 35 (Spring–Summer, 1977),
    224–36; Janet Sharistanian, "Afterward," Slesinger, *The Unpossessed* (New
    York: Feminist Press, 1984); Alan Wald, "The Menorah Group Moves Left,"
    Jewish Social Studies 38 (Summer–Fall, 1976), 289–320; for McCarthy,
    McCarthy, *On the Contrary* (New York: Farrar, Straus, 1962); Carol
    Gelderman, *Mary McCarthy: A Life* (New York: St. Martin's Press, 1988);
    for Piercy, Celia Betsky, "A Talk with Marge Piercy," *New York Times Book
    Review*, 24 February, 1980, 36–38; Piercy, *Parti-colored Blocks for a Quilt*
    (Ann Arbor: University of Michigan Press, 1982); Todd Gitlin, *The Sixties*
    (New York: Bantam, 1987), 371–73.

2   Tess Slesinger, *The Unpossessed* (New York: Simon and Schuster, 1934),
    32.

3   Mary McCarthy, *The Oasis* (New York: Random House, 1949), 8–9.

4   Marge Piercy, *Vida* (New York: Summit Books, 1979), 110.

5   *Ibid.*, 411–12.

6   McCarthy, *The Oasis*, 4.

7   Slesinger, *The Unpossessed*, 33–34,

8   *Ibid.*, 31.

9   *Ibid.*, 29.

10   *Ibid.*, 31.

11   *Ibid.*, 326–30.

12   *Ibid.*, 40–41.

13   *Ibid.*, 53.

14   *Ibid.*, 61.

15   *Ibid.*, 231.

16   McCarthy, *The Oasis*, 35.

17   *Ibid.*, 89.

18   *Ibid.*, 19, 21–22.

19   *Ibid.*, 88.

20   See Gelderman, *Mary McCarthy: A Life*, 142–48. Also see general assess-
    ments: William S. Graebner, *The Age of Doubt: American Thought and*

Culture in the 1940s (Boston: Twayne, 1991); Paul Boyer, *By Dawn's Early Light: American Thought and Culture at the Dawn of the Atomic Age* (New York: Pantheon, 1985).

21   *Ibid.*, 32–33.

22   *Ibid.*, 109.

23   *Ibid.*, 178.

24   Thought not McCarthy's intention, one is led to wonder if this "new" alternative is not a return to capitalism.

25   Marge Piercy, *Vida*, 312.

26   *Ibid.*, 311.

27   *Ibid.*, 310–11.

28   This dichotimization of men as power seekers and women as life enhancers was extensively explored in the feminist utopian novels of the 1970s (to which Piercy contributed with her *Woman on the Edge of Time*). Newness here reached its apex with the virtual elimination of men from society. See: Kristine Anderson's astute analysis: "The Great Divorce: Fictions of Feminist Desire" in Libby Falk Jones and Sarah Webster Goodwin, eds., *Feminism, Utopia, and Narrative* (Knoxville: University of Tennessee Press, 1990), 85–90.

29   Marge Piercy, "The Grand Coolie Damn" in Robin Morgan, ed., *Sisterhood is Powerful* (New York: Vintage, 1970), 430.

30   Slesinger, *The Unpossessed*, 97.

31   *Ibid.*, 350.

32   Piercy, *Multi-colored Blocks for a Quilt*, 177.

33   Philip Rahv (book review), *New Masses* 11(1934), 26–27.

34   Allan M. Wald, *The New York Intellectuals* (Chapel Hill: University of North Carolina Press, 1985), 40.

35   Richard H. Pell, *Radical Visions and American Dreams* (Middletown, CT.: Wesleyan University Press, 1973), 404.

36   Donald Barr (book review), *New York Times*, August 14, 1940. Also see: Alex Gottried and Sue Davidson, "Utopia's Children: an Interpretation of Three Political Novels," *Western Political Quarterly* 15 (March, 1962), 17–32.

37   Sidney Hook, *Out of Step* (Harper and Row, 1987), 524.

38   Elinor Langer, "After the Movement," *New York Times Book Review*, February 24, 1980.

39   John Leonard (book review), *New York Times*, January 15, 1980.

40   Irving Howe, *Politics and the Novel* (New York: Meridian, 1957), 163.

41   On the concept of invented communities, see: Robert Nisbet, *The Twilight of Authority* (New York:Oxford University Press, 1975) and Philip Abbott, *Seeking New Inventions* (Knoxville, Tenn.: University of Tennessee Press, 1989).

42   Ralph Waldo Emerson, "New England Reformers" (1844) in Reginald L. Cook, ed., *Selected Prose and Poetry* (New York: Holt, Rinehart and Winston, 1950), 145, 147.

43   *Ibid.*, 147.

44   Writing in another generation, Jane Addams, early in her career, contended that a "fast growing number of cultivated people" were so infected with a sense of loneliness that they were being "buried beneath mental accumulation." Thus "subjective necessity" required devotion to public problems. *Philantropy and Social Progress* (New York: Crowell, 1893), 20.

45   Jane J. Mansbridge describes this structure expertly in her *Beyond Adversary Democracy* (Chicago: University of Chicago Press, 1980). Also see Robert D. Holsworth's summary of "personalist politics" in *Let Your Live Speak* (Madison, Wisconsin: University of Wisconsin Press, 1989), pp. 179–200.

46   Erving Goffman, *Relations in Public* (New York: Harper and Row, 1971), 7.

47   Slesinger, *The Unpossessed*, 39.

48   See the comments of collective members in Annie Popkin's account of early feminist radical organization. For example: "My whole lifestyle was completely determined by the movement. . . Bread and Roses became the newer form and it was better for me." "An Early Moment in Women's Liberation," *Radical America* 22 (1989), 19–35. See Todd Gitlin on the centifrugal impact of feminism on the radical project of the sixties. *The Sixties* (New York: Bantam, 1987), 375–76.

49   For a helpful review of problems in recent social movement theory, see Carl Boggs, *Social Movements and Political Power* (Philadelphia: Temple University Press, 1986), ch. 1.

50   Slesinger had recently become estranged from the independent radicalism of the Menorah group that was led by her former spouse, Herbert Solow. See: Alan M. Wald, *The New York Intellectuals*, pp. 64–74.

51   Warren Sussman, *Culture as History* (New York: Pantheon, 1984), 173.

52   Harvey Klehr, *The Heyday of American Communism* (New York: Basic Books, 1984), p. 367

53   Mark Gottdiener, *The Social Production of Urban Space* (Austin: University of Texas Press, 1985), pp. 284–86.

54   Henri Lefebvre, "Space: Social Product and Use Value" in J. W. Frieberg, ed., *Critical Sociology* (New York: Irvington, 1979),p. 292; Robert Bellah, *Habits of the Heart* (Berkeley: University of California Press, 1985), 71–75.

Chapter 10

Conclusion
Ducks, Sheds, and Freeways

We have now discussed thirteen exemplary texts in American political thought by chronicling their employment of the old and the new to defining and redefining American identity. The authors have used old/new with great skill and often with great success. And while the dichotomy itself has a monumental repetitiveness about it, the combinations and reinterpretations of this pairing are not only intricate and but also inventive. Can, however, this light of old/new that we have shone upon these texts provide a basis for a general account of American Exceptionalism? In chapter one, focusing largely upon contemporary views, we noted that American political theorists also seemed to adopt dichotomous positions in regard to the question as to whether America was exceptional. An ideological orientation emphasized the limits of American discourse and a utopian one emphasized its possibilities. In extremis (which appears to be its common form), nothing in the way of significant change seems possible in America or everything is possible. Overlaid with these orientations were positions of criticism and celebration. If nothing was possible in the ideological formulation, then this was a condition to be praised or condemned, and if everything was possible so too was this a condition that called for negative or positive assessments. Thus if we placed these positions in a matrix with a few contemporary exemplary examples, it would look like this:

	UTOPIAN	IDEOLOGICAL
CRITICAL	Jameson	Hartz
CELEBRATORY	Shklar	Boorstin

Is it possible, however, to place the texts we have discussed in this matrix? Suppose we tried to do so in a preliminary fashion with at least some of the works we have reviewed. The matrix might look something like this:

	UTOPIAN	IDEOLOGICAL
CRITICAL	ML King	Dubois
CELEBRATORY	Jefferson	Publius

Does this lead us to the conclusion that authors who emphasize the old are ideological exceptionalists of either celebratory or critical types and those who emphasize the new are utopians of the same types? Would the matrix look like this?

	NEW	OLD
CRITICAL	ML King	Dubois
CELEBRATORY	Jefferson	Publius

Certainly there is a preoccupation in the texts we have examined with America in terms of its range of limits and possibility, and new-ness/oldness does provide the framework for verifying what is American. This configuration by itself, however, misses the complexity of both the uses of the old/new and the definitions of each in American political thought. For example, Publius frequently warns against reliance upon the old when he speaks of the tragic course of republican foundings (the "dark and degrading pictures") but also recommends the second founding as one consistent with a science of politics based upon the "tried course of human affairs." The new is to be avoided when it does not recognize the constraints of human nature (No. 10), and the new is to be embraced when circumstances make experimentation desirable (No. 14). Thus Publius, through various definitions of the old and new, provides a map of American Exceptionalism that tells us when to avoid the old and when to acknowledge it, when to grasp the new and when to shun it.

Publius' map contains signposts that permit us to maneuver through the old and the new. We are "lost" when we fail to follow his way and in a central sense are in danger of losing America by following roads that lead to unexceptional histories already traveled by past republics.

Jefferson too offers a map, but it is not one that artfully combines the old and new because his exceptionalism is based upon systematic delineations of the new in the form of separate genres. What is possible in Jefferson's terms is determined by traversing his different genres of America. Racial equality is precluded in the scientific analysis of America and racial conflict is resolved and critiqued in the "old" republican text. But "old" genres, like republicanism and the pastoral, are transformed into new ones when they are pasted upon the American context. The Faustian implications of the scientific text are negated by the "reappearance" of the pastoral. Thus one form of newness negates or transforms or parallels another. Jefferson's "multiple newness" functions much like the new and the old for Publius because Jefferson is the authority of the new though not because he can distinguish between "good" and "bad" forms of both but because he shows us how to travel from one form of the new to another.

In this respect, Tocqueville's analysis of the new is similar to Jefferson's. But while Jefferson's delineates the new in terms of distinctive texts of the new, Tocqueville does so in terms of the dichotomies between the exceptional and the *exceptional* and the exceptional as unique and the exceptional as first instance. While the positive unique and positive in the first instance correspond generally to Jeffersonian sensibilities, though without the filter of his genres, there is a dread of the new in Tocqueville's analysis of the new despotism that democracies can produce and a sense of regret in the negative unique in regard to race that are both absent in Jefferson's exceptionalism. It is this perspective as "outsider," which is captured by Tocqueville's focus on the issues of replicability and uniqueness in regard to America, that authorizes *Democracy in America* as an exceptional text of American Exceptionalism.

The two texts of "exceptionalism-within-exceptionalism" we have examined offer a significant variation from Publius', Tocqueville's, and Jefferson's. Both Dubois and the Southern Agrarians embrace oldness as a vehicle for their exceptional grievances against an exceptional nation that will not or cannot listen in large part because of its infatuation with newness. DuBois' insistent reminder, "We were here before you," is one the Agrarian would readily agree too as well, though the African American is erased from his own "settlement" of America. Indeed there is an obsessive fear in these texts with envelopment by the new epitomized by the Hippomenes and Remington narratives of DuBois and Kline respectively. The "new Negro" and the "new South" reverberate with dread in both these exceptionalist texts. Yet the new has a way of making its presence felt in both these challenging exceptionalisms. Not only do the Southerners have difficulty in ignoring the eclecticism of their invented culture but they experience difficulty in being prideful of their own newness. Dubois delineates a new kind of American who is defined by his twoness and his "gift" of second sight, which he fears will be obliterated by a new kind of newness. And, of course, there is a grandiose newness in the dual imaginings of new foundings by both texts of exceptionalism-within-exceptionalism. DuBois and the Southern Agrarians resist the nationally recognized foundings, which constitute America's oldness, as aborted or perverted foundings respectively and replace them with "new" foundings that constitute their *own* form of newness that is immune to the newness of America. These exceptionalist-within-exceptionalist texts are undoubtedly critical in their perspective and identify America in terms of its iron constraints upon the possible. But their own celebration of oldness is designed to distinguish them from the rest of America, and their conception of newness is bifurcated between the newness that is America and the newness that is their own.

The estrangement from America in *Walden* and *Winter in Taos* is just as severe as it is in *The Soul of Black Folk* and *I'll Take My Stand*. But the alienation is so acutely personal that the objections of Thoreau and Luhan seem to become absorbed in the individualist ethos of America despite their best efforts. The suffocating consequences of a parochial and materialist individualism still finds a home in America as long as their texts are interpreted as attempts to seek liberation through their reexamination of selfhood. Thus *Walden* and *Winter in Taos* are valorized as texts of utopian exceptionalism of the critical kind. Only if Americans learned how to live—which they could if they followed these two experiments in living—could they reach their potential. Thus the place of the two experiments is an attempt to escape place. The best place is, in Emerson's interpretation of Thoreau, "where he stands." But if we read these two texts as efforts to create an exceptional place rather only than exceptional efforts to flee place (a place which is not really a place at all since it is as "pure" as a state of mind), we find Thoreau and Luhan exploring a place that might be as unsettled as individual salvation but one that attempts an actual sense of place as *oikos*. In order to describe this exceptional American sense of place—partly an escape from place but also partly an attempt to find one, Thoreau and Luhan explore the old and the new. Walden and Taos are open rejections of established (old) places (Concord, Buffalo, and even the "new" Greenwich Village), but they are intimately tied to their new places since they constitute an act of (re)placement. Both new places are built upon alternate conceptions of a household (one based upon bachelorhood and one upon matriarchy) and alternate conceptions of farming and culture (the new "agriculture"). But their newness extends from (re)placement because these new settlements lift from Americans the moral burden that all old places bear (unless, of course, the skeptical reader foregrounds the sequestered old settlers in their new communities). Thus the attempt to retrieve the old is managed through the most assertive exploration of the new (for both Walden and Taos as texts record utopia), and the same skeptical reader as well might be forgiven if she reads only personal identity (re)made as the only settlement in these acts of (re)newal. Whatever is one's reaction to *Walden* and *Winter in Taos*, there still stands the notion that what is exceptional about America is that it is a place in which one can always (re)new one's self or (re)new self as place or perhaps even (re)new place itself.

(Re)newal too is the central, perhaps the only generic trope of the *Declaration of Independence*. The *Declaration* at Philadelphia can of course be regarded as the original, the "first" new. No subsequent reading can quite replicate this newness as long as the American regime remains intact since the performative element of the *Declaration* is even stronger than the *Federalist Papers* which after all is said by Publius still leans upon the Constitution as its authority. But if we view the Declaration as a merged text, that is, as a text that includes the Declarations at Gettysburg and Birmingham, (re)newal fills the entire document. Lincoln used "rededication" as his act of (re)newal, which at once authorized the new and secluded it. In fact, until the moment at Gettysburg, Lincoln's merger remained contested as "new" and hence unmerged, and it could be said that it was Lincoln's sacralization of battlefield death that sealed the merger. His argument at Chicago that the *Declaration* needed to be read as a textual authority for equality competed, not only with the rebellion proposition, but with Douglas' ethnic exclusionism until the moral resolution of fratricide through a narrative of national (re)birth was delineated. The Declaration at Gettysburg so effectively merged with that of Philadelphia that King could only (re)open the Lincoln reading with the threat (modified by the concept of civil disobedience) of rebellion that the discredited Southerners had so fervently attempted to center. King's strategy of enclosing his reading paralleled Lincoln's as he marked the struggles and martyrdom of civil rights "soldiers" as acts of national redemption. Certainly both Lincoln and King represent a critical utopian exceptionalism in which the new forms an avenue for making claims about the feasibility of (re)newal. But as we have seen, these claims were deeply imbedded in insistences based upon oldness either through the "embalmed" nature of the Declaration at Philadelphia or the "promissory note" unredeemed at Gettysburg.

The texts of regret we have examined are generational reassessments of what participants regarded as truly novel attempts at capturing the new since the experiments fictionalized were designed to inaugurate a post-exceptional America. Thus we see the failure of the radical dream (as opposed to the American one) collected and collectivized into two postmortems, which are themselves based upon newness. Had the participants thought fully in novel terms they would have avoided the old fetishism of ideas and/or the old trappings of patriarchy. The observation made by one of Piercy's radicals, "We have to change or we're relics," is meant to convey the necessity of revolutionary flexibility, but it also reveals a proclivity to search for reasons for failure in lack of newness. Thus the self-critiques anticipate the radical departures of the future and keep alive the dream of post-exceptionalism. These generational searches for the new that will truly be new is not the only source of revolutionary elan in America, but these systematic self-critiques show how the dream of post-exceptionalism is another replication of the texts that are less open to this alternative.

Moreover, while for these generations of radicals a post-exceptional America is the newness they seek before which everything else is old, the question of a post-exceptional America is always present in American political texts. Most often, it is the inverse of the radical perspective. For to be without exception is to be "old." For Publius, a post-exceptional America is one like Europe with all its ancient animosities. Indeed, a post-exceptional America would represent the subjugation of the old over the new for as Europe replicated in America, America would be erased as a distinct identity. That same concern is reiterated by Lincoln, who defined the Civil War as a test of whether America "so conceived and so dedicated, can long endure." Even the exceptionalism-within-exceptionalism theorists, who were so anxious to deny the exceptionalism of the nation at large, seemed reluctant to pursue projects that might threaten their own imperiled and maligned exceptionalism. Thus post-exceptionalism becomes the kind of oldness that does not preserve the new but is unable to generate the new. This sterility, which is the reverse of the themes of birth and rebirth that form the structure of exceptionalism from which appeals to oldness can be framed, constitutes an irreversible closure. No doubt speculation about the threat of the post-exceptional is a tactic of the American as exceptionalist as a way to protect his present project, but its presence in all variations of exceptionalism—ideological/utopian and celebratory/critical suggests that the possible absence of exceptionalism would constitute not only sterility but an inevitable death of national identity itself. The complete collapse of the new into the old would entail a complete negation from which all thought would be silenced. Post-exceptionalism then hovers over all American texts as a grand erasure. Given this consequence, the constant flirtation with the post-exceptional is always potentially a source of extreme dread and it is thus an intriguing feature of American political culture that its authors should still be so willing to gaze upon the possibility even when tempted to do so for immediate gain.

We should not, however, draw a picture of American political culture as a James Dean mentality writ large, as a culture careening down the road risking obliteration. The threat of post-exceptionalism may heighten the pursuit of American identity, but this does not mean that Americans ignore signposts along the highway. In fact, as we saw so vividly in Jameson's and Mather's analyses, the continual preoccupation with newness always places the post-exceptional abyss in different sites so that its presence is variable.

Let me offer then an alternative interpretation of American Exceptionalism, one that attempts to avoid replication of a particular exceptionalist position but which acknowledges the general stress placed upon exceptionalist theorists in gauging the possible. I first borrow as a source an innovative account of modern (and post-modern) architectural theory. *Learning from Las Vegas* by Robert Venturi, Denise Scott Brown, and Steven Izenour is helpful in a general way because the authors attempt to confront the phenomenon of newness (a new type of emerging urban form emanating largely from America) in a context in which the new is the preferred (modern architects value the "revolutionary, utopian, and puristic"). Thus the modern architect must be especially responsive to newness and at the same time retain a framework that distinguishes the new as the "ugly

and ordinary" and the new as "heroic and original." The project of
Venturi et al., in fact, looks very much like those of the American
authors we have surveyed, though with a candor that is largely absent
from American texts. We "hope to make the case for a new but old
direction in architecture . . ." is their stated project.[1]

Central to their effort is their presentation of two different kinds of
architecture.[2] One, which they name "the duck" in honor of a huge
duck-shaped drive-in photographically captured by Peter Blake in his
God's Own Junkyard, submerges architectural rules of form and space
in favor of "overall symbolic form." America is strewn with examples
of this outlandish architecture which includes restaurants and motels
in the shape of elephants, whales, and teepees. The other, which
Venturi et al. call the "decorated shed" (which also informs their own
conceptualization of Las Vegas) makes architectural decisions as starkly
dramatic as those of the duck model. The decorated shed places space
and structure directly at the service of the program. The Las Vegas
strip is a pure example of decorated sheds since it consists of a series
of "conventional shelters" surrounded by elaborate signs (huge and
colorful for the daytime auto traveler and electric for the nighttime
one). In duck architecture the symbol is more important than the structure, indeed it is the structure, and in the decorated shed architecture,
on its $10,000 supports rest $100,000 signs, the symbols are an
elaborate adornment.

American Exceptionalism in general, and specifically for its critics,
is frequently portrayed as a huge, ugly (or heroic) duck. For example,
Jameson insists that unless the decorative sheds fit into some common sign they exhibit all the characteristics of the post-modern mor-
bidity he describes. In point of fact, Jameson's own theory, much like
Mather's, fits the model of Venturi's duck. His periodization of the
sixties is actually an elaborate duck in which the chaotic and contingent features of the period, including America itself as symbol, are
housed in this grand symbol of late capitalism. It is important to note,
however, that when we examined the duck it seemed to become transformed into a set of decorative sheds. Jameson's detours are much
like Venturi's cloverleaf design of modern airports in which one must
turn right to turn left. Similarly, while Shklar initially speaks of the
varied character of the American political tradition, illustrated by its
three founding sciences of politics, and posits a Manichean battle of
liberal and illiberal cultural forces in American history, the essence of
America emerges in the form of one heroic duck of democratic
experimentation.

Using Venturi's analysis we can say that the exceptional texts we have examined look very much like decorated sheds. For example, the various narratives (travel, science, republicanism, pastoralism) offered by Jefferson are symbolic ornaments attached to sheds, multiple significations if you will, of America. Leo Marx's analysis of the *Notes* read one of Jefferson's signs as other commentators have described different ones. Or consider other "decorations": Publius' sorting of the Constitution in terms of the acceptably old and new; Lincoln's erasure of the rebellion proposition from the *Declaration* and King's replacing of it. It is certainly the romance of America as sign that it contains many signs. But Jefferson's decorative sheds do function much like the roadside stands that Venturi et al. have valorized, for they tell the American where to go and how to get there. As Venturi's auto driver confronts "a dangerous, sinuous maze" and "relies on signs for guidance—enormous signs in vast spaces at high speeds,"[3] so does Jefferson provide the American with advise on where to go and how to stop. The basic structure of American Exceptionalism, with its admonitions as to what is possible and what is not, and the guides who comment on the quality of the landscape, can be seen, in fact, as the template for this tour. Thus the guide who tells us to stop at this shed or ignore it because it is "old" (that is, sacred or venerable or outdated) or "new" (innovative or untested) can regard the whole as infinitely various or treacherously narrow. He can complain along the way about the ride or act as an enthusiastic booster. All the time the driver is himself rearranging the sheds, providing different decorations to existing ones and altering the paths among them and of course, considering the possibility that a wrong turn will lead to nowhere (a post-exceptional state).

There are certainly pathological aspects to this kind of theorizing, not the least of which is that readers of signs can become more lost than they might be without the instructions. In fact, Jean Baudrillard provides us with another image of American Exceptionalism that is especially useful since it strips away the populism of Venturi's analysis yet keeps the metaphor. For Baudrillard finds the essence of American culture too in the freeway and its signs:

> To the person who knows the American freeways, their signs read like a litany. 'Right lane must exit.' This 'must exist' has always struck me as a sign of destiny. I have to go, to expel myself from this paradise, leave this providential highway which leads to nowhere, but keeps me in touch with everyone. This is the only real society or warmth here, this collective propulsion, this compulsion—a compulsion of lemmings plunging suicidally together. Why

should I tear myself away to revert to an individual trajectory, a vain sense of responsibility? 'Must exit'; you are being sentenced. You are a player being exiled from the only—useless and glorious—form of existence. "Through traffic merge left": they tell you everything, everything is announced. Merely reading the signs that are essential to your survival gives you an extraordinary feeling of instant lucidity, of reflex 'participation', immediate and smooth. Of a functional participation that is reflected in certain precise gestures. The lines of traffic diverging towards Ventura Freeway and San Diego Freeway do not leave one another, they must separate out. At every hour of the day approximately the same number split towards Hollywood or towards Santa Monica. Pure, statistical energy, a ritual being acted out—the regularity of the flows cancels out individual destinations. What you have here is the charm of ceremonies; you have the whole space before you, just as ceremonies have the whole of time before them.[4]

Baudrillard's conclusion is stated thusly: "Drive ten thousand miles across America and you will know more about the country than all the institutes of sociology and political science put together."[5] If we look at Baudrillard's freeway as the exceptionalist text writ large, the reader is left not with a deciphered maze to follow but with contradictory reactions. Is to be on the freeway (that is, to be an American) to be in a state of constant possibility or is it a state of aimlessness? Are the freeway drivers in a condition of collective freedom or imprisonment? No doubt for Baudrillard it is both but for the reader of exceptionalist texts, he is being herded to various exits (here is the equivalent to Venturi's decorated sheds) that create both a sense of regret and exhilaration. Thus the American political theorist who creates the signs must confront a specific destiny for a people who are ambivalent or hostile to direction. When Publius says "Harken not to the voice" or Thoreau says "Simplify!" or Lincoln says you cannot live in a "house divided," each is saying "Turn Left!" "Merge Right!" and they color the signs with oldness or newness to make us change direction. If we are hypnotized by these signs we turn and we feel a sense of exhilaration at our collective movement.

Do these freeways, even with their decorated sheds and exits and entrances, go nowhere except to encircle and reloop? Baudrillard certainly thinks so but then he is, of course, himself an American Exceptionalist (of the stridently critical variety). The key, however, for the student of American Exceptionalism may be to keep both possibilities before us. That is, that the frenetic recombinations of the old and the new offered to us as exceptional texts together contain the *exceptionalism* we crave as well as the exceptionalism from which we seek redemption. To recognize exceptionalism as both a form of freedom *and* a form of enslavement is a conception of American identity that eludes each exceptional text we have examined, but it is possible to capture it collectively. With the risk of recollapsing this insight into *exceptionalism* once more, this may be the most glorious form of the exceptional of them all.

Notes

1   Robert Venturi et. al., *Learning from Las Vegas*, rev. ed. (Cambridge: MIT Press, 1977), 87.

2   *Ibid.*, 87–100.

3   *Ibid.*, 9.

4   Jean Baudrillard, *America*, Chris Turner, trans. (New York: Verso, 1988), 53–4.

5   *Ibid.*, 56.

Selected Bibliography

Abbott, Philip. *The Exemplary Presidency: Franklin Roosevelt and the American Political Tradition*. Amherst: University of Massachusetts Press, 1991.

—————. *Seeking New Inventions. The Idea of Community in America*. Knoxville: University of Tennessee Press, 1987.

Adair, Douglas. "Experience Must Be Our Only Guide." In *Fame and the Founding Fathers*. Trevor Colbourn ed. New York: Norton, 1974.

Baker, Houston. *Blues, Ideology and Afro-American Literature*. Chicago: University of Chicago Press, 1987.

Ball, Terence and J.G.A. Pocock. eds. *Conceptual Change and the Constitution*. Lawrence, KS: University of Kansas Press, 1988.

Baudrillard, Jean. *America*. Chris Turner, trans. New York: Verso, 1988.

Beard, Charles. *An Economic Interpretation of the Constitution*. New York: Macmillan, 1913.

Bedini, Silvio A. *Thomas Jefferson: Statesman of Science*. New York: Macmillan Press, 1990.

Bell, Daniel. "The End of American Exceptionalism." *Public Interest 4* (Fall, 1975): 193–224.

Bellan, Robert N. et al. *Habits of the Heart*. New York: Harper & Row, 1985.

Bennett, Jane. *Thoreau's Nature: Ethics, Politics, and the Wild*. Thousand Oaks, CA: Sage, 1994.

Bercovitch, Sacvan. ed. *Reconstructing American Literary History*. Cambridge, Harvard University Press, 1986.

Boorstin, Daniel. *The Genius of American Politics*. Chicago: University of Chicago Press, 1956.

————. The Lost World of Thomas Jefferson. New York: Henry Holt, 1948.

Buckley, William F. ed. *American Conservative Thought in the Twentieth Century.* Indianapolis: Bobbs-Merrill, 1970.

Burbick, Joan. *Thoreau's Alternative History.* Philadelphia: University of Pennsylvania Press, 1987.

Cavell, Stanley. *The Senses of Walden.* New York: Viking, 1972.

Chinard, Gilbert. *Thomas Jefferson: Apostle of Americanism.* Boston: Little, Brown, 1929.

Commager, Henry Steele. *Jefferson, Nationalism and the Enlightenment.* New York: George Braziler, 1975.

Cooke, Jacob E., ed. *The Federalist.* Middletown, CN: Wesleyan University, 1961.

Dahl, Robert. *A Preface to Democratic Theory.* Chicago: University of Chicago Press, 1956.

Diamond, Martin. "The Federalist." In Morton J. Frisch and Richard G. Stevens. eds. *American Political Thought.* Itasca, IL: Peacock Press, 1983.

Drescher, Seymour. "More than America: Comparison and Synthesis in *Democracy in America.*" In Abraham S. Eisenstadt, ed. *Reconsidering Tocqueville's Democracy in America.* New Brunswick: Rutgers University Press, 1988.

————. "Tocqueville's Two Democracies." *Journal of History of Ideas* 25 (April–June, 1964: 206–15.

Du Bois, W.E.B. *The Souls of Black Folk.* New York: New American Library, 1969.

Dumbauld, Edward. *Thomas Jefferson: American Tourist.* Norman: University of Oklahoma Press, 1946.

Engelhart, Tom. *The End of Victory Culture: Cold War America and the Disillusionment of a Generation.* New York: Basic Books, 1995.

Evans, J. Martin. *America: The View from Europe.* New York: Norton, 1976.

Franklin, Jimmie Lewis. "Black Southerners, Shared Experience, and Place: A Reflection." In Larry J. Griffin and Don H. Doyle, eds. *The South as an American Problem.* Athens: University of Georgia Press, 1995.

Furtwangler, Albert. *The Authority of Publius.* Ithaca: Cornell University Press, 1984.

Genovese, Eugene. *The Southern Tradition.* Cambridge: Harvard University Press, 1994.

Gitlin, Todd. *The Sixties.* New York: Bantam, 1987.

Grant, Ruth W. *John Locke's Liberalism.* Chicago: University of Chicago Press, 1984.

Hartz, Louis. *The Liberal Tradition in America*. New York: Harcourt, Brace, Jovanovich, 1955.

Hegel, G.F.W. *Lectures on the Philosophy of History*. New York: Colonial Press, 1900.

Hofstadter, Richard. *The American Political Tradition*. New York: Vintage Press, 1948.

Hook, Sidney. ed. *The Essential Tom Paine*. New York: New American Library, 1969.

Howe, Daniel Walker. *The Political Culture of the American Whigs*. Chicago: University of Chicago Press, 1979.

Huntington, Samuel. *American Politics: The Promise of Disharmony*. Cambridge: Harvard University Press, 1981.

Jameson, Frederic. *The Ideology of Theory: Essays 1971–1986*. Minneapolis, University of Minnesota Press, 1988.

———. *Postmodernism or The Cultural Logic of Late Capitalism*. Durham: Duke University Press, 1991.

Jefferson, Thomas. *Notes on the State of Virginia*. William Peden, ed. New York: Norton, 1954.

Jordan, Winthrop. *The White Man's Burden*. New York: Oxford University Press, 1974.

Kammen, Michael. "The Problem of American Exceptionalism: A Reconsideration." *American Quarterly* 45 (1993): 1–43.

Kenyon, Cecilia. ed. *The Antifederalists*. Boston: Northeastern University Press, 1985.

King, Martin Luther, Jr. *I Have a Dream*. (New York: Harper San Francisco, 1992.

Koch, Adrienne and William Peden, eds. *The Life and Selected Writings of Thomas Jefferson*. New York: Modern Library, 1944.

Kolodny, Annette. *The Lay of the Land*. Chapel Hill: University of North Carolina Press, 1975.

Kroes, Rob. *If You've Seen One, You've Seen the Mall: Europeans and American Mass Culture*. Urbana: University of Illinois Press, 1996.

Lamberti, Jean-Claude. *Tocqueville and the Two Democracies*. Cambridge: Harvard University Press, 1989.

Lasch, Christopher. *The Culture of Narcissism*. New York: Warner, 1979.

Lebeaux, Richard. *Young Man Thoreau*. New York: Harper & Row, 1975.

Lerner, Ralph. *Revolution Revisited*. Chapel Hill: University of North Carolina Press, 1994.

Lewis, David Levering. *W.E.B. Du Bois: Biography of a Race.* New York: Henry Holt, 1993.

Lienesch, Michael. *New Order of the Ages.* Princeton: Princeton University Press, 1988.

Lipset, Seymour Martin. *American Exceptionalism: A Double Edged Sword.* New York: Norton, 1996.

Lively, Jack. *The Social and Political Thought of Alexis de Tocqueville.* Oxford: Oxford University Press, 1961.

Locke, John. *Of Civil Government.* Chicago: Regnery, 1971.

Luhan, Mabel Dodge. *Intimate Memories: Background.* New York: Harcourt, Brace, 1933.

———. *Lorenzo in Taos.* New York: Knopf, 1932.

———. *Winter in Taos.* New York: Harcourt, Brace, 1935.

Lutz, Donald S. *Popular Consent and Popular Control.* Baton Rouge, LA: Louisiana State University Press, 1980.

McCarthy, Mary. *The Oasis.* New York: Random House, 1949.

McGerr, Michael. "The Price of International History." *American Historical Review* 96 (1991): 1056–70.

Martin, Edwin T. *Thomas Jefferson: Scientist.* New York: Schuman, 1952.

Marx. Leo. *The Machine in the Garden.* New York: Oxford University Press, 1964.

Mather, Cotton. *Magnalia Christi Americana.* Kenneth B. Murdock, ed. Cambridge: Harvard University Press, 1977.

Matthews, Richard K. *The Radical Politics of Thomas Jefferson.* Lawrence, KS: University Press of Kansas, 1984.

Miller, Charles A. *Jefferson and Nature: An Interpretation.* Baltimore: Johns Hopkins University Press, 1988.

Miller, Chester. *The Wolf by the Ears: Thomas Jefferson and Slavery.* New York: Macmillan, 1977.

Miller, James. *Democracy is in the Streets.* New York: Simon and Schuster, 1987.

Miller, Joshua. *The Rise and Fall of Democracy in Early America.* University Park: Pennsylvania State University Press, 1991.

Miller, Perry. *Consciousness in Concord.* Boston: Houghton Mifflin, 1958.

Morgan, Edmund S. *The Puritan Dilemma.* Boston: Little, Brown and Co. 1958.

Murray, Albert. *The Omni-Americans.* New York: Outbridge and Dienstfrey, 1970.

Nadel, Alan. *Containment Culture: American Narratives, Post-Modernism and the Atomic Age.* Durham, N.C.: Duke University Press, 1995.

Neufeldt, Leonard. *The Economist: Henry David Thoreau and Enterprise.* New York: Oxford University Press, 1989.

Nisbet, Robert. "Many Tocquevilles." *American Scholar.* 46 (Winter, 1977): 59–75.

Nolla, Eduardo. "Democracy or the Closed Book." In Peter Augustine and Joseph Alulis, eds. *Tocqueville's Defense of Human Liberty.* New York: Garland Press, 1993.

Onof, Peter S. ed. *Jeffersonian Legacies.* Charlottesville: University of Virginia Press, 1993.

Ostrom, Vincent. *The Political Theory of the Compound Republic.* Lincoln: University of Nebraska Press, 1987.

Pangle, Thomas L. "The Federalist Papers' Vision of Civic Health and the Tradition Out of Which That Vision Emerges." *Western Political Quarterly* (December, 1986): 577–602.

———. *The Spirit of Modern Republicanism.* Chicago: University of Chicago Press, 1988.

Pell, Richard H. *Radical Visions and American Dreams.* Middletown, CT: Wesleyan University Press, 1973.

Peterson, Merrill D. *The Jeffersonian Image in the American Mind.* New York: Oxford University Press, 1960.

Piercey, Marge. *Vida.* New York: Summit Books, 1979.

Orren, Karen. *Belated Feudalism: Labor, Law and Liberal Development in the United States.* Cambridge: Cambridge University Press, 1991.

Paul, Frederic R. Paul. *Modern and Modernism: The Sovereignty of the Artist, 1885–1925.* New York: Atheneum, 1985.

Paul, Sherman. *The Shores of Walden: Thoreau's Inner Exploration.* Urbana: University of Illinois Press, 1958.

Pierson, George Wilson. *Tocqueville in America.* Garden City: Anchor Books, 1959.

Potter, David M. *People of Plenty.* Chicago: University of Chicago Press, 1954.

Randolph, Sarah N. *The Domestic Life of Thomas Jefferson.* New York: Harper, 1871.

Reeher, Grant. *Narratives of Justice: Legislators' Beliefs About Distributive Fairness.* Ann Arbor: University of Michigan Press, 1996.

Reich, Charles. *The Greening of America.* New York: Bantam, 1970.

Reisman. *The Lonely Crowd: A Study of the Changing American Character.* New Haven: Yale University Press, 1950.

Reynolds, Charles H. and Ralph V. Norman, eds. *Community in America.* Berkeley: University of California Press, 1988.

Roper, Jon. *Democracy and Its Critics: Anglo-American Democratic Thought in the Nineteenth Century.* London, Unwin Hyman, 1989.

Ross, Dorothy. *The Origins of American Social Science.* Cambridge: Cambridge University Press, 1991.

Schleifer, James. *The Making of Tocqueville's Democracy in America.* Chapel Hill: University of North Carolina Press, 1980.

————. "The Problem of the Two Democracies." In Eduardo Nolla, ed. *Liberty, Equality, Democracy.* New York: New York University Press, 1992.

Shaffer, Byron E. ed. *Is America Different?* New York: Oxford University Press, 1991.

Sheldon, Garrett. *The Political Philosophy of Thomas Jefferson.* Baltimore: Johns Hopkins University Press, 1991.

Shklar, Judith. *American Citizenship.* Cambridge, Harvard University Press, 1991.

————. "Redeeming American Political Theory." *American Political Science Review* 85 (September, 1993): 3–15.

Skocpol, Theda. *Protecting Soldiers and Mothers: The Political Origins of Social Policy in the United States.* Cambridge: Harvard University Press, 1992.

Slesinger, Tess. *The Unpossessed.* New York: Simon and Schuster. 1934.

Smith, Rogers M. "Beyond Tocqueville, Myrdal and Hartz: The Multiple Traditions in America." *American Political Science Review* 87 (September, 1993): 549–66.

Stepto, Robert B. *From Beyond the Veil: A Study of Afro-American Narrative.* Urbana: University of Illinois Press, 1991.

Stout, Harry, S. *The New England Soul: Preaching and Religious Culture in Colonial New England.* New York: Oxford University Press, 1986.

Thomas, Owen. ed. *Walden and Civil Disobedience.* New York: Norton, 1966.

Thoreau, Henry David. *A Week on the Concord and Merrimack Rivers.* Carl F. Howde, ed. Princeton: Princeton University Press, 1980.

————. *The Writings of Henry David Thoreau.* Boston: Houghton-Mifllin, 1906.

Tocqueviile, Alexis de. *Democracy in America.* George Lawrence, trans. London: Fontana Press, 1969.

Twelve Southerners. *I'll Take My Stand.* New York: Harper and Row, 1962.

Tyrell, Ian. "American Exceptionalism in an Age of International History." *American Historical Review* 96 (1991): 131–155.

Van Doren Stern, Philip, ed. *The Life and Writings of Abraham Lincoln.* New York: Modern Library, 1940.

Venturi, Robert, et al. *Learning from Las Vegas.* Cambridge: MIT Press, 1977.

Wilentz, Sean. *Chants Democratic: New York City and the Rise of the American Working Class, 1788–1850.* New York: Oxford University Press, 1984.

Wills, Gary. *Inventing America: Jefferson's Declaration of Independence.* New York: Vintage, 1979.

Wood, Gordon S. *The Creation of the American Republic, 1776–1787.* Chapel Hill: University of North Carolina Press, 1969.

———. *The Radicalism of the American Revolution.* New York: Knopf, 1992.

Wrobel, David M. *The End of American Exceptionalism: Frontier Anxiety from the Old West to the New Deal.* Lawrence, KS: University of Kansas Press, 1993.

Young, Thomas Daniel. *Waking Their Neighbors Up.* Athens: University of Georgia Press, 1982.

Zetterbaum, Marvin. *Tocqueville and the Problem of Democracy.* Stanford: Stanford University Press, 1967.

Index

MAJOR CONCEPTS IN POLITICS
AND POLITICAL THEORY

This series invites book manuscripts and proposals on major concepts in politics and political theory—justice, equality, virtue, rights, citizenship, power, sovereignty, property, liberty, etc.—in prominent traditions, periods, and thinkers.

Send manuscripts or proposals, with author's vitae to:

Garrett Ward Sheldon
General Editor
Clinch Valley College
of the University of Virginia
College Avenue
Wise, VA 24293